Economic Liberalisation, Social Capital and Islamic Welfare Provision

Also by Jane Harrigan:

Paul Mosley, Jane Harrigan and John Toye
AID AND POWER
The World Bank and Policy-Based Lending: Volume 1 and 2

Ernest Aryeetey, Jane Harrigan and Machiko Nissanke (editors)
ECONOMIC REFORMS IN GHANA
The Miracle and the Mirage

Jane Harrigan
FROM DICTATORSHIP TO DEMOCRACY
Economic Policy in Malawi 1964–2000

Also by Hamed El-Said:

(1992). *Unemployment in Jordan*. Amman-Jordan: The Economic Research Centre, The Royal Scientific Society. Co-author with M. Kassawneh and M. Ahmera.

(1992). *The Position of Women in the Jordanian Labour Market*. Amman-Jordan: The Economic Research Centre, The Royal Scientific Society. Co-author with M. Ahmera and A. Qassem.

(2002). *Management and International Business Issues in Jordan: The Potential of an Arab Singapore?* New York: Haworth Press. Co-edited with Kip Becker.

Economic Liberalisation, Social Capital and Islamic Welfare Provision

By

Jane Harrigan

and

Hamed El-Said

palgrave
macmillan

Softcover reprint of the hardcover 1st edition 2009 978-0-230-20219-1

First published 2009 by
PALGRAVE MACMILLAN
Houndmills, Basingstoke, Hampshire RG21 6XS and
175 Fifth Avenue, New York, N.Y. 10010
Companies and representatives throughout the world

PALGRAVE MACMILLAN is the global academic imprint of the Palgrave Macmillan division of St. Martin's Press, LLC and of Palgrave Macmillan Ltd. Macmillan® is a registered trademark in the United States, United Kingdom and other countries. Palgrave is a registered trademark in the European Union and other countries.

ISBN 978-1-349-30033-4 ISBN 978-1-137-00158-0 (eBook)
DOI 10.1057/9781137001580

This book is printed on paper suitable for recycling and made from fully managed and sustained forest sources. Logging, pulping and manufacturing processes are expected to conform to the environmental regulations of the country of origin.

A catalogue record for this book is available from the British Library.

Library of Congress Cataloging-in-Publication Data

Harrigan, Jane.
Economic Liberalisation, Social Capital and Islamic Welfare Provision/ by Jane Harrigan and Hamed El-Said.
p. cm.
Includes bibliographical references and index.

1. Public welfare—Islamic countries. 2. Social capital (Sociology)—Islamic countries. 3. Economic development—Islamic countries. 4. Islamic countries—Economic policy. I. El-Said, Hamed. II. Title.
HV435H37 2008
361.917'67—dc22

2008021222

10 9 8 7 6 5 4 3 2 1
18 17 16 15 14 13 12 11 10 09

Transferred to Digital Printing in 2011

This book is dedicated to Jane's nephew and niece, Jo and Alex Yates and Hamed's two nephews Omar and Hamzah El-Said.

Contents

List of Tables ix

Acknowlegements x

Foreword xii

1 Islamic Social Welfare and Political Islam in the Arab World 1

2 Social Capital, Faith-Based Welfare and Islam 8

3 'You Reap What You Plant': The Historical Evolution of Social Networks in Jordan 27

4 Faith-Based Welfare and Jordan's Muslim Brotherhood Movement 56

5 Economic Liberalisation, Poverty and Faith-Based Welfare Provision in Egypt 1991–2006 78

6 Economic Reform, Social Welfare, Civic Society and Islamists in Morocco 111

7 Structural Reform and the Political Economy of Poverty Reduction in Tunisia: What Role for Civil Society? 145

8 Conclusion and Synthesis: What Can be Learnt from our Four Country Studies? 176

Notes 185

Bibliography 195

Index 213

List of Tables

1	Mosque related groups in Egypt, Jordan, Morocco and Algeria	14
2	Jordan: Key social indicators 1980–2002	61
3	Jordan: Educational and health programmes and projects carried out by the Islamic Society Charity Centre (end of 2005)	63
4	Jordan: Charity projects carried out by the Islamic Society Charity Centre of the MBM (end of 2005 US$)	64
5	Jordan: Professional activities of the Islamic Society Charity Centre (2005)	64
6	Jordan: Main sources of income of the Islamic Society Charity Centre (2004 and 2005) (US$)	73
7	Attitude towards religious leaders in Jordan	73
8	Poverty trends in Egypt 1958–82	81
9	Poverty trends in Egypt 1990–2000	87
10	Egypt: Health and education indicators 1990–2003	89
11	Egypt: GDP growth 1990–2004	94
12	Morocco: Comparative social welfare indicators	118
13	Morocco: National poverty headcount	121
14	Politics and religion in Egypt, Jordan, Morocco and Algeria	135
15	Tunisia: Social spending as a percentage of GDP, 2001	147
16	Tunisia: Government spending as a percentage of total spending per sector, 1961–80	148
17	Tunisia: Social indicators, 1961–85, selected years	149
18	Tunisia: Social transfers, 1986–2002 (millions of constant 2002 dinars)	152
19	Tunisia: National Solidarity Fund main achievements 1993–2006	155
20	Poverty incidence in Tunisia (Regional Headcount 1980–2000)	156
21	Tunisia: Human development indicators, 1980–2004, selected years	159

Acknowledgements

We would like to thank the UK Department for International Development (DFID) who gave us a grant to undertake the research and field work for this book. DFID supports policies, programmes and projects to promote international development. DFID provided funds for this study as part of that objective but the views and opinions expressed are those of the authors alone. We would also like to thank Dr Chengang Wang who acted as a research assistant in the early stages of the research work and gave us much valuable assistance in data collection and analysis and Dr Myriam Blin who carried out field work and wrote chapter 7 on Tunisia.

Thanks to Kitty Carruthers who did an excellent and swift job sub-editing and setting the manuscript.

Finally, we would like to thank all those who gave us their time for interviews during our field work in Egypt, Jordan, Tunisia, Morocco, Beirut and Washington DC. They are too numerous to mention but without them this book would not have been possible.

The authors and publishers also wish to thank the following for permission to reproduce copyright material:

Government of Tunisia, Institut National de la Statistique for Table 16: Government spending as a percentage of total spending by sector, 1961–80.

International Journal of Comparative Sociology for Table 1: Mosque related groups in Egypt, Jordan, Morocco and Algeria and Table 14: Politics and religion in Egypt, Jordan, Morocco and Algeria.

Palgrave Macmillan Ltd for Table 18 from Ben Romdhane (2006) Tunisia: Social transfers 1986–2002 (millions of constant 2002 dinars) in Karshenas, M. and Moghadam, V. (Eds) *Social Policy in the Middle East.*

Swiss Journal of Economics and Statistics for Table 20 from Poverty incidence in Tunisia (Regional Headcount 1980–2000), Ayadi et al (2001).

The World Bank for the following:
Table 8 from Poverty trends in Egypt 1958–82, Table 2.1.
Table 9 from El-Saharty, S., Chase, S. Richardson, G. (2005), Egypt and the Millennium Development Goals: Challenges and Opportunities in Report no. 31705.

Table 10 from WDI: Egypt Health and education indicators 1990–2003.
Table 12 from WDI: Morocco: Comparative social welfare indicators.

Every effort has been made to trace rights holders, but if any have been inadvertently overlooked, the publishers would be pleased to make the necessary arrangements at the first opportunity.

Foreword

This book is the culmination of five years' research work on a project entitled 'From Economic to Human Crisis: Policy-Based Lending in the Middle East and North Africa'. The research work was funded by the UK Department for International Development as project R8251.

The project set out to examine one facet of globalisation in the Middle East and North Africa (MENA), namely, policy-based lending by the International Monetary Fund (IMF) and the World Bank. Such lending consists of financial flows from the two Washington-based institutions which have policy reforms attached as conditions. These reforms consist of an opening up of the recipient economies to the global economy via liberalisation policies. Within this context we explored five hypotheses. The hypotheses are as follows: 1) The flow of international finance from the IMF and World Bank to the Arab region has been partly determined by geo-political factors, namely Washington's desire to support pro-Western regimes; 2) the economic reform conditions attached to IMF and World Bank policy-based loans have often had disappointing outcomes; 3) the economic reform conditions attached to this finance have resulted in a decline in state provision of social welfare, increased poverty and increased inequality; 4) this form of globalisation has been increasingly challenged by Islamist groups that have moved in to provide social capital and fill the welfare gap created by the gradual withdrawal of the state from economic and social affairs.; 5) globalisation, by restricting the ability of the state to protect the poor, has strengthened the hand of political Islam and undermined the political legitimacy of incumbent regimes and so increased their authoritarianism.

We used a variety of methodologies to examine these five hypotheses. Econometric work was used to test the extent to which financial flows to the Middle East and North Africa (MENA) were determined by geopolitical factors as well as to estimate growth accounting models for our four country case studies. The countries chosen as case studies were Egypt, Jordan, Tunisia and Morocco. They were chosen on the basis that they have a long history of IMF and World Bank policy-based lending and because they are often held up by the two Washington institutions as success cases. In addition to the econometric work we carried out extensive field work in the four case countries as well as in Beirut (a regional headquarters for World Bank staff) and Washington DC, the headquarters of the IMF and World Bank. This field work consisted of conducting semi structured interviews with a range of different people – government officials, IMF and World Bank staff, staff from other donor agencies, politicians, academics, members of the business community, Islamists and NGO staff. In addition, the field work was used for data collection and collection of official reports.

The original intention was to present the findings of the research and the testing of the five hypotheses in a single volume. However, the material we collected was so rich and extensive that two separate books have been the result. The first of the two books, which is a companion volume to this book, is entitled *Aid and Power in the Arab World: IMF* and *World Bank Policy-based Lending in the Middle East and North Africa* (Harrigan and El-Said, 2008) and is also published by Palgrave Macmillan. It examines the first two hypotheses centred on the flow of finance to the MENA region and the effects of economic liberalisation in our four chosen country studies. This is the second book, and it examines the remaining three hypotheses, namely: the extent to which economic liberalisation in our four countries has resulted in a decline in state welfare provision; the extent to which this space has been filled by faith-based welfare provision, especially by Islamic groups; and the nature of the state response to this phenomenon.

Although the two books stand alone, it is recommended that they are read together to gain a fuller insight into various facets of globalisation in the Arab world.

1

Islamic Social Welfare and Political Islam in the Arab World

Introduction

Many countries in the Arab world, especially the resource-poor countries of the Middle East and North Africa (MENA), have undertaken economic liberalisation programmes over the past ten to twenty years. Often these programmes are supported by the International Monetary Fund and the World Bank through policy-based loans such as stabilisation and structural adjustment loans. In many other regions of the world, especially in Latin America and sub-Saharan Africa, such programmes which were undertaken in the 1980s and early 1990s, have resulted in a decline in social welfare (Cornia, Jolly and Stewart 1987, Mosley, Harrigan and Toye 1995). This book explores the trends in social welfare in four countries in the MENA region which have undertaken extensive economic liberalisation programmes under the auspices of the IMF and the World Bank, namely, Jordan, Egypt, Tunisia and Morocco, to see whether economic liberalisation has been associated with a decline in social welfare. These countries were chosen not just because of their prolonged adjustment efforts, but also because they are often put forward by the international financial institutions as cases of successful reformers, with regimes in Jordan, Morocco and Tunisia generally perceived as the 'most advanced' and 'successful reformers' in the region (Shafiq 1998 p. 8), 'good pupils of the IMF' who followed its 'commandments religiously' (Pfeifer 1996 p. 40).

The prescriptions of the IMF and World Bank, designed in a package of policy reform known as stabilisation and structural adjustment programmes, in the Arab World were typical of the IMF and World Bank, embracing policies not much different from the ones prescribed by these international institutions to developing countries in other regions, such as Latin America and sub-Saharan Africa. In the Arab World, as elsewhere, the 'Washington Consensus' demanded stabilisation measures calling for massive cuts in public spending, new and broader taxes, and high and positive interests rates. They also called for immediate trade liberalisation combined with large currency devaluations and massive reduction in tariffs and elimination of non-tariff barriers. Privatisation of state-owned enterprises, price and financial deregulation also figured prominently in every SAL package signed with local governments (Niblock and Murphy 1993, Harik and Sullivan 1992, Vandewalle 1996, Shafiq 1998, El-Erian et al 1996).

We wish to explore whether the above types of economic reform conditions have resulted in a decline in state provision of social welfare, increased poverty and increased inequality. A second hypothesis we wish to explore is whether civic groups, especially Islamic groups, have moved in to fill a gap left by the retrenchment of the state in terms of welfare provision, and if so, what form such activity takes. Throughout the past two decades Islamic voluntary groups and charities have sprung up in the MENA region providing a vast array of services, including health services, education, literacy training, job training, social groups and financial help for the vulnerable and disadvantaged, amongst other things. We employ the concept of social capital to help analyse these phenomena.

Globalisation and economic liberalisation, by restricting the ability of the state to protect the poor, has strengthened the hand of political Islam[1] and undermined the political legitimacy of the very same incumbent regimes Washington sought to support, forcing these regimes to become increasingly authoritarian. We analyse these trends for our four countries, Jordan, Egypt, Morocco and Tunisia to assess the extent to which this has taken place.

International finance, poverty and inequality

In our analysis of the social effects of economic liberalisation we hope to fill an important gap in the literature. Compared to other regions there has been a dearth of work on the impact of stabilisation and structural adjustment programmes in the MENA region. While economic reform programmes implemented in sub-Saharan Africa in the 1980s and 1990s have been extensively researched (Mosley, Harrigan and Toye 1995), the same programmes in the MENA, except in Turkey and to a lesser extent in Egypt, have not received the attention they deserve. Not only is the available literature limited, but what is available tends to evaluate the experience of economic reform in the MENA in an individualistic approach, focusing mainly on the experience of one country or another with little regional linkage (Lofgren 1993).

The scant empirical evidence so far available suggests that the IMF and World Bank-sponsored economic reform in the MENA has not been the total success claimed by these organisations. The social and welfare implications of reform in the Arab world, despite their injection with a strong poverty focus in the 1990s, have been disappointing. This impact, particularly when implemented suddenly and prematurely, has already been extensively discussed elsewhere for other regions of the world. Theory and evidence show that when these policies are implemented in association with and on the terms of the IMF and World Bank the outcome is often a drastic increase in poverty, unemployment and inequalities (Stiglitz 2002, Dunkley 1997, Goldstein 2000, Stewart 2000, CAFOD 1998).

The available empirical evidence suggests that the social impact of hitherto reform in the MENA region has been disappointing. For example, the 2002 UN Arab Human Development Report argued that, although the Arab World has less abject poverty (income of less than $1 a day) than other developing regions, poverty in the region, along with unemployment and inequalities have all risen rapidly in recent years: around 12 million Arab people, or 12 per cent of the labour force are unemployed; of every five Arabs, one lives on less than $2 a day; among 280 million Arabs, 65 million adults are still illiterate, two-thirds of them are women; 10 million children have no schooling at all; and only sub-Saharan Africa registered lower annual growth in income over the past 20 years than the Arab world. Although the Arab World does not lack resources, the report added, it is 'richer than it is developed' (UNDP 2002, *The Economist* 2002a).

While surveying eight countries that accepted co-operation with the IMF and World Bank in the 1980s (Egypt, Morocco, Tunisia, Jordan, Sudan, Turkey, Algeria and Mauritania), El-Ghonemy (1998) also maintained that, despite improvement in macroeconomic indicators, the social situation in each reforming country got 'worse than before reform'. Not only did unemployment and poverty increase, but also inequality of income worsened in all of them, except in Tunisia, which managed to reduce poverty in the mid-1990s by violating IMF conditionality and refusing to compromise on social welfare and protection of the poor. Another more recent study (El-Said 2002a) found that not only had the social impact of reform in the Arab World been disappointing in the 1990s, but that it had been more severe in countries which were subject to international pressure to globalise rapidly, the 'good pupils' of the IMF, particularly Morocco, Jordan and Egypt (as well as Algeria which had been suffering from political instability). In those four states, unemployment, poverty and inequalities had not only been much worse in the late 1990s than in the early 1990s, but also much worse than in other states that either followed the commandments of the IMF and World Bank less religiously, such as Yemen, for example, or did not cooperate with them at all, such as Syria.

The overall situation in the Arab states that are described as 'successful reformers', or IMF's 'good pupils', is indeed, puzzling for some observers. 'How', Pfeifer asked, despite disappointing social impact of restructuring, 'did Tunisia, Morocco, Jordan and even Egypt become IMF success stories in the 1990s in the first place'? (Pfiefer 1999 p.23). Put differently, why, despite the fact that efforts to globalise were lubricated by massive capital inflows, has the social outcome been disappointing?

We intend to build upon the above works by further exploring the social effects of IMF and World Bank financially supported economic reform programmes in our four case country studies. In Chapters 4 to 7 we examine the impact of World Bank and IMF reforms on poverty and social welfare in our four country studies and find that only in Tunisia was there an unambiguous improvement.

Social welfare and political Islam

A second theme we wish to explore in this book is the idea that in response to declining state provision of social welfare, Islamic groups, many with growing political aspirations, have stepped in to fill the gap by providing various forms of welfare and contributing to the development of social capital. Becker (1993) defines social capital as any social, or non-market, interaction with a continuing effect. Fine (2000) argues that the World Bank regards social capital as interventions in civil society which constitute non-market responses to market imperfections where 'civil society' can be seen as the space between family and State. Social capital either complements the state when the latter is performing well, or substitutes for it when it is in retreat as under austerity and liberalisation programmes.

The provision of welfare and charity by religious groups is a well-known but under-studied phenomenon in the MENA region (Woltering 2002), and we wish to assess whether faith-based welfare provision has been strengthened during the period of economic reform and liberalisation in MENA. Globalisation has been occurring at a time when the international financial institutions are insisting on policies that restrict the ability of the state to provide adequate social welfare and social safety nets to protect the poor. Such policies include cuts in public sector expenditure and more general policies to roll back the state. We find that the resulting decline in the quality of state welfare provision has prompted Islamist groups with political aspiration to fill the welfare gap, particularly in Egypt and Jordan, and become the main champions of the poor, providing them with food, clothing, cash transfers to pay for health, education and even marriage ceremonies as well as directly providing health and education services. They also provide credit for businesses via their specialised Islamic banks that have proliferated throughout the region and are more in line with local tradition and culture. Islamists have been in the forefront of defending the welfare of the poor and organising charities to collect donations for them. As Richards and Waterbury in their extensive work on the region put it: 'While government dithers, the Islamists move in and win support by providing their own assistance' (Richards and Waterbury 1996 p.228).

Through their welfare activities Islamists have been able to enhance their political legitimacy at the expense of incumbent regimes (Ayubi 1995a). A consensus is rapidly emerging among scholars and observers both inside and outside the region to the effect that 'Islam has been nurtured by the failure of current, authoritarian regimes to achieve economic equality ... [and] also by the US policy of supporting corrupt, authoritarian dictatorship' combined with unconditional support to Israel (Niva 1998 p.28). When Hamas eventually decided to enter the Palestinian elections in early 2006, its landslide victory, ironically, stunned the Western world. From the outset, Islamists dominated the Jordanian parliament in 1989. It was only after the regime, with US backing, changed the elections law in 1993 that their influence in the Jordanian parliament was reduced, though not eliminated. Despite the fact that the Muslim Brotherhood Movement is still banned in Egypt, its individual candidates did far better than expected in the last partially-free elections. Lifting the ban on the Moroccan Justice and Development Party in the late 1990s has also led to important Islamist gains in the Moroccan Parliament. In Egypt, Morocco, and Jordan Islamists are confident of their eventual overwhelming victory. They equivocally maintain that their strategy has so far not focused on dominating the political theatre, knowing very well that the local authorities, backed by the US and EU, will not allow such a scenario, and that the outcome will therefore be more reminiscent to the Algerian fiasco. If this is the case, then there is little doubt that Hamas's landslide victory will embolden Islamists in other Arab states and will cause a strategic change in their political thinking. During our field work in Jordan, Egypt, Tunisia and Morocco, we explored the extent to which religious groups have provided welfare and social capital in response to the changes in social welfare under liberalisation, and the extent to which they overlap with groups that have political aspirations in the form of opposition to incumbent regimes.

Repression, authoritarianism and the political backlash: the price of maintaining 'friendly' regimes

The final theme we wish to explore is that rather than enhancing the stability of pro-Western regimes, the US-led policies of globalisation and economic liberalisation supported by international finance have actually undermined and destabilised the very regimes the USA sought to protect. As a result of growing poverty and inequality in the region, Islam has been gaining strength, not just in its provision of welfare and social capital but also as a political movement and as a vocal opponent to globalisation and western capitalism. Many radical Islamists view globalisation as a new form of imperialism, aimed at dominating Islamic countries' resources and people (Schirato and Webb 2003). It is against this background that the Egyptian President, Hossni Mubarak, used the May

2006 World Economic Forum in *Sharam El Alsheik* to appeal to the world community, particularly the industrialised countries, to help in creating 'globalisation with a human face', and to warn against the widening gap between the rich and poor within and between countries of the region and the rest of the world.

The importance of equality for stability, investment and, hence, for growth and development has long been stressed and emphasised by various scholars. A high level of inequality makes it difficult to reduce poverty, weakens incentives and increases both stress among workers and market uncertainties. These inequalities destroy cohesion of a society, leading to political and social instabilities that are detrimental to investment, growth and development (DFID 2000). Further reform expected under the IMF, World Bank and WTO, if not accompanied by a mechanism to protect and compensate the losers from globalisation, could lead to a far reaching and devastating distributive conflict in the region, not unlike the one that has plagued Indonesia since the late 1990s or ravaged the Algerian economy and society for more than a decade. The 1990s and the first years of the 21st century have already experienced a rise in the number and forms of distributive conflicts in the Arab World, including riots, demonstrations, strikes, violence, assassinations, clashes with labour unions and university students in addition to an increase in the crime rate (Ayubi 1995b, Richards and Waterbury 1996, El-Ghonomy 1998, Shafiq 1998, *Economist* 2002b).

The response of incumbent Arab regimes to growing Islamic influence and opposition to the political and economic policies of the 'Washington Consensus' has been a marked increase in repressive measures. Washington and the EU not only 'decided to suddenly turn a blind eye to what is going on, perhaps because of a need to clamp down on Islamists' (Shahine 2005), but also gave their tacit approval for such repressive measures. Yet Prime Minister Tony Blair and President George Bush publicly declared that we 'share a vision of a free, peaceful, a democratic broader Middle East'. (Full text of Bush and Blair Press Conference, *Guardian*, 12 November, 2004, on website http://news.bbc.co.uk/go/pr/fr//1/hi/world/americas/4008071.stm) Such contradictory stances have led Carothers to argue that America's foreign policy in the Arab World suffers from schizophrenia, a 'split personality'. On the one hand, it is committed to good governance and democracy abroad, on the other, its war on terror has increased its reliance on corrupt and authoritarian regimes (Carothers 2003). Gerges, while working on Egypt, revealed that stability of pro-Washington regimes 'clearly overrides other consideration … in US eyes' (Gerges 2000 p. 607). In Egypt, Jordan, Morocco, Tunisia, and even Yemen and Saudi Arabia, incumbent regimes were explicitly encouraged by Washington and other European states to brutally repress all shades of anti-Western Islamist activism in return for keeping their countries allied with the West at any cost.

International organisations, including Amnesty International and the International Crisis Group, have repeatedly warned against increased repressions in such states, which has undermined nascent domestic political reform initiated in the region in the early 1990s, in addition to putting the US-backed international financial institutions in a rather difficult and hypocritical position (International Crisis Group 2003a and b).

Since the early 1990s the international financial institutions have paid increased lip service to the concept of 'good governance' in developing countries. Particularly in sub-Saharan Africa the provision of finance has been made conditional on good governance, including the elimination of corruption and the introduction of Western style multi-party democracy.[2] However, increasingly the same institutions are providing financial support to corrupt and undemocratic Arab regimes labelled as Western 'allies'. The latter are not the democratic or 'good governance' that Washington and the IFIs portray them to be.

Long before the September 11 attacks on the USA, political liberalisation, initiated in the late 1980s by some states like Tunisia, Morocco, Jordan and Egypt was arrested shortly after its introduction under the pretext of fighting terrorism. The September 11 attacks only provided a more pertinent pretext, with Western tacit support and funding, to repress not only Islamists, but also all other forms of opposition (Garnham and Tessler 1995). For the first time in decades, Islamists and nationalists have been united in their (ambivalent) attitude towards their regimes and their Western backers.

Lack of real democracy has also hampered the ability of domestic regimes to rein in corruption, and has also encouraged them to maintain and nurture an old form of politics; corrupt 'patron-client relationships' upon which their legitimacy and survival came to depend (Richards and Waterbury 1996). It is not surprising, therefore, that a vicious cycle has emerged whereby reform in the region has failed to protect the poor and instead benefited only a small élite, one that is strongly linked to the state officials, bureaucrats and army generals. In Algeria, this élite came to be known as the 'new bourgeoisie' (Pfeifer 1996 p.3), in Morocco the 'agrarian élite' (Knauss 1989 p.437), in Tunisia the 'economic and political élite'(King 1999 p.421), in Egypt 'crony capitalists' (Sadowsky 1991), and in Jordan it refers to the 'progeny' of the men which King Hussein of Jordan relied on to implement his policies since the early 1970s (El-Said 2002b p.271). Corruption and authoritarianism have been the price of preserving 'allies' and friendly regimes in power in the region, a price that Washington firmly believes it is worth paying in order to enhance the stability of 'existing regimes' (Klare 1998 p.15).

2

Social Capital, Faith-Based Welfare and Islam

Introduction

Over recent years, the concept of Social Capital (SC) has attracted great scholarly and academic awareness. Despite the rise in the prominence of SC analysis, 'relatively little scholarly attention has been given to the role of religion in social capital formation' (Smidt 2003 p.2). The upshot has been an insufficient and unconvincing explanation for the phenomenal, recent and rapid rise of political Islam in most Muslim societies. It seems that thirty years since Iran's Ayatollah Khomeini brought to the modern world the idea that Islam might be a formula for governance, political Islam has gained vast momentum in almost every Muslim and Arab state. From Morocco through Jordan to the Gulf, Islamists' voluntary charities and networks seem to have transformed themselves into successful political parties and congregations, winning parliamentary elections or registering important victories in local, municipalities and professional associations. For most scholars and observers in the West, the recent political elevation of Islamic charity organisations is seen as a 'surprise' (BBC News 2006), unexpected, and even 'ambiguous' (Abdel-Latif 2005). Muslim societies are going through a crisis; 'The crisis of Islam' is reflected in political Islam itself and the political rise and prominence of voluntary religious organisations demanding large sacrifices.

In fact, contemporary images of Islam have come to be dominated by militants and fundamentalists. Islamic charitable, and mostly non-political organisations, are invariably seen as 'radical religious militias ... tak(ing) their religious faith to violent extremes', and using their resources to finance 'effective ... suicide attacks' (*The Economist* 15 Jan 2004). Such a view has had predictable and obvious implications. It not only called for, but also led to sturdy measures aimed at curbing formal 'subsidies' and other sources of finance to faith-based organisations, particularly Islamic charities, because they 'induce extreme increases in sacrifice' (Morford and Berman 2003 p.15). In one country after the other, from Washington to Europe to the Middle East,

Islamic charities have been either closed down or their operations restricted and hamstrung severely (Stoddard 2007). The invariable view of Islamic voluntarily organisations as terrorists using their resources to induce suicide and violent attacks is not really helpful in understanding the unfolding of political Islam, because it ignores the other side of good Islam. It also fails to highlight the experience of the contemporary moderate, pragmatic, or parliamentary Islamic movements, which have been overshadowed by the invariable view of all Islamic organisations as terrorist radical movements. This resulted in a 'lack of research available about the growth of these religious-oriented political movements in the Arab World and Muslim societies', which are deeply embedded in society's rank and file (AUJRC 1997 p.7). This chapter seeks to fill an important gap in the literature. It seeks to enhance understanding of Islam by highlighting the cultural, civil, and associational traditions of Islamic religion. Specifically, we analyse the link between religion and social capital in general and Islamic faith and social capital in particular. It evaluates the key role played by Islamic voluntary associations, particularly the Muslim Brotherhood Movement (one of the oldest, most organised, and successful organisations in the region) in the formation of both social capital and human capital which are held today as prerequisites for promoting civil society, political and social stability, and liberal democracy. The view that all Islamic movements are radical and terrorist provides no rational explanation for the recent surge in political Islam by Islamic charity organisations through ballots, not bullets. This chapter argues that faith-based organisations represent the most important form of social and human capital in Muslim societies. The recent political elevation of such organisations is thus attributed to their ability to foster social capital in their societies, internalise their religious norms and values, and hence to evoke positive attitudes and actions from both their members and supporters.

Social capital framework

Social capital has been given many definitions and applied to study various phenomena (Grootaert and Van Bastelaer 2002a, Dasgupta and Serageldine 1999). Most of these definitions and applications refer not to SC itself, rather 'to manifestations of social capital' (Fukuyama 2000 p.3). Putnam (1995 p.167), for example, an acknowledged original source in the rise of SC, defines SC as 'features of social organisation ... that can improve the efficiency of society by facilitating coordinated actions'. Similarly, Smidt, (2003 pp.2 and 4) referred to SC as 'any facets of social relations that serve to enable members of society to work together to accomplish collective goals'.

The SC framework thus focuses on the socialisation process of individuals and groups and the alleged beneficial economic and political impact of such socialisation, not only to participants but also to the corporate body (society). This is exactly how some of the very early applications of the term SC, by Hanifan in 1916,[3] for example, were understood and intended to be used, namely, to draw attention to the beneficial effects of social ties to individuals and corporate bodies. As Hanifan wrote in 1916:

> The individual is helpless socially, if left to himself. If he comes into contact with his neighbour, and they with other neighbours, there will be an accumulation of social capital, which may immediately satisfy his social needs which may bear a social potentiality sufficient to the substantial improvement of living conditions in the whole community. The community as a whole will benefit by the cooperation of all its parts, while the individual will find in his associations the advantages of the help, the sympathy, and the fellowship of his neighbours.
>
> (Quoted from Putnam 2000 p.19)

What distinguishes SC from other forms of capital is that it is 'relational', in that it only exists when shared with others (Narayan 1999 p.20). 'To possess social capital, a person must be related to others, and it is these others, not himself, who are the actual source of his or her advantage' (Narayan and Cassidy 2001 p.60). This is unlike other traditionally defined forms of, say, economic capital, which usually reside in people's bank accounts, or human capital, which exists inside people's heads.

The focal point of SC theory therefore is that social ties and networks have both economic and political functions (Putnam, 1995 and 2000). 'The economic function of SC is to reduce the transaction costs' associated with formal contracts and thus to facilitate transactions among individual and groups within a society (Fukuyama 2000 p.6). This effect is achieved as a result of at least three features of the socialisation process itself caused by membership in social networks (Grootaert and Van Bastelaer 2002a pp.8–9). First, since membership means belonging to a social network, participation in such networks not only increases the availability of and access to information, but also lowers its costs. The type of information generated and accessed by members varies, and can relate to significant matters like location of new markets, suppliers, prices, sources of credit, and treatment of livestock. For those who feel that they have some kind of moral or divine commitment to care for others and assist the needy, social networks can provide important information on the location of the poor and their needs. SC hence can, and has been used to address the problem of market imperfection, particularly in credit markets where the lack of information on borrowers' credit worthiness and loan-use has limited the access of the poor to credit in many developing countries (Grootaert and Van Bastelaer 2002a).

Second, being part of a social network increases face to face interactions. Individuals learn more not only from each other, but also about one another. These interpersonal interactions might progress into personal exchange, leading to the development of trust among group members. Trust is an important component of SC because it facilitates and lubricates cooperation: more trust leads to more cooperation, which makes it easier for any group to take a collective decision and implement collective action (Grootaert and Van Bastelaer 2002a p.8). As Thomas Greene, while describing a community of lyceum which he found in 1829 wrote:

> While we mingle together … we shall learn to know each other more intimately; we shall remove many prejudices which ignorance or partial acquaintance with each other had fostered. In the parties and sects into which we are divided, we sometimes learn to love our brother at the expense of him whom we do not in so many respects regard a brother … We may return to our homes and firesides with kindlier feelings toward one another, because we have learned to know one another better.
>
> (Quoted from Putnam 2000 p.23)

SC, therefore, compared to other formal institutions formed by the state, like stock or labour markets, for example, is not very costly (Fafchamps 2006): SC promotes 'spontaneous cooperation' among group members (Putnam 1995 p.170), and connects together 'autonomous individuals into communal relationships' (Smidt 2003 p.11). It serves as a transformation mechanism; self-interested individuals with weak social conscience and obligation are 'transformed into members of a community expressing shared interests and a sense of common good' (Smidt 2003 11).

Finally, while forging social trust inherent in interpersonal relationships, social networks promote sturdy norms of reciprocity, expectations, obligations and even sanctions that reduce the free rider problem and opportunistic behaviour. Social networks set certain norms and rules of behaviour which members are expected to follow and conform with. Being a member in a network implies recognition of (and acceptance of) the rules and norms of reciprocity of that particular network. Social sanctions (such as gossip, exclusion and ostracism) are usually effectively employed to reinforce conformity with norms of behaviour in a social network (Barr 2002). This reinforces the social support system inherent within a social network and reduces opportunistic behaviour. As Colman (1988 p.102), another acknowledged original source in the rise of SC, put it: 'If A does something for B and trusts B to reciprocate in the future, this establishes an expectation in A and an obligation on the part of B'. In the same way, Sobel (2002 p.150) describes how the anthropological literature on gift giving and exchange has nicely captured this rationale of reciprocity, mutual trust, and obligation: Giving a gift creates both an obligation to accept and reciprocate; 'To the extent that using social capital operates like gift exchange, taking advantage of social capital creates an obligation to honor future requests for assistance and increases the value of individual's connections.'

The political function of SC flows from a similar logic. It was long explicated from Alexis de Tocqueville's analysis of political life in modern liberal democracies (Smidt 2003 p.1, Fukuyama 2000 p.7). A prerequisite for successful liberal democracies, he argued, is a vigorous associational life or civic associations. Even if they are not political in nature, civic associations still serve an important function by providing meanings and sources of social engagement. Civil associations serve as a mediator, a balancing mechanism between the coercive powers of the state and excessive individualism in society, both of which can undermine political freedom within the community. Fukuyama (2000 p.7) nicely captured the political function of SC in the following words:

> It was only by coming together in civil associations that weak individuals became strong; the associations they formed could either participate directly in political life (as in the case of a political party or interest group) or could serve as 'schools of citizenship' where individuals learned the habits of cooperation that eventually carry over into public life.'

The link between associational life and political and economic functions of SC begs an important question related to the role of the state in promoting or weakening civic associations and associational life. This link was captured by Gellner's (1994) famous phrase: 'no civil society, no democracy'. By extension, no associations, no SC. This is an issue we return to in later sections.

Religion and social capital

While voluntary civic associations serve an important economic and political function, little attention has been given to religious SC or the role of faith-based organisations in forming SC. This is mainly due to the fact the SC framework itself has so far been more engaged in a discussion over the role and consequences of the socialisation process and associational life in general, regardless of its form. In this respect, religious associations have been one form, among many, of voluntary associations and thus treated in a similar way (Smidt 2003 p.2). While both Putnam (2000) and Fukuyama, for example, recognise the fact that SC can also be produced by 'major religions, like Buddhism, Hindusim, Christianity, and Islam, or a large cultural system like Confucianism' (Fukuyama 2000 p.13), they make no attempt to differentiate between religious SC and other forms of SC.

The available empirical evidence suggests that faith-based organisations or Religious Social Capital (RSC) play a distinctive and 'unique role', not only in constructing SC but also with regard to its wider implications (Smidt 2003 p.2). At least three key factors are given for why religious SC deserves special attention (ibid., Cnaan et al 2003). First, religious congregational life has traditionally been a primary component of associational life in almost all societies regardless of their religion, cultural systems, or level of development and industrialisation. In fact, in capitalist industrialised countries, like the US, which are characterised by individualism and self-interest, 'faith communities in which people worship together are arguably the single most important repository of social capital' (Putnam 2000 p.66). In developing, authoritarian countries where civic associations are legally prohibited and associational life restricted, (for example, the Arab World is a prototype example here), faith-based organisations are among the very few organisations that escaped the state's dictatorial control, and, in many cases, are the only form of voluntary associations available for citizens. The Arab World is distinctive in the extent of SC generated through faith-based organisations. Social networks and associations, including in particular Islamic voluntary associations, are today widely recognised as the primary source of congregational life in the Arab World, with a remarkable capacity to provide a unifying factor, a sense of identity and rootedness for both individuals and groups. Table 1 clearly demonstrates that mosque-related groups are currently a common type of organisation that most Arabs in Egypt, Jordan, Morocco and Algeria join. This is particularly the case today after decades of failure (political, social and economic) by secular, leftist and nationalist developmentalist ideologies that dominated the political scene in the Arab World in the post-independence period.[4] As Richards and Waterbury (1996, p.348) observed, 'Islamism is ... [today] conceived as the new nationalism in Arab countries ... [it] arose out of the failure of the old order'. (Also see Owen 1992, Wickham,2002; and Singerman 1998.)

Table 1: Mosque related groups in Egypt, Jordan, Morocco and Algeria

	Egypt	**Jordan**	**Morocco**	**Algeria**
How often do you spend time with people at your mosque?:	%	%	%	%
Weekly	37.9	39.1	23.5	29.3
Monthly	19.5	18.3	10.5	10.2
Less		29.2	9.3	14.4
None at all	42.6	38.3	56.7	46.1
Apart from weddings, funerals and christenings, how often do you attend religious ceremonies?:				
More than once a week	22.4	28.9	32.4	25.2
Weekly	19.8	15.2	11.8	18.6
Less	32.8	13.3	19.1	37.5
Never	25.1	42.6	37.7	17.7
Index of mosque involvement:				
Very high	24.9	41.4	29.8	33.8
High	17.4	2.3	5.0	6.4
Low	45.4	12.5	21.3	22.5
Very low	12.3	43.8	43.9	37.3

Source: Tessler 2003 p.15.

Secondly, RSC is also distinctive in its contribution to SC formation in that its voluntary activities provide primary safety nets to the weak, poor and needy in society. All major religions have a 'moral foundation', and have thus developed divinity for compassion, care and the welfare of society: they all emphasise social justice, collective responsibility for the welfare of society, the legitimate claims of the weak upon the community and the duty to help the poor and strangers at all times and regardless of economic and social circumstances (Cnaan et al 2003 p.29). It is no coincidence that, even in the most industrialised societies, religious associations are almost always involved in voluntary, charitable and other 'acts of mercy ... that help to provide a safety net for members of society who are at risk' (Smidt 2003 p.2). In the

Arab World, the Washington Consensus' developmental ideology, along with economic mismanagement and rent-seeking, led to frail public sector services, thus creating a vacuum that has naturally been filled by faith-based organisations (Morford and Berman 2003). The size, extent and reach of such activities and 'programmes have left many observers baffled' (Abootalebi 1999 p.1). Faith-based, particularly Islamic, social welfare programmes and provisions in the Arab World have outdone, outperformed and, in some cases, exceeded by far the size of official safety nets provided by their states (Hamas in Palestine, Hizb Allah in Lebanon, the Muslim Brotherhood Movement in Jordan and Egypt, the *Dahiras* in Senegal, to mention but a few examples). These forms of RSC 'have numerous positive externalities and very few negative ones. They save public sector money because they encourage the provision of numerous services to persons in need ... form[ing] a nucleus of conformity, stability, and social order in communities that would otherwise be volatile' (Cnaan et al 2003 p.20). Over the past two decades, there has been an exponential growth in the size and extent of voluntary, charitable and other 'acts of mercy' by Islamic associations in the Arab World, a phenomenon which some observers recently referred to as 'The Parallel State' or 'The Shadowy State', composed primarily of sophisticated voluntary, charitable faith-based network of social provisions (Nowarah 2007 p.1).

In other words, faith-based organisations are distinctive not only in terms of their contribution to the formation of SC, but also with regards to its benefits and implications for the wider community. RSC is neither formed on the basis of the coercive means of the state, nor motivated by personal self-interest of the market. It is produced and used to achieve divine and religious motives, that is, to be 'useful to a fellow disciple for God's sake' (Babou 2002 p.170).

The final way in which RSC is distinctive is in terms of the norms, values and teachings that it fosters, and which promote civic skills and civic culture, or what Tocqueville described in a different context as 'the art of association' (quoted in Fukuyama 2000 p.7). Through education and emphasis on cultural aspects of religion, faith-based organisations promote religious norms and values that teach members habits of cooperation, and norms of compassion and care. These habits are internalised by members in their dealings with both other members and non-members. Even if a community is not religious, 'these norms still become part of the socialisation process of younger generations into adults in society and serve as instructions for desired behaviour of compassion and social care' (Cnaan et al 2003 p.29). Communities with more active faith-based organisations were found to be more sociable, more charitable and possess more vibrant voluntary social welfare programmes. For example, in their analysis for the impact of faith-based organisation in the US, Cnaan et al (2003 p.23), observed that 'church-goers are more likely to volunteer than those who do not attend church'. These results are reinforced by Campbell and Yonish's 2003 study which found that American faith-based communities volunteer more not only for religious but also for non-religious and secular endeavours, and that church attendance rivals education as a predictor of the extent of volunteering. Not only were faith-based communities found to be more enthusiastic when it came to volunteering, they were also found to be more charitable. Nemeth and Luidens (2003) show that members of faith-based organisations in America are more likely than others to be generous, and to contribute more broadly and generously than non-members (regardless of income levels) to both religious and non-religious aspects.

In a modern, open, and 'borderless world' with states with diminished social and economic capacities in the life of their communities (Ohmae 1990 and 1995), faith-based organisations know very well that their credibility, and even survival, have come to depend on their ability to continue to access trust and wider social networks in communities where they live and operate. This makes them accountable to their donors and forces them to develop leadership skills to recruit new members, attract new sources of finance, and expand their community and welfare services. Faith-based organisations, including Islamic associations, are thus an important source of not only SC, but also of human capital and skills too; they are a 'key element for acquiring human and social capital, the necessary tools for civic engagement' (Smidt 2003 p.20).

Yet, it is important not to fully romanticise the effects of RSC. Fukuyama (2000 p.4) makes the case that, because it 'tends to produce more in the way of negative externalities' than either human capital or physical capital, SC seems less perceptively a 'social good'. Putnam (2000 p.22) eloquently described the effects of SC when he stated that 'Social capital ... can be directed at malevolent, antisocial purposes, just like any other form of capital' (Putnam 2000 p.22). It was SC, for example, which enabled a group of what Prince Hassan of Jordan in 2007 described as 'misguided men' who share common distorted and 'misinformed' norms, values and ideologies to attack the US in 2001, Madrid in 2005, London in 2006 and several other places such as Casablanca, Amman, Bali and Nairobi. Al-Qaeda also relies on both physical capital (planes, trucks or Tie-sacs laden with explosives) and human capital (highly trained pilots or explosive-making expertise) to achieve anti-social and malicious acts. It is probably safe to conclude that if religious associations produce more SC than any other form of civic association, they can also produce more negative externalities than any other source of SC too. Just as it is seen to unify, religion can also vastly divide, with devastating effects for the whole community and society. Iraq, Sudan, Lebanon's civil war in the 1970s and 1980s, Algeria in the 1990s and the former Yugoslavia are but a few examples of devastating effects of religious divisiveness. It is therefore misleading not only to assume that all forms of associations lead to the same level and extent of SC, but that they will also have similar effects and social consequences. The debate then turns to what type of institutions (and social, political and economic circumstances) can lead to and produce socially and economically desirable outcomes?

To capture the negative and positive externalities of SC, Gittell and Vidal (1998 p.8) introduced the concepts of bonding and bridging SC. Bonding SC promotes trust and exchanges among a narrow circle of individuals and groups. It reinforces exclusive identities and homogeneous groups, whether ethnic, religious, tribal or racially based. The outcome is specific reciprocities and solidarities, which are important for the less fortunate members. Bonding SC is good for 'getting by' in life. It serves as a coping and risk management mechanism during deprivation and scarcity. However, because it is intra-group or inward looking, bonding SC can generate animosity against non-members, bar members from access to outside opportunities and resources, and deepen social cleavages and conflicts thus undermining development. The same bonds that include can also exclude. Associations and networks which foster bonding SC suffer from the absence of what Granovetter (1973) called 'weak ties' that link us to distant acquaintances who are able to move between groups' various social networks and therefore become transferors of various assets, information and ideas. Such 'weak ties' promote generalised, as opposed to specific, trust and reciprocities, and are seen by most political scientists as prerequisite for political stability and sustainable economic development (Francis 2002). While bonding SC is good for 'getting-by', bridging SC is good for 'getting ahead', and can thus enhance the poor's access to wider assets and resources than bonding SC, which creates 'strong ties' that link members to relatives and intimate friends who usually move in the same social circles and often have similar assets (Granovetter 1973).

More recently, Colletta and Cullen (2000) have explored a third form of SC, namely, linking SC.[5] Linking SC refers to the relationship between citizens and their formal institutions. More specifically, linking SC refers to ties people have with state officials who are in charge of decision-making processes and resource allocation. Linking SC can thus provide the poor and the needy with additional resources from the state, and, more importantly, with a political voice to represent their interests and needs. While bonding and bridging SC are usually at a micro level, linking SC takes place at a macro level, and reflects the degree of trust and confidence people have in their formal institutions and state officials. While exploring how bonding, bridging and linking social capital interact in situations of violent conflicts in Cambodia, Rwanda, Guatemala and Somalia, Colletta and Cullen (2000) found that unequal distribution of political power and resources can decrease trust among various (ethnic) groups, causing them to foster bonding SC and turn away from bridging social capital.

In reality, however, it is difficult neatly to classify associations and networks as ''either-or' categories' since some networks and associations 'bond along some intra-group social dimension and simultaneously bridge across others' (Putnam 2000 p.23). Each form of SC can affect political and economic development and poverty in different ways. In the same study cited above Colletta and Cullen (2000) concluded that the nature of bonding social capital is ambiguous: 'even if other forms of capital are replenished, economic and social development will be hindered unless social capital stocks are restored'. Similarly, while analysing the link between SC and religion in small Iowa communities in the US, Jan Curry (2003) found that only those communities which combined bridging SC with sufficient bonding SC were healthy communities exhibiting sustainable institutional, social and economic development. The key challenge therefore is in finding the right balance or 'mix' between these various forms of SC (NESF 2003 p.34).

To sum up the main point in this section, not all associations promote SC to the same extent or level. Nor do they foster civic culture, civic action and promote cooperation across communities to the same extent. Whether an association or social network promotes bonding, bridging or linking SC depends on the particular views, ideologies and resources of members. The relevance of various forms of SC itself depends on the historical, social, political, and cultural context within which groups, associations and social networks are embedded (Smidt 2003).

Islam and social capital

As a religion, Islam is 'poorly understood in America', just as American culture is poorly understood in the Arab World (Sachedina 2002 p.22). During a 1995 presentation at a conference on 'The Moral Economy of Islamism', Fred Lawson of Mills College argued that 'successful development requires a single-minded focus on growth' and that Islam's excessive focus on 'moral codes (perhaps social capital)' prohibits the achievement of this objective. Therefore, Islamic economic thought is flawed, he implied, because it 'does not offer any internally coherent and consistent theory of economics founded on reasonable assumptions about human behaviour', which must 'take human viciousness as given; we try to design institutions, to create "rules of the game", that assume that many of us most of the time and all of us some of the time will behave selfishly, perhaps even callously'.[6]

Although all major religions developed a moral theology that emphasises social justice, and collective responsibility for the welfare of others, Islam emphasised the significance of the socialisation process, along with peace, justice, social harmony and collective responsibility for the poor and needy perhaps more than any other religion. According to the Koran, justice is the main source of good governance. The call to address social justice and the needs of the poor is part of and goes hand in hand with personal redemption. To ignore them is to ignore the main thrust of the Islamic faith (Sachedina 2007a and 2007b). For example, the Koran, the primary source of Islamic law, 'uses the word 'justice' more than a thousand times', and 'repeatedly legitimises trade' (and, by extension, privatisation, deregulation and stabilisation) 'based on goodwill' and benefit to Muslim society (Richards and Waterbury 1996 p.351). While religion in the West is generally understood to refer to a set of beliefs or practices that spiritually link autonomous individuals to God, for Muslims religion is a way of life; it is 'a blueprint for an ideal society ... a blueprint that organises all aspects of social and political life', for nurturing a trusting and trustful society, with 'a universal mandate ... to create an ideal society on earth' (Sachedina 2002 p.23).

Islam's second primary source of law, the Shari'a, provides the paradigm of a civil religion. After defining the God-human relationship, interpersonal social transactions are the Shari'a's second major area of concern. 'This area of the law is known as *Mu'amalat* – that is, social transactions that must be conducted between individuals and groups, including the state, in keeping with the demands of justice in all areas of human existence' (Sachedina 2007b p.19). Almost every economic transaction, since it depends on the actions of and interaction with others, relies on trust resulting from interpersonal interactions. As the laureate, Arrow (1972 p.357), wrote:

> Virtually every commercial transaction has within itself an element of trust, certainly any transaction conducted over a period of time. It can be plausibly argued that much of the economic backwardness in the world can be explained by the lack of mutual confidence.

Moral and ethical societies, or trusting and trustful societies, to use some key terminologies employed by the SC literature, resort less to formal institutions to enforce agreements. Not only are litigations likely to be less frequent in such societies, but written contracts, as a result, will not be needed – nor do they have 'to specify every contingency that may arise between the parties; most presuppose a certain amount of goodwill that prevent the parties from taking advantage of unforeseen loopholes' (Fukuyama 2000 p.6). This is the core thesis of SC economic function discussed earlier. That is, to reduce transaction costs associated with formal coordination mechanisms, thus inducing individuals and entrepreneurs to focus more on innovation and productivity rather than worry about diverting a great deal of their resources to monitor, litigate, negotiate and enforce formal contracts with their agents and protect their property rights from their unlawful violations (Knack and Keefer 1997 p.1251-2).

Islam's excessive focus on morality and ethicality, or the creation of an 'ideal society', also has a political function. Trust has an accumulative effect. Being a compassionate and caring person increases the propensity of individuals and groups to join collective action, and involve themselves in more charities and voluntary undertakings. This generates SC by fostering interaction with other like-minded members of the society, and increases the likelihood that trust will be generated through interpersonal interactions. Over time, and as the society becomes more complex and modern, the accumulation of these forms of specific and interpersonal trusts among various members of society (through social networks and associations) become a 'form of generalised social trust', spilling over to trust in state officials and formal institutions (Smidt 2003 p.3). In trusting and trustful societies, government officials and institutions 'may be perceived as more trustworthy, and their policy pronouncements as thus being more credible ... trigger[ing] greater investment and other economic activity' (Knack and Keefer 1997 p.1253). This is also why there is a strong link between associations and SC on the one hand, and between civic life and liberal democracy on the other.

This has always been Islam's position, which views trust, harmony and social order as both necessary and sufficient conditions for economic and political development. They can only 'be achieved through the promotion of individual virtue – by individuals altering their behaviour to conform with Divine Revelation' (Fred Lawson in Richards and Waterbury 1996 pp.353-4). Islam's solution to the core problem of political economy, namely, scarcity, is not simply getting prices right and getting government out,[7] rather to correct individual virtue and alter selfish behaviour of individuals.

Islamic economic thought never really believed that growth alone is sufficient to achieve sustainable growth and development or to bring about a just and harmonious social order. Up until the mid-nineteenth century, the Islamic empire insisted on not separating public policies, including economic policies, from the state itself, or even accepting the principle of ceding the state's monetary policies to an independent state institution, to something equivalent to a central bank in modern times. Such a policy would be antithetical to poverty reduction, social harmony, and social justice. This is despite the fact that the Islamic tradition did empower human beings to create, regulate, and maintain all necessary human institutions to further human relationships (Sachedina 2001). Today, there is a consensus, even inside the IMF, World Bank and other official Washington institutions, that growth is important, but alone is insufficient (Stiglitz 2002).

The Mosque and the Brotherhood: background

Wuthnow (2003) argues that, to capture the full impact of religion on civic society, it is not enough to focus on voluntary associations and social networks alone without paying equal attention to the institutional role of religion. The mosque is one of the earliest and most enduring institutions in the Islamic faith: it is a 'lived tradition' which plays a significant role in Muslim society (Owen 1992 p.168). The mosque itself traditionally served several functions, including as a school or education centre, a clinic, training and playing ground, and simultaneously a place where members of local community gathered to study local problems and find collective solutions. The mosque always played a key role in social services provision to community members, and mosque or religious congregational life has always been a key component of associational life in every Muslim society.[8] What is new, however, about the role of the mosque in the modern era is the scale and extent of its involvement (through faith or Islamic-based organisations) in social welfare provisions and mechanisms of delivery.

The most enduring, powerful and influential Islamic faith-based organisation in the contemporary era is the Muslim Brotherhood Movement (MBM), which was established in 1928 in Egypt by a teacher-activist, Sheikh Hassan al-Banna. Al-Banna sought to protect Muslims from what he perceived as an increased threat from Western secularisation to the Muslim community following political and economic reforms (*Tanzimat*) introduced by the state (and Ottomans) in the second half of the nineteenth century. For most Western observers, the *Tanzimat* (which included new measures that called for the administration of courts by the Ministry of Justice rather than by the Sultan himself as had always been the case, and the introduction of Western commercial and penal codes) marked 'the beginning of the modern world as far as the practice of Islamic politics was concerned' because it made it 'possible to make the distinction between religion and the state' (Owen 1992 pp.169–70).[9]

The MBM was itself based on the notion of separating politics from religion. One of the MBM's primary objectives was to 'create protective umbrella institutions' to protect 'mercy acts' of religious organisations and to facilitate the practice of faith without political interferences (Owen 1992 p.170). Of course, the MBM was not the only faith-based organisation at the time of its creation. Many other faith-based organisations, some non-Islamic, also existed and were engaged in various 'mercy acts' and voluntary operations. But they were small, fragmented and decentralised. Al-Banna sought to centralise all Islamic organisations under the umbrella of one, dynamic national leadership guiding the activities of self-sustaining local neighboured groups geared to the aspirations and particular needs of their members and local community. In that endeavour, he succeeded tremendously and rapidly, not only in Egypt but also in the whole region. Indeed, the MBM's success in attracting followers was so impressive that it began to spread throughout the entire Arab World. By the end of the Second World War, or shortly thereafter, a branch of the MBM existed in almost every Arab country, including in Jordan.

Although the roots of most MBM's branches in the Arab World are linked to the Egyptian parent organisation, each Arab regime 'dealt differently with internal Islamist movements', and therefore 'each of these states developed its own model for handling Islamism' (Enhaili and Adda 2003 p.1). As a result, the experience of each Islamist movement not only varies 'between', but also 'within' countries and regions of the Arab World – Maghreb or Mashriq (Weitzman 1997 p.1). Each has its own contextual specificity, which must be studied and analysed separately.

The World Bank and faith-based welfare provision

In our analysis of the impact of globalisation and economic liberalisation on the MENA region we concentrate on the roles of the IMF and World Bank in their policy-based lending activities. One facet of the analysis has been the extent to which economic liberalisation has been accompanied by the growth of faith-based welfare provision, primarily Islamic welfare provision. In this section we attempt to explicitly draw these two strands of analysis together by exploring the attitude of the World Bank to faith-based welfare provision. We concentrate on the World Bank rather than the IMF because the latter is primarily concerned with macroeconomic variables in member countries, particularly the middle income countries such as most of those in the MENA region. There is little scope here for integrating faith-based welfare into the activities of the IMF. The World Bank on the other hand, is concerned with the broader process of development in middle income countries, including dimensions of social welfare and poverty. Given that faith-based groups can and do play an important role in social welfare provision and poverty alleviation, it would seem that there is considerable synergy between the Bank's mission and that of religious groups. However, our interviews with Bank staff, both in Washington DC and in our four countries of analysis, showed a surprising lack of awareness of the growing phenomenon of faith-based welfare provision and a reluctance to engage with it. This was also the case with many staff in other donor agencies that we spoke with. For example, in the field work in Egypt, one donor is quoted in the case study as saying:

> Donors don't want a dialogue with non-violent religious groups. There are limits to this as we have a different world view. European aid is secular at the

institutional level but Islam thinks secularism is wrong and donors don't understand Islamic welfare.

(Personal interview Cairo August 2005)

The 2004 World Bank publication *Mind, Heart, and Soul in the Fight Against Poverty* by Katherine Marshall and Lucy Keough (Marshall and Keough 2004) argues that although development institutions and faith-based institutions often share common goals of addressing poverty and social inequities they usually inhabit separate worlds:

> The worlds of faith and development might seem, at first glance, natural allies in efforts to combat poverty, to fight social injustice, and to improve the daily lives of the world's poor and marginalised people. The connections between these two worlds, however, have been fragile and intermittent at best, critical and confrontational at worst.

(Marshall and Keough 2004 p.1)

They argue that the relationship between faith and economic and social development is a topic that has received limited attention, despite the fact that faith-based welfare provision, especially in the fields of health and education, has a long history. They speculate that the traditional divisions of state and religion, especially in the areas of public policy, has spilt over into development institutions such as the World Bank, which by mandate must work through member states:

> The result is that the world of religion has been largely unacknowledged and often unseen among many development practitioners, both in writing and on the ground.

(Ibid. p.2)

Another factor which helps explain this separation of the two worlds of faith and development and the relative neglect of the former by the latter, is that for many religious groups, the provision of social welfare and help for the needy is something that is done for God, and as such is not heavily publicised. This is particularly so in the Islamic tradition, where the saying goes that 'the right hand should not know what the left hand is doing'. One negative upshot of this is that there has been limited evaluation of faith-based welfare provision. Although anecdotal evidence from the benificaries of faith-based welfare of various kinds often suggests that it is provided efficiently and honestly, there are few formal evaluations to back up this claim.

The World Bank is not a homogeneous institution and one would expect to find different views on faith-based welfare provision within the Bank. Engagement with faith-based welfare varies by country and by region and is often a reflection of different personalities and beliefs amongst Bank staff. However, historically, from an institutional perspective, the Bank has been fairly oblivious to, and uneasy with, faith-based welfare provision. This is reflected in the fact that World Bank publications seldom address the role of faith-based institutions in the development process or draw lessons from their experience. This is also true of most other multi-lateral and bi-lateral development organisations. This changed to some extent under the World Bank Presidency of James Wolfensohn, who attempted to tackle the subject of faith and development and its implications for the Bank in a very public manner. In 1998 Wolfensohn initiated a development dialogue with faith groups in a meeting chaired by himself and the Archbishop of Canterbury, George Carey. Central to the discussion was what was meant by 'poverty'. From this meeting emerged a sense of common goals in working with the poor, a greater awareness of the different views on poverty and development both between and within faiths, and a consensus that faith and development was a topic which required more dialogue. The meeting also gave birth to a movement known as the World Faiths Development Dialogue (WFDD) based in Canterbury, UK, with Wolfensohn and Carey as its founders. The WFDD aims to facilitate a dialogue on poverty and development among people from different religions and between them and the international development institutions.

Within the Bank this agenda was taken forward by the Development Dialogue on Values and Ethics, a unit within the Human Development Network Vice-Presidency. The unit is primarily responsible for engaging with faith institutions around development issues and working with other institutions and leaders who are addressing ethical issues around globalisation. Wolfensohn's initiatives were regarded by many in the Bank as controversial and the Board of Directors expressed some unease at the Presidential dialogue with religious leaders. Nevertheless, as an input to the 2000 World Bank's World Development Report on the topic of poverty the WFDD made a concerted effort to consult with representatives of the major faiths on the topic of poverty and their assessment of the World Bank's activities in this area (WFDD 1999).

However, despite Wolfensohn's initiative their remains a tendency within the Bank not to regard faith-based groups as part of civil society, even though in many countries, especially in the Arab world, they dwarf the rest of civil society. Under the subsequent Presidency of Paul Wolfowitz, the faith and development initiative at the World Bank is withering. The current President has not articulated a position on faith and development and although he has occasionally expressed an interest in moderate Islam, this has not resulted in any institutional initiatives.

Several other multi-lateral development institutions have, like the World Bank under Wolfensohn, had limited engagement with the topic of faith and development. Perhaps the best example is the Initiative on Social Capital, Ethics and Development launched by the Inter-American Development Bank (IDB) in 1999 in collaboration with its member states and the government of Norway. This took the form of a series of consultations with leaders of different faith traditions and the IDB President, Enrique Iglesias, and staff focusing on social capital and ethics. As a result faith leaders are now represented in most of the IDB dialogue at country and regional levels giving them the opportunity to voice their views on development issues and the work of the IDB. The IDB has also extended specific support to a number of faith-based communities in the region. Similarly, the International Labour Organisation (ILO) launched a dialogue with the World Council of Churches (WCC) in 2002 to address the meaning and issues of 'decent work' which places human dignity as central to work (Peccoud 2004).

All of the above initiatives, including that of the World Bank, are largely ad hoc and do not represent a full integration of faith-based initiatives into the institutions in question. This is despite the fact that where faith-based and development institutions have worked together for the common aims of poverty reduction and welfare enhancement 'remarkable results have been achieved' (Marshall and Keough 2004 p.xii). The book by Marshall and Keough published by the World Bank documents case studies of instances where faith-based organisations have teamed up with institutions from other realms and sectors to fight poverty and improve the lives of poor communities. Interestingly however, there are no examples taken from the Arab world and only a limited number of examples involving Islamic groups from other regions of the world. The latter include the initiative by the Aga Khan Foundation and local Islamic communities to promote early childhood learning through Madrasas throughout East Africa via the Madrasa Early Childhood Programme; the leading role played by the Islamic Medical Association of Uganda in education and community action concerning HIV/AIDS; and the role of Islamic groups in contributing to the work of the World Bank funded Social Fund for the development of the conflict torn southern regions of the Philippines.

The lack of World Bank engagement and documentation of the welfare work of Islamic groups in the Arab World, which we will show to be both significant and growing, can perhaps be explained by two facts. Firstly, unlike low income countries, the predominantly middle income countries of the MENA region are not required by the Bank and the IMF to draw up Poverty Reduction Strategy Papers (PRSPs) in consultation with civil society. This means that there is no natural avenue through which civil society, including faith-based groups, can participate in a country's development dialogue. Secondly, both the IMF and World Bank, along with many other international development institutions, have a governance structure that revolves around governments as both shareholders and governors. This means that their approach to civil society often has to mirror that of the member government in question. As we show in our case studies in this book, many Arab governments are hostile to Islamic groups providing welfare and do not treat them as full members of civic society to be supported and encouraged. The relative neglect of faith-based welfare in the Arab world by the World Bank can thus be explained by the fact that it is mirroring the attitude of incumbent regimes in the region. This is unfortunate as we have shown that religious components of civil society in the MENA region have a potentially important role to play in providing social welfare and social capital.

3

'You Reap What You Plant': The Historical Evolution of Social Networks in Jordan

Introduction

During the past 15 years, the Hashemite Kingdom of Jordan (hereafter referred to as Jordan) has experienced an increase in poverty, inequality, and unemployment; volatile economic growth and low productivity; a significant increase in nepotism and corruption in public institutions; a rise in the rate of crime and civil violence; and pervasive lack of trust not only between citizens themselves but also between them and their formal institutions. This lack of general trust, 'a central element of social cohesion, or social capital' (World Bank 2002a p.iii), is one of the main constraints to sustainable economic growth and development in Jordan. It is also potentially threatening to the country's social cohesion and political stability.

This chapter contributes to the growing body of literature on social capital by focusing on the role of public policy and other main factors that affect the level, type, and nature of SC observed in a society, an area where 'efforts have been successful only to a very limited degree' (Grootaert and Bastelaer 2002a p.77). It thus attempts to answer questions that still loom high in the literature on SC: 'where does social capital come from and how might public policy affect it?' (Miguel 2003 p.196).

Jordan has been chosen as a case study in order to fill a gap in the existing literature, namely the fact that 'the concept of social capital has been little used explicitly in the Middle East Region' (Francis, 2002 p.8). Not unlike other Muslim societies of the region, Jordan is a country traditionally vibrant with social networks that operate on the basis of trust and reciprocity. As Singerman (1997 pp.xi, 4 and 49) noted in her work on the region, social capital or 'Informal networks and informal institutions' remain particularly vibrant and effective 'avenues of participation ... [in] Muslim societies ... [with] political import and aggregate power for collective benefit.' In their work on Middle Eastern societies, Cunningham and Sarayrah (1993 p.1) also concluded that informal and social networks remain a major 'force in Middle Eastern societies', determining most economic and political outcomes. Hence, this chapter makes a useful contribution to the literature on social capital by analysing a country in a region of the world where there is sparse literature that examines how social capital can explain social, economic, and political outcomes. Jordan is also usually cited by the international financial institutions, particularly the International Monetary Fund (IMF) and World Bank, as a star-plus student, a showcase of reform and globalisation (Harrigan El-Said and Wang 2006). Yet it is a country experiencing increasing levels of inequality and poverty to a point where more than a third of the population today live below the poverty line. Jordan therefore provides an interesting case to study factors that affect SC and how the latter affects and is affected by social and economic factors.

This chapter argues that public policy and general political and economic conditions are crucial factors affecting the level and nature of SC in a country. Abrupt market reform and increased poverty can force the poor to withdraw from vibrant social networks that provide important opportunities and resources. We will argue that this plus public policy, influenced by the demands of local nationalists particularly after the 1971 civil war, played a significant role in undermining cross-cutting ties in Jordan, thus weakening general trust, contributing to increased poverty, social and economic polarisation, and political instability.

Theoretical framework

The focal point of the theory of SC[10] is that 'social networks', which provide important assets and resources to their members, 'have value' that tend to improve productivity of both individuals and groups in similar ways to physical capital and human capital (Putnam 2000 pp.18–9). Just as a tractor (physical capital) and a training course or years of experience (human capital) can yield more output (both individual and collective), so too social contacts affect individual and collective productivity.

While contentious debate remains over whether SC can be called capital,[11] very few doubt its value and importance, and all agree that SC is 'relationale' (Narayan 1999 p.20), and 'truly social' (Grootaert and Bastelaer 2002a p.70). Put differently, the existence of networks and associations is necessary for the creation of SC. The World Bank defines SC as 'institutions, relationships, attitudes, and values that govern interactions among people and contribute to economic and social development' (Francis 2002 p.5). These interactions can affect economic and social development, including poverty reduction, in several ways (Grootaert and Bastelaer 2002a pp.8–9). For example, social networks create and also reduce the cost of accessing important information that directly and indirectly affect the welfare of individuals and groups. Such information can relate to jobs, contracts, inputs or suppliers and prices, location of new markets and new technologies, sources of credit, or treatment for diseases. A wide range of studies have empirically supported this argument by emphasising the role of social networks in facilitating access to such vital information.[12]

At a community level, mutual trust and reciprocity are of primary importance particularly in countries and communities where property rights are weakly developed or enforced, as is the case in Jordan and most other Arab Middle Eastern states (El-Said and McDonald 2002). Knack and Keefer (1997 p.1260) argue that the impact of social capital or trust on growth should be higher in countries with weak property rights, especially 'if trust is more essential where contracts are not reliably enforced by the legal system, and where access to formal sources of credit is more limited due to an underdeveloped financial sector'. Under these circumstances, mutual trust and reciprocity can facilitate both collective decision and action for public benefit. Examples include mobilisation to effectively manage common resources and maximising their yield. Kahkonen (2002) shows how SC was used by local communities to build consensus on the design, construction, and maintenance of complex rural drinking water delivery, urban sanitation, and agricultural irrigation in several developing countries.

Similar findings were noticed in a recent assessment of an 11-year poverty alleviation project in rural Jordan, carried out jointly by the German Technical Cooperation Agency (GTZ) and the Ministry of Agriculture: 'Project experience showed that with the mobilisation of self-help efforts remarkable results can be achieved.' The assessment also concluded that an approach based on local level participation, ownership, and strengthening of self-help efforts can improve performance of local organisations and networks (*Jordan Times* 2006a). This improvement in performance stems from sensitivity to local conditions and ability of SC to balance conflicting delicate interests between various individuals and groups (Ostrom 1999).

However, SC alone does not ensure better performance in economic and social outcomes. A host of other factors, including in particular the degree of group and community homogeneity, government actions, and the overall governance structure and environment, 'have been shown to have a critical bearing on the performance of collective action' (Kahkonen 2002 p.266). In fact, the broad definition of SC used in this chapter serves to bring the concept of SC into the purview of New Institutional Economics (NIE). The latter posits that the strength or weakness of community networks are primarily determined by the incentives provided by the political, legal, and formal institutional environment that sets the rules of the game (North 1990). Modern states, like modern societies, are heterogeneous. They differ in their effectiveness, performance, regime type, and capacity to influence their societies and communities (Migdal, 1988). SC develops under all types of states. But weak, hostile, corrupt states that restrict associational life have a profoundly different impact on community life and development projects than states that are transparent, fight corruption, uphold the rule of law, honour contracts, have fair and independent judiciary, promote associational life, and respect civil liberties. The former, by restricting associational life and not providing legal recognition for civil society organisations, undermine the SC of their communities. They also undermine their own accountability and credibility by preventing the emergence of vibrant civic society that demands transparency, better governance structure, and monitors the actions of state officials and therefore helps in reducing corrupt behaviour (Narayan 1999). As Knack and Keefer (1997 p.1252) observed, social capital dimensions, particularly trust and civic cooperation, are not only associated with stronger economic performance, but they are also stronger in and encouraged by states 'with formal institutions that effectively protect property and contract rights', monitor and constrain arbitrary policies and activities of state officials, 'and in countries that are less polarised along lines of class or ethnicity'.

In other words, SC and the state can complement each other. Local development programmes and projects were found to have a much higher rate of success in well-functioning central governments (Grootaert and Bastelaer 2002a p.4). The outcome of SC is found to be more effective and beneficial in countries that enjoy good governance (Putnam 2000). Governments that make information about jobs and its own actions available to citizens, establish educational systems and values that promote mutual respect and tolerance, create inclusive political systems, and encourage associational life can enhance the quantity and quality of interaction of local networks and reduce further transaction costs. These states have also proven to have more social cohesion, political stability, sustainable growth, and higher welfare indicators enjoyed by their citizens (World Bank 2002a, Kuehnast and Dudwick 2004, Narayan 1999, NESF 2003). Fafchamps (2006 pp.1187, 1191 and 1196) has recently summarised the relationship between SC and state in the following words:

> Depending on the context, social capital can either complement or substitute for formal institutions ... without some form of voluntary acceptance by the public, government efforts to provide public goods are likely to fail. Social capital is thus probably essential for public good delivery... If the state is broken, why not fix it ... Investing in social capital should be seen as a complement to investing in government capacity. The two cannot and should not be separated.

Because formal institutions are legally recognised and rule bound, while informal institutions have no legal status and are characterised by face-to-face relationships (for example, ethnic, kinship, clan, familial, friends, or tribal networks), the initial NIE literature tended to focus mostly on the former at the expense of the latter. While this literature provides graphic details on how the state can shape social interactions and networks, little is known about how societies and communities can also shape the state (Migdal 1988, Kuehnast and Dudwick 2004 p.9). O'Donnell's work (1993) shows how social relations, norms, and informal networks explain the performance of very different regimes in Latin America. Similar work has recently been focusing on the Middle East region, where informal networks remain vibrant despite market-led reforms (Cunningham and Sarayrah 1993, Fukayama 1995, Al-Braizat 2002, El-Said 1996, UNDP 2004a). In fact, much of the appeal of the SC concept comes from its capacity to bring-in and reflect the importance of the informal/normative aspects (Fafchamps, 2006, p.1182). This provides a unique opportunity to focus on both formal and informal institutions, and how they interact to shape and be shaped by one another (Grootaert and Bastelaer 2002a p.3, Ghecham 2005).

The SC framework in general is also accredited with enhancing our understanding not only of the positive effects of SC, but also of its negative and less beneficial ones.[13] To capture these effects, Gittell and Vidal (1998 p.8) introduced the concepts of bonding and bridging SC as discussed in Chapter 2. We have argued in that chapter that bonding SC can be associated with negative consequences, such as restricting access to resources and opportunities, restriction of individual freedom, excessive claims on successful group members, and the emergence of powerful, tightly knit social groups that are not accountable to society and who can capture state institutions, use them to further their own interests, and practice corruption, nepotism and cronyism. Hence, Narayan (1999 p.12) argues that:

> For societal well being or the collective good, a transition has to occur from exclusive loyalty to primary social groups to networks of secondary associations whose most important characteristics is that they bring together people who in some ways are different from the self.'

It is within this framework that the issue of group homogeneity gains special interest. The empirical evidence on the impact of social heterogeneity on SC and networks is 'mixed' (Kahkonen 2002 p.290, Krishna and Shrader 2002 p.21). What is evidenced however is that while homogeneity makes it easier to share and exchange information, facilitates trust and collective action among specific groups, homogeneous groups may have similar information and limited resources. Because they provide access to a larger pool of information, opportunities, and resources, heterogeneous groups and networks 'yield higher level of benefits', are better at pooling risks, and can therefore provide better mechanisms to cope with social and economic risks and crises (Grootaert et al 2004 p.11). In fact, SC, particularly bridging SC that is promoted via generalised trust in government institutions as well as interpersonal trust mobilised via clubs and networks, is among 'fundamental determinants' of social cohesion and political stability in heterogeneous societies (Fafchamps 2006 p.1182, Fukayama, 1995).

To sum up, the main issue here is not one of an 'either/or' form of SC (Putnam 2000 p.23). Both are important and serve different objectives. Bonding SC is crucial for reducing personal vulnerability, while bridging SC is important for empowerment, social cohesion, and political stability. The main aim of this chapter is to trace developments in these two particular types of social capital in Jordan (bonding and bridging), and to shed some light on the factors that can affect their evolution, nature and extent in a country. There is a consensus today among observers and scholars that while both bonding and bridging social capital are important and provide different benefits to members, too much bonding social capital, or specific trust placed in limited groups based on kinship, ethnic, or special interest ties will have potentially large negative consequences on economic performance, social cohesion and political stability. This type of organisation will facilitate rent-seeking activities among members and lead, especially under high poverty and scarcity, to violent distributional conflicts (see Knack and Keefer 1997). The key challenge therefore is in finding the right balance or 'mix' between bondingness and bridgingness (NESF 2003 p.34), a balance which has gone drastically wrong in post-1971 Jordan.

Measuring social capital

SC is not easy to measure. It is local and culture-specific, and therefore its assessment is usually beset by data difficulties on the nature of local associations and networks (Grootaert and Bastelaer 2002). Intensive efforts have been underway to develop measures of SC, with World Bank staff being at the front of these efforts. This has led to the emergence of a general agreement on some important dimensions to evaluate SC. Many of these dimensions were tested both qualitatively and quantitatively across countries and were found to have positive and significant correlations in most cases. The following were found to be the most common and frequent dimensions of SC across societies: satisfaction with life; formal and informal associations and membership in and quality of participation in local community; generalised norms of trust and reciprocity; political engagement and perception of government institutions; communications (including variables related to media and proximity variables), everyday sociability; family, friends and neighbourhood connections; and the level of safety and crime in a country[14] (Narayan and Cassidy 2001, Narayan 1999, Grootaert and Bastelaer 2002, Dasgupta and Serageldine 1999, Putnam et al 1993, Putnam 2000, Knack and Keefer 1997).

Several questions have also generally been employed to assess these various dimensions of SC in a society. For example, the question used to assess satisfaction with life is, 'How happy are you in life?'; to assess the level of trust in a society, 'Generally speaking, would you say that most people can be trusted?'; to assess membership in formal or informal associations, 'Are you … a member of any groups, organisations, or associations?'; to assess the level and perception of trust in state officials and institutions; 'Do you trust state officials?', 'Police and security?' (see the 'Social Capital Assessment Tool' in Grootaert and Bastelaer 2002a, and Knack and Kefeer 1997). Such questions have been found to be helpful in gauging and generating useful information to assess the level and nature of SC in a society. Putnam's seminal work on SC (1995 and 2000) relied heavily on such measures as membership in voluntary associations, voting and how generally people feel about their lives.

Unfortunately, time and financial constraints prevented the authors themselves from generating data on the main dimensions of SC cited above in Jordan. However, some of these data are now available as a result of several surveys and polls carried out recently, and in some cases regularly, by independent sources in Jordan.We rely overwhelmingly on these sources in our attempt to provide some assessment of the recent developments in the level and extent of SC in Jordan.

Social networks in Jordan during the rre-independence period

Informal social-based networks and relationships – in the form of family, kinship, and clan – have always played an important role in Jordan's social life. Although the region saw several empires come and go, including the Greek, Roman, Byzantine, and Ottoman, these powers showed interest in, and extended influence only to those rain-fed cultivated areas that could be taxed more easily. Nomad tribes were kept independent of central authority. To lessen tribal raids on settled areas and main trade routes, heads of tribes (*shaykhs*) were paid a tribute (*surrah*) by foreign powers (Gubser 1973, Peake 1958, Cunningham and Sarayrah 1993). Tribal values of family and social solidarity were reinforced by Islam's strong emphasis on the significance of family, social solidarity (*takaful al ijtima'i*) and mutual assistance. They thus remained a powerful social force even after these powers departed.

Today this social network-based system is referred to in Jordan, and the wider Middle East, as *wasta*, and it remains in the present day an important feature of social, economic, and political life of modern Jordan just as it was decades ago. *Wasta* exemplifies the personalised approach to social and political life. It literally means 'to employ a middle man, a broker, a go-between or an intermediary – usually a person of high social status and accepted rank – to achieve one's ends' (Fathi 1993 p.61). In modern language, *wasta* means a connection or influence.

People resorted to *wasta* as a mechanism to solve local and community disputes, facilitate the management of common scarce resources, and for negotiation with and intercession in dealings with central authorities under the Romans, Byzantines,[15] and Ottomans. Under the British rule between 1921 and 1946, several factors reinforced *wasta* at both the macro (state) and micro (society) levels. At the state level, the new ruler of the country, Prince Abdullah, sought advice from tribal leaders on the educational and skill levels as well as qualifications of their tribe members. Literate tribe members were used to staff his nascent administration. These new officials became an important source of influence and connection for their families and tribes inside the state apparatus, interceding on their behalf for state benefits, like jobs, public services, and infrastructure (Cunningham and Sarayrah 1993 Chapter 1).

At the society level, the tribes, who remained suspicious of the British-backed central authorities, kept the formal governmental system out of their affairs. They continued to solve their disputes and manage their common resources informally and through traditional social customs and norms (Braizat 1998). This was reinforced, especially in rural areas, by the inherited Ottoman *mushi* system of collectively-owned land. The *mushi* ensured that members of the same family and kin lived and worked together, thus facilitating cooperation and maintaining the durability of family ties and social networks[16] (Amadouny 1994). Such ties provided important psychological assistance, political security, and social and economic resources and benefits to members such that it was difficult to 'imagine living in a different land' or place without such forms of social ties:

> [Social and] Tribal affiliation is the source of safety and, conversely, expulsion from the tribe for some grievous offence is the gravest sentence. Law and morality are also defined in tribal terms … I will never leave this country because I will not think of becoming a foreigner to my tribe and their camp … having to travel far from one's country and relatives and friends is a curse that descends from the forefathers to the child.
>
> (Lerner 1958 pp.318 and 319).

Through *wasta*, local citizens not only bonded together along social and geographic lines (same tribe, clan, region or people of the same background), but also simultaneously bridged others. Members of certain clans, tribes or regions resorted to *wasta* to intermarry with clans and tribes, solve disputes, and even to build alliances and social and economic networks with other, more differentiated groups. *Wasta* thus helped people to cope with the harsh conditions of the desert environment and scarce resources.[17] It also substituted for the lack of a formal welfare system, thus playing an important informal social safety net role (Cunningham and Sarayrah 1993).

Norms of reciprocity play an important role in *wasta*. This reciprocity was not based on an immediate tit-for-tat exchange between the beneficiary and provider of *wasta* ('I'll do this for you only if you do that for me'). Rather, it was based on the expectation that either the beneficiary himself or one member of his family would one day return the favour. Cunningham and Sarayrah (1993 p.8) captured this definition of reciprocity in their description for a *wasta* performer in a common accident or conflict resolution in Jordan:

> Today I or one of my relatives is the victim; tomorrow, or a year from now, we may become the defendant. If we do not show forgiveness, mercy and tolerance to others in their difficult times, we will not be shown tolerance by others when we are in distress. [Hence the popular] Arabic saying, 'You reap what you plant'.

Although the components of a *wasta*-based settlement include an important gift giving and exchange element, the latter was not based on material rewards. It was considered *ayeb* (shameful) to demand and accept material rewards for helping others (Gubser 1973 p.37). Respect from the community was the highest reward sought by a *wasta* performer, mainly from tribal *shaykhs* and notables. Success in solving a conflict led to mutual praise and enhanced the popularity and social and political status of the whole tribe. Mediating and interceding on behalf of others was thus essential to Jordan's social identity (Fathi 1993).

Transjordan, compared with its neighbours (Palestine, Syria, Lebanon, and Iraq), enjoyed tremendous political stability and economic prosperity. This was partly caused by centralisation and security extended first by the Ottomans during the last four decades of the nineteenth century and continued under the British Administration between 1921 and 146 (Rogan and Tell 1994; Robins 2004, Braizat 1998). Social capital also played an important role in Transjordan's enhanced political stability, economic prosperity and social cohesion. A survey conducted by Lerner in the late 1940s and early 1950s (Lerner 1958 p.328) showed that the majority of the population 'described themselves as very happy' with their lives.

Even before the outbreak of the 1948 war, Transjordan's political stability and economic prosperity began to attract a relatively large number of immigrants from neighbouring states, particularly Syria, Palestine, and Lebanon. *Wasta* facilitated their integration into the Transjordanian society (Amawi 1994; El-Said 1996, Gubser 1973, Mackenzie,1946). But immigration into Jordan vastly increased after the war of 1948, bringing tens of thousands of Palestinian refugees into an overwhelmingly tribal society. Since wasta was, and still is, a shared concept operating throughout the entire Arab region (Cunningham and Sarayrah 1993), the political and economic environments that prevailed in the 1950s and 1960s allowed for bridging SC to form quickly between Transjordanians and their new Palestinian guests.

Social capital and population movement: the 1950s and 1960s

Following the 1948 war against Israel, more than 820,000 Palestinians were forced to leave their homeland, 320,000 of whom stayed in the West Bank as refugees, 210,000 in the Gaza Strip, 180,000 went to other Arab sates while 100,000 came to the newly-independent Hashemite Kingdom of Jordan (Zureik 1996 pp.2–12). In 1951, King Abdullah I formally annexed the West Bank to Jordan and gave all Palestinians Jordanian citizenship, hitherto the only Arab leader to do so in the region.

For most observers, the 1950s, and to a lesser extent 1960s were decades of political turmoil, unrest, and tension between state and society in Jordan (see, for example, Robins 2004, Lerner 1958, Joffee 2002, Dallas 1999, Piro 1998, Brand 1994). This focus on the political was at the expense of the social. Little attention has been paid to the equally important issue of intercommunal relationships, particularly the relationship between 'Palestinians-Transjordanians [which] remain largely unexplored, except, to a limited extent, as a direct function of the PLO-Jordanian relations' in the Post-1971 period (Brand 1995 p.46).

Although the first few years of the late King Hussein's reign, specifically the period between 1953 and 1957 'was an extremely unstable time for Jordan politically ... during the 1950s and 1960s Jordan experienced sustained growth in its gross domestic product of about 8 per cent per annum' (Piro, 1998, p.30).[18] Notwithstanding economic factors (including labour migration to the Gulf, ensuing increase in remittances, and surge in US grants to Jordan), social capital had also contributed to Jordan's prosperity and even political stability after 1957.

It is unquestionable that the period between 1953–7 was characterised by political tension and unrest, culminating in the regime's decision to ban all political parties, dissolve the parliament, and even to impose martial law in 1957. But this was not regarded as 'communal tensions' (CERMOC 1997 p.111).

Rather, it reflected many Jordanians' dissatisfaction with their then young King's foreign policies, and was instigated chiefly by external and regional factors[19] (Dallas 1999, Richards and Waterbury 1996, Snow 1972). In fact, some observers, like Uriel Dann (1989), for example, argued that there was little evidence that the Palestinians played any role in the street demonstrations and riots of that period.

Following the formal annexation of the two Banks of the River Jordan in 1951, Jordan became a state with two countries. The newly-annexed West Bank was much more naturally endowed than the East Bank. Whether a citizen saw him/herself as a Palestinian or a Jordanian did not really matter. To a large extent, the regime itself followed a more or less balanced political approach: 'The state's goal was less to impose on Palestinians a Transjordanian identity than to create a hybrid Jordanian identity for both communities' (Brand 1995 p.50). This was also reflected in the cabinet as well, which was 'well balanced: every region was represented; half the ministers were from the East Bank and half from the West Bank; there were two Christians and one Circassian' (Dallas 1999 p.47).

In a recent analysis for the Zimbabwean villagers who resettled in new areas, Abigail Barr (2002) noticed that, when faced with low stocks of traditional kin-based social capital, resettled villagers use their resettlement in new areas to build social networks and stock of social capital with their new neighbours. They do this by encouraging themselves and their offspring to intermarry and form civil associations in their new environment: 'Intermarriages facilitate informal insurance, while the emergent civil society provides an environment within which trust can develop' (ibid. p.2). This analysis is consistent with the resettlement experience of Palestinian influx in Jordan during the 1950s and 1960s.

Seeking a fresh start, the new immigrants immediately began a process of building new stocks of social capital in their new environment, and became cooperative and socially and economically active. They immediately began the process of building trust, informal insurances, and a stock of SC through intermarriages and participation in civil society organisations. The latter was facilitated by the new 1951 constitution which boosted, albeit temporarily until 1957, political freedom and right to associate, leading to a proliferation of political parties and other civic associations that had been well documented elsewhere (see El-Said 1996, Joffe 2002, Richards and Waterbury 1996, Dann 1984, Satloff 1994, Vatikiotis 1967, Wilson 1987). While analysing the Jordanian-Palestinian relationship in this period, Brand (1995 p.50) concluded that 'Not surprisingly, intermarriage between Palestinians and Transjordanians ... [was] more common than previously' expected.

The immigrants, although mostly refugees, brought with them new skills, experiences, and above all, a lot of capital. According to Piro (1998 p.28), the influx of Palestinians brought more than 20 million Palestinian pounds, which exceeded, by far, the total money supply in Jordan at the time. This was invested locally in new, small industry, real estate, and services. Many large Palestinian businesses, including the giant Arab Bank, relocated to Amman (Robins 2004 p.84). The result was a remarkable building and business boom.

The international community also assumed its responsibilities. UNRWA (United Nations Relief and Works Agency) was established in late 1949 and created four main camps[20] to provide international relief efforts and address the needs of the refugees. It provided basic services and staples, including health, education, and food therefore enabling the refugees to better cope with the trauma of dispossession and easing the pressure on the state's limited resources. UNRWA's efforts were supported by a rising level of international grants to Jordan, thus enabling the government to better cope with the large influx of refugees (Al-Jumrid 2000). The government was even encouraged to establish the Ministry of Refugees and the Ministry of Welfare in 1949 and 1951, respectively, to deal with the economic hardship of the refugees and to provide a formal safety net and protection to the Jordanian population as a whole (Mishal 1978).

High growth rates, availability of jobs at home and abroad,[21] and the prevalence of an egalitarian social stratification led people to bridge communal or specific social dimensions. *Wasta* played an important role in allowing bridging SC to form very quickly between Jordanians and their Palestinian guests. Both communities resorted to *wasta* in order to cope with the pressures of daily life in an environment characterised by general scarcity. For example, through *wasta* a large number of Palestinians managed to acquire important jobs in civil administration and expanding public sector enterprises (Fathi 1993). Palestinians also established strong business and social networks with Jordanians, where *wasta* also played an important role in facilitating the choice of business partners and even labours. Supported by a strong feeling of Arab identity and nationalism atypical of the 1950s and 1960s, Jordanians and Palestinians perceived their predicaments as one. They thus borrowed money from one another, and jointly worked in bureaucracy and public administration. Asking favours from each other was common, and was not considered shameful or a source of embarrassment. Availability of jobs meant stable incomes, a fact which not only encouraged groups and individuals to ask for favours from one another whenever the need arose, but also allowed recipients to repay in kind in the future. Day (1986 p.64) noted that these networks were also reinforced and cemented by a rising number of intermarriages between the two communities.

Jordanians then sympathised tremendously with the plights of their new guests. The establishment of UNRWA and the Ministry of Refugees was seen not only as necessity by most Jordanians, but also became a symbol of unity and support, not jealously and envy. According to Abu-Odeh (1999), the 1951 formal unification of the East and West Banks was accompanied by the emergence of an informal alliance between the Palestinians and Jordanians; they 'worked voluntarily together ... Their ideology and programs were cross-communal, helping to unite the two peoples [leading to] unofficial routes toward integration-namely, the socio-economic and political paths [which] went unscathed.'

Even when the late King Hussein took a decision in 1957 to ban all political parties and impose martial law, he was encouraged – even urged – to do so by many members of the Palestinian business community and conservative landed élite who felt threatened by the proliferation of communist and socialist-Ba'athist ideologies calling, among other things, for the redistribution of wealth (Singh 2002). It was hardly surprising therefore that the more business and professionally oriented (then also pro-regime) civil organisations, particularly the Muslim Brotherhood Movement and the Professional Associations, (themselves established by Jordan's early immigrant's community in the pre-independence period and with overwhelming membership from Palestinians), were the only movements to survive the ban (Friedrich-Ebert-Stiftung 1997, Singh 2002, p.76).

After 1957, prominent members of the Palestinian community focused their efforts on 'stav[ing] off a vibrant Palestinian nationalist movement against the Hashemite rule' (Piro 1998 p.29). They established, sometimes in their own private houses and properties, important, informal civic institutions and networks to replace the undermined formal institutional networks. Such institutions, which became popular in Jordan as *al-jam'iate* (societies) or '*diwans*' (Al-Oudat 1999 p.44), met regularly and brought together members from both communities (Jordanian and Palestinian) to discuss, debate, and provide solutions to daily and common problems. Their efforts 'moderated beyond recognition' the political environment of the 1950s, and were largely responsible for promoting political stability in the post-1957 era, albeit temporarily (Singh 202 p.77).

In sum, strong bridging social capital developed in Jordan during this period and was associated with economic growth and political stability, particularly after 1957. But this was to be severely undermined by the activities of Palestinian guerrillas between 1966–9 that terminated in a civil war in 1970–1, and was further undermined by the ensuing state policies.

Planting the seeds of discord: post-civil war reconstruction – 1971–89

Prior to the 1967 war, the Jordanian regime could still take pride in having managed to keep the West Bank, Jerusalem and other religious sites in Arab hands. But the 1967 war with Israel dealt a 'death blow' to this claim, as well as to the country's economy (Salibi 1998 p.222). The war deprived the country not only of its most fertile land, but also its most developed sector and foreign exchange earner, namely, tourism. As the late King Hussein put it: 'the loss of the West Bank endangered Jordan's very existence' (Braizat 1998 p.131).

The war also brought another large wave (400,000) of displaced Palestinians, thus severely straining the country's limited natural resources and infrastructure (World Bank 2004a p.1). The creation of the Palestinian Liberation Organisation (PLO) in 1964, with the aim of librating all of Palestine from Israeli occupation through armed struggle, ushered in a new era of tense societal relations between Jordanian and Palestinian communities and meant the inevitable destabilisation of Jordan's political regime. The PLO relied on a network of individuals and groups bound together by a common ideology and norms of reciprocity to achieve its goals. To this end, their guerrillas resorted to unpopular tactics, including kidnapping, plane hijackings, rule and regulation bypassing, and executing insignificant military operations against Israeli targets that led to harsh and disproportional Israeli reprisals against Jordanian towns and villages. The situation culminated in an armed civil conflict in 1970–1 between the Jordanian armed forces and Palestinian guerrillas that resulted in the ousting of guerrillas and their sympathisers to Lebanon in 1971.

SC is increasingly recognised as an essential element of peace-building and post-war (including civil war) reconstruction (World Bank 2002a). Under these circumstances, special mechanisms and processes are needed to promote tolerance and reconciliation among former warring groups and individuals. Building a new consensus requires improvement in governance structure, clean and efficient bureaucracy, fair and effective courts and judicial system. It also requires effectual mass media and an educational system that endorses mutual trust, provide support needed to heal wounds and increase the probability of social connectivity by re-knitting social fabric. All of this calls for and can be facilitated by political competition and liberalisation to support associational life, and to provide equal access to state facilities, services, resources, and opportunities (Narayan 1999, pp.10 and 36). This did not occur in Jordan.

To be sure, the armed conflict itself did not cause 'cracks in the Jordanian-Palestinian relationship at community level;' the SC that had developed between the two communities during the earlier period protected and facilitated 'their continued co-existence'.[22] Nevertheless, the activities of the guerrillas and the ensuing conflict created a psychological rift between the two communities, and 'awakened, for the first time, a strong and vocal patriotism among the many Jordanians who remained loyal to the Hashemite throne' (all quotations from Braizat 1998, pp.143 and 231).

For Jordanian nationalists,[23] the issue of origin became of paramount importance. Palestinians came to be seen as guests whose presence in the army, security, and public sector represented a threat to Jordanian national identity. Local nationalists began viewing Palestinians as perfidious, and were determined to exclude them from access to state apparatus and opportunities.

A process of 'Jordanisation' started in earnest. It was facilitated by the mopping up operation which followed the 1970-1 clashes and aimed at purging dissident elements, both Palestinians and Jordanians (Yorke 1988 pp.13 and 41). It was also made possible by the triangular alliance which emerged between the three main state departments that monopolise coercive powers in the country: security, *Mukhabarat* (secret intelligent department), and the army. With new regulations making the attainment of all posts in the state sector contingent on a recommendation letter, a seal of approval of the *Mukhabarat*, a process of 'Jordanisation' was set in motion and was to prove effective in achieving its goals, with far-reaching social and economic implications[24] (Abu-Odeh 1999).

King Hussein was well aware of the importance of social capital for social cohesion, political stability and hence for growth and development. He wanted to heal the wounds after the civil war ended and achieve national unity.[25] But he could not row against the tide of East Bank Jordanian nationalists, who now became the backbone of the regime and demanded an exclusive Jordanian state sector. Hence, 'King Hussein started to reduce the Palestinian presence in his regime and administration' and began relying more heavily on Jordanians (Braizat 1998 p.157). Leading representatives of loyal Jordanian families were co-opted into influential positions in the cabinet, civil administration, army, and security.

Other regime policies have also directly and deliberately undermined bridging SC in the country and have instead strengthened bonding SC. To prevent the possibility of an independent, more broadly based opposition from emerging, or simply any 'significant challenges to his authority,' the regime played a game of stoking communal tension between the two communities[26] (Singh 2002 p.76). As Brand (1995) wrote:

> Anecdotal evidence over the years suggest that the regime is not above exploiting such tensions (generally by encouraging the expression by Transjordanians of various forms of anti-Palestinianism) when it sees fit. By the same token, the regime is equally conveying the message to curb such expressions when they risk getting out of hand. Thus when tensions had reached new heights in mid-June 1994 … King Hussein railed against those

working to plant the 'seeds of discord in this country among its people' and vowed that 'any person who attempts to harm national unity will be my enemy until judgment day'.

At the same time, Jordan's associational life was formally restricted after 1971. For example, the Parliament was suspended indefinitely in 1974, and remained so until 1989. Martial law, in place since 1967, was maintained and new emergency measures kept in place the ban on political parties. Even the only legal forms of civil association permitted by the government, namely, the professional associations and the Muslim Brotherhood, were also tightly controlled and monitored by the state (Friedrich-Ebert-Stiftung 1997 El-Said 1996).

While Hussein co-opted loyal elements of Jordanian families into influential state positions with little regard to merit or competence, they in turn co-opted their family members, relatives, and close friends too. Tribal and regional ties (bonding SC) were promptly revitalised at the expense of bridging SC:

> 'When the Jordanian bureaucracy expanded… after the 1960s, an agency head would fill positions with employees from his extended family of origin. For example, a cabinet minister would appoint many people from his town. Their qualifications and job performance would be questionable … Gradually, Jordanian public institutions have come to constitute different groups and power centers, such as '*Shamalat* (Northerners), *Saltiyyiah* (Saltit), *Sharkus* (Circassians), *Janoub* (Southerners), and *Mesihiyyih* (Christians)'
>
> (Cunningham and Sarayrah 1993 pp.10 and 46)

By the late 1970s and early 1980s, a division of labour, based on ethnic lines, developed in Jordan. Jordanians came to dominate the public sector, including public enterprises, civil administration, security, and the army. On the other hand, Palestinians, whose legal and political rights had been undermined by the post-1971 measures, came to dominate the private sector.[27]

Abu-Odeh (1999), the former political adviser to King Hussein, provides graphic detail of the evolution of social and state-society relations in Jordan during this period.[28] The formal state system became completely skewed, totally tilted in favour of Jordanians, and very suspicious of Palestinians and vice versa. 'Problems of mutual confidence … [thus] emerged … between the Jordanian political elite which includes a respectable number of Jordanians of Palestinian origin[29] – and the Palestinian political elite (mainly the … PLO)' (Al-Hamarneh 2002 p.174).

Under these circumstances, tribal origin and affiliation became the ticket to state resources and opportunities, as well as positions of decision-making and influence. Personal connections, or *wasta*, came to determine almost everything from jobs in the state sector, to access to élite education and quality health services to simple rights and entitlements such as the acquisition of a passport or a driving license. Even the state's judicial system, the main guarantor of justice, became more sympathetic, biased and even lenient with crimes, violations, and offences committed by Jordanians, including the abuse of public office for private gains (Abu-Odeh 1999).

It is interesting to compare the change which occurred in the nature and extent of *wasta* in the post-1970 period, a point which will also be expanded on in later sections. The change in public policy in particular which took place after the civil war, along with rise in poverty and unemployment since the mid-1980s, affected the functioning of *wasta* itself. While *wasta* seemed to be helpful in building bridging social capital in good times and supportive public policy environment, it came to play a harmful role, a tool to strengthen bonding social capital at the expense of bridging social capital in bad times characterised by biased and corrupt public policy.

Ali and Crain (2002) argued that economic freedom might be more important for economic growth and innovation than political freedom. But even in the case of the Jordanian private sector, Palestinians were beleaguered, and their innovative and entrepreneurship spirit undermined[30] by suspicious public sector officials. Abu-Odeh (1999 p.197) documented 'stories of civil servants who obstruct Palestinian official transactions… in Jordan'. This led Brand (1994) to describe the relationship between the Jordanian public and private sectors as parasitic, not only distrustful of each other but also predating on one another, thus undermining general trust, collective decisions, and actions for common interests. This situation created an insider and outsider phenomenon in the economy. Civil servants and state officials (insiders) predate on and obstruct the activities of the private sector (outsiders and overwhelmingly Palestinian). The outcome is high transaction costs, stifled private initiative and copious obstacles to investment (El-Said and McDonald 2002).

To reduce transaction costs and/or facilitate their private activities, Palestinian businessmen had to develop various strategies and tactics (*see* El-Said 1996 Chapter 5). One such strategy was to bribe state officials in order to grease the wheels of businesses. Another was to employ, or even to give shares to, a prominent Jordanian whose main job was to make sure that their company's official transactions circumvented obstructive bureaucracy. These appointments depended on the Jordanian's connections, not his personal merits: 'The higher [the] Transjordanian connections, the better ... ironically,' the discriminatory stance of Jordanian bureaucracy created new job opportunities, and perhaps a new way of distributing income in favour of their higher connected cronies (Abu-Odeh, 1999 p.197, also see El-Said and McDonald 2001 and 2002).

Some individuals with original roots outside Jordan went further to 'Jordanise' their names, that is, 'to changing their name to reflect a tribal origin' in order to cement their links and form working alliances with top state officials[31] (Fathi 1993 p.249). This, they hoped, would improve their chances of acquiring a state contract, employment or other state benefits. Yet, a large number of those who lacked a tribal affiliation and/or resented the culture of *wasta* (including some Jordanians themselves) opted for an exit strategy. They simply sought work abroad, particularly in the Arab Gulf oil rich states. By the early 1980s, more than 400,000 Jordanians, mostly of Palestinian origin, were working in the Gulf, remitting back to their families and to the Jordanian economy more than US$1 billion annually[32] (Anani 2002, Kanaan and Kardoosh 2002).

To be sure, the intercommunal divide was also fashioned by the Palestinian political élite, if with different input and for different reasons. After the ousting of the PLO from Jordan in 1971, competition between Palestinian authorities and the Jordanian regime over the loyalty of Palestinians in the Arab World, including in Jordan and the West Bank increased disturbingly. This competition was intensified following an Arab league resolution in 1974 that recognised the PLO as the sole legitimate representative of the Palestinian people, 'a move that directly challenged King Hussein's claim to the loyalty of West Bank Palestinian citizens, not only heightened intercommunal tension but also played a role in the king's decision to suspend indefinitely the activity of the Jordanian parliament, where half the seats had been apportioned to West Bank representatives' (Brand, 1995 p.53). The PLO started to exploit the rising communal tension to its own advantage. To gain support among Palestinian refugees, the PLO began making large 'social service provisions in camps' inside Jordan, including direct cash handouts to many of its supporters (Al-Hamarneh 2002 p.176).

The post-1970 political, social, and economic environment stands in stark contrast to that which prevailed in the 1950s and 1960s. After the 1970–1 civil war, the negative bonding aspects of social capital came to outweigh the positive bridging elements. As Al-Hamarneh (2002 p.187) wrote: 'The earlier years of political cooperation in government between Jordanians and Palestinians in the 1950s and 1960s had been completely forgotten.' Worse, bribery, corruption, and nepotism sapped the capacity of the state, and created a wasteful and inefficient public sector that drained the treasury.[33] The new political environment has been dominated by narrow primordial relations that were not conducive to sustainable growth and development.

However, it was not until the second half of the 1980s that the negative effects of eroded SC were felt. In the 1970s and early 1980s, Jordan was awash with foreign aid, particularly from the Arab oil-rich states, which temporarily 'soothed the rawness of conflicting identity and interests' (Robins 2004 p.3). Along with a high level of remittances, this fuelled economic activities, leading to an unprecedented high real GDP growth rate of 7.9 per cent between 1972–82 before declining to 5.7 per cent during 1982-86 (Harrigan, El-Said and Wang 2006). As soon as external rents began drying up in the early and mid-1980s, Jordan's economic and social problems began to surface. Following a twin banking and currency crisis in 1989, the government of Jordan turned to the IMF and World Bank for support. The year 1989 also marked the eruption of Jordan's first large civil unrest in almost three decades. Ironically, the rioters were Jordanians, the backbone of the regime, not Palestinians. The erosion of generalised mutual trust and bridging social capital had undermined the social cohesion and political stability of the country.

Social capital and state policies in the post-1989 economic crisis

In economic terms, the 1989 reform programme, which ended almost 15 years later in 2005, was met with mixed success. The early and late 1990s were characterised by economic recession whilst the mid-1990s and the early 2000s saw spurts of growth. However, the growth was largely extensive growth caused by increasing factor inputs especially returnee labour, Iraqi immigrants, and the savings of both groups rather than intensive growth caused by productivity gains (Harrigan El-Said and Wang 2006). As such, the reform programme failed to tackle the country's growing unemployment and poverty problems and the period since 1989 has been characterised by increased unemployment, poverty, and inequality. Between 1997 and 2002 unemployment rose from 8.0 per cent to estimates which range from 13.7 per cent to 27.0 per cent and the poverty headcount from 3.0 per cent to estimates which vary from 15 per cent to 30 per cent (ibid. Table 1).[34]

The process of Jordanisation was not only maintained, but was also accelerated and intensified following the 1990/91 Gulf war, which forced the return of more than 300, 000 Jordanians formerly working in the Gulf and mostly of Palestinian origin.[35] One of the main aims of the structural adjustment program promoted by the IMF and World Bank since 1989 was to reduce the economic role of the state, including public employment, expenditure and subsidies, and to strengthen the role of the private sector. Given a Jordanian-public sector/Palestinian-private sector divide, 'Transjordanians felt threatened by the economic restructuring from which Palestinians seemed poised to benefit,' while Transjordanians seemed to be 'gradually losing control of their country to successive waves of outsiders' (Brand 1995 pp.55 and 56). These fears were primarily responsible not only for accelerating the Jordanisation process, but also for triggering a 'de-Palestinianisation process' aimed at undermining the presence of Palestinians in key private sector enterprises and projects, including particularly the press and public universities, thus depriving

Palestinians of 'cheaper and more prestigious state universities'[36] (Abu-Odeh 1999 pp.215 and 227).

It was not surprising therefore that the returnees, who brought back with them billions of dollars from their life savings in the Gulf and invested them in Jordan, found it difficult to adjust to living in Jordan: The returnees 'feel little sense of attachment to or understanding of Jordan as a country' (Brand 1995 p.49). They are seen as 'outsiders,' competing for already scarce employment and limited resources, and blamed for 'increasing the prices of everything,' particularly rented accommodation, food, and energy (UNDP 2004a pp.43 and 62).

The communal division of labour between a Jordanian public sector and a Palestinian private sector itself became a source of tension and envy between the two communities. While Jordanians envy Palestinians' dominance of more dynamic and higher-wage private sector activities, Palestinians envy Jordanians' dominance of the public sector and 'the fringe benefits that go with government jobs, such as health insurance and subsidised goods (food, clothes, and appliances)' (Abu-Odeh, 1999, p.198). By the mid-1990s, both communities were dissatisfied with the status quo. Opinion polls suggest that neither Palestinians nor Jordanians are happy with what they do, and both were reminiscing 'those days … [when life] was good' (DFID 2001 p.11).

Measuring social capital in Jordan

As elsewhere, measuring SC in Jordan is not easy. Assessing the full impact of SC decline is beset by problems related to the quantity and quality of data. Several qualitative studies on poverty and social relations were carried out in Jordan since the early 1990s (for example, see Fathi, 1993, Cunningham and Sarayrah 1993, El-Said 1996, Abu-Odeh 1999, Reiter 2002, International Crisis Group 2003a, International Crisis Group 2003b, Centre for Strategic Studies 2003a and 2003b, Shaban et al 2001, DFID 2001,UNDP 2004a). Ironically, none of these studies cited earlier work on or used the term SC as a theoretical framework in their attempt to encapsulate the vitality of social and community relations, or as an analytic framework to study increased poverty, corruption, nepotism, and weak enforcement of the rule of law and regulations. The only exception is the 2004 UNDP Jordan Human Development Report, whose main aim was not really to investigate or measure SC, but rather to analyse the impact of the economic and political shocks of the past fifteen years on the poor and on their coping strategies. This report, nevertheless, provides important information on the nature and function of SC and social networks in an environment characterised by scarcity and increased poverty. It is also the only study that refers to the term SC, albeit very briefly and in a short section that does not exceed one and a half pages.

The report is based on consultation with over 800 rural and urban community members, in seven different communities and with around 25 local and national institutions. The 2004 UNDP Report will therefore provide a reference point for most of the analysis in this section, unless otherwise stated. Another important source used intensively in this section is opinion poll surveys initiated in the mid-1990s and maintained by the Centre for Strategic Studies (CSS) at the University of Jordan. These valuable surveys provide important proxies to measure and analyse various dimensions of SC in Jordan.

The above studies and others clearly point to a decline in social capital in Jordan since the beginning of the post-1989 economic reform programme. The qualitative poverty studies carried out since the early 1990s coincide in their finding that social relations have experienced significant changes and that the country's SC has deteriorated rapidly since 'the recession in the second half of the 1980s,' and particularly after the 1989 financial crisis (Centre for Strategic Studies 2003a p.16). These studies also reveal that Jordanians at large are no longer satisfied with their lives and that they are unanimous and affirmative in their belief that 'No, the past was better' (DFID 2001 p.11).

Another important visible manifestation or dimension of declining SC in Jordan is the small and falling membership of voluntary civil organisations. A recent survey by the Centre for Strategic Studies (2005, p.15) found that only 15 per cent of all Jordanians in 2005 were members of voluntary civil society organisations, such as trade unions, professional associations and clubs, down from 17 per cent in 2004. The 2005 annual 'Run or Walk' charity organised by the Care of Neurological Patients was marked by a steady decline in the number of participants over the past six years, a phenomenon observed in other charity campaigns as well (*Jordan Times* 2005c). A recent study on voluntary civil actions found that work of 'committees, societies, clubs, and working camps showed deterioration in the value and results of their operations.' This deterioration, the study noticed, is caused by 'the lack of real desire to serve others, lack of responsibility towards serving the society, and a preference for non-participation' among the youth as well as increased 'responsibilities' of life (all quotations from Swalem et al 2005 p.2).

Even the simplest form of political participation, namely elections, has also been dwindling. For example, while 62 per cent of eligible Jordanians went to the polls in the 1989 first parliamentary elections in almost three decades, this declined to 59 per cent in the last elections of 2003 (Centre for Strategic Studies 2003a). Another survey by the Centre for Strategic Studies (2003b p.24) found that only 1.5 per cent of all Jordanians belonged to a political party in 2003. Jordanians are also disillusioned with their democratic process. In the same survey, 77.6 per cent and 83.2 per cent of Jordanians respectively stated that they could not take part in peaceful political activities or criticise the government publicly because they fear being tortured, either themselves or members of their families, by the government's security forces. This reflects deterioration in the quality of political life in the 1990s. The hard won gains of political reforms achieved in 1989–91 were reversed, and the regime resorted back to its old tactics of restricting freedom of press, speech, and associations (International Crisis Group 2003a and 2003b). The pro-regime *Jordan Times* local newspaper (2005b) recently warned that political 'concerns cannot be addressed at the expense of freedom of association.'

The effects of hardship, poverty and economic reforms on bridging and bonding social capital

We focused earlier on the effects of public policy, namely, Jordanisation, in eroding bridging SC across communities in Jordan. We now show how increased hardship, poverty, and worsening inequities along with more capitalist orientated attitudes, have not only further undermined bridging SC in Jordan, but what was left of bonding SC within communities.

In addition to public policies, increased hardship and poverty have also exacerbated the decline in cross-cutting bridging SC. Jordan's leading sociologist, Professor Seri Nasser, attributes most of Jordan's social plights to the rise in poverty and the 'encroachment of materialistic values' (Khalifah 2005). When asked about their most serious problems in the latest opinion polls carried out by the CSS, most Jordanians, 54 per cent, ranked poverty and unemployment respectively as their most pressing problems, calling upon the government to find immediate solutions for them (Centre for Strategic Studies 2005 p.14).

Under economic stagnation and poverty, some of the issues which facilitated social integration during the good times in the 1950s and 1960s became a source of tension and polarisation over the past decade. For example, the programme introduced by UNRWA[37] following the 1948 war to assist Palestinian refugees, began to arouse the resentment of Jordanian lower middle class families:

> They can buy whatever they want. They receive help from the international agencies, while we don't receive similar assistance.
>
> (A focus group discussion with the poor UNDP 2004a p.43)

The bicommunal divide fashioned by Jordanian nationalists over the years has also had other far-reaching economic and social implications, and, ironically, has posed more problems for Jordanians themselves in times of hardship. 'The exchange value of social capital depends very much upon the resources to which social networks give access to ... previously well connected individuals whose networks are embedded in a declining sector ... may find their social capital has completely eroded' (Kuehnast and Dudwick 2004 p.v).

Since 1989, the Jordanian public sector has been put under severe pressure as a result of market-oriented policies recommended by the so-called Washington Consensus. The fiscal and monetary constraints imposed by these institutions and the immediate freeze on public sector wages and salaries as well as on employment have significantly reduced job opportunities in certain categories of employment where the poorest and least qualified Jordanians were traditionally absorbed. Privatisation not only reduced further employment opportunities, but also increased unemployment, and poverty. Those who lost their jobs in the public sector were thus deprived of their former workplace in which materially important social networks can be formed and maintained (UNDP 2004a).

The fact that most Palestinians opted to work in the private sector, either by choice or lack of it and either in Jordan or abroad, made them more dynamic and exposed to entrepreneurial skills. Therefore, despite rising poverty and unemployment generally in Jordan, the Palestinians were more prepared to face the new global economy than their Jordanian counterparts, who relied mostly on easy and uncompetitive jobs in the public sector that require little skill (Anani, 2002). As a prominent Palestinian businessman put it:

> We gave them [Jordanians] what they wanted, namely politics, and we [Palestinians] focused on what we can do best, that is, private activities. Today, I feel sorry for most Jordanian towns and villages because they are very poor.
>
> (Personal interview Amman September 9 2005)

Indeed, there is alarming empirical evidence (from the point of view of the regime) which suggests that today villages and towns that not only are inhabited overwhelmingly by Jordanians but also rely overwhelmingly on public sector jobs, such as those in 'south Jordan consistently rank at the bottom of the national list in terms of most of the basic indicators,' including poverty, unemployment, living standards, literacy, and education (International Crisis Group 2003b p.7). These areas, once known for their unconditional support for the regime, have also experienced the highest rate of violence and political instability over the past fifteen years. Between 1989 and 2002, these areas experienced at least four major political crises, all of which involved acts of violence and rioting. 'Unlike the 1970–1972 conflict with the Palestinian Liberation Organisation, it was home grown, pitting security services against indigenous Transjordanians – or as one of many several prominent political leaders put it, against the regime's oldest and strongest constituents' (International Crisis Group 2003b p.4).

Hardship and poverty has not only deepened the pre-existing bi-communal cleavages in Jordanian society, but have also undermined intra–community ties or bonding social capital amongst the poor and within communities themselves. While analysing social networks in post-Communist Kyrgyz Republic, Kuehnast and Dudwick's (2004), drawing on the work of a long line of anthropological studies, showed that under scarcity and poverty, reciprocal social networks contract with various degrees of rapidity to the detriment of the poor and needy (Sahlins 1972). This analysis fits well the experience of the poor and social networks in Jordan over the past fifteen years. The available empirical evidence suggests that poverty has impacted on the nature and function of social relations between the poor and the better off within the same community or ethnic group.

Social networks are traditionally and historically an important feature of Jordanian society. Reciprocal solidarity (*takaful*) among community members is best demonstrated during social events such as weddings, births, funerals, and *eid* celebrations. Consultation process with the poor in rural and urban communities suggests that increased poverty and economic dislocation is causing them to withdraw from such important traditional ceremonies and social-based reciprocal networks:

> Change in the economic situation ... has affected social relations ... poor families, unable to offer tangible items, prefer not to participate ... because the dignity of a man is based on his ability to repay the debt of social events.
>
> (A focus group discussion with the poor UNDP 2004a 62)

DFID's study of Poverty Assessment in Jordan (2001, pp.18 and 22) also reported similar findings when it noted that the 'poor families ... could not afford having a social life or attending social events like wedding parties or exchanging visits with their neighbors ... because [they cannot] afford it.' Such ceremonies and life rituals provide important opportunities to cultivate and develop more resourceful networks and connections. The withdrawal of the poor from them leads to their further deprivation, isolation, and exclusion.

This is not to say that social networks cease to function or that people are no longer relying on support from family, friends or neighbours. Social-based networks continue to be an important survival strategy for the poor. 'People in [poor] and low-trust environments will transact more with close friends and relatives than with strangers' (Knack and Keefer 1997 p.1256). Put differently, the nature of social networks often changes during times of hardship. In Jordan, poverty revitalised 'tribal ties' among Jordanians in an attempt 'to protect themselves from the hardship of life' (Centre for Strategic Studies, 2003c, p.20):

> In all communities, the poor noted that they rely on connections (wasta) to facilitate procedures and access to entitlements. Urban residents … describe wasta as a magic wand promising job opportunities, access to loans, cash assistance from NAF and access to better, discounted health services. Those without wasta expressed their frustration and helplessness … without wasta, we cannot live.
>
> (A focus group discussion with the poor UNDP 2004a p.63)

However, the networks of the poor and better off are separating and polarising, with the social networks of the poor becoming more horizontal, 'work[ing] together to share resources' and connecting the poor with other poor that have fewer resources and potential to support each other (UNDP 2004a p.8). As Bel-Air (2002 p.156), while describing the change in social structure and relations in Jordan since the late 1980s noted, 'as the vertical ties of domination fade, horizontal ties of solidarity [have been] strengthened among brothers, cousins and other members of the same.'

Another important development relates to the nature and function of *wasta* or connection itself in a more capitalist-based society. While accessing rights and entitlements are increasingly mediated by personal connections, money has come to play a vital role in such transactions. Today, a *wasta* performer no longer seeks social recognition and respect as the main reward for his or her efforts: 'These ties are no longer based on commitment to abstract principles or codes. Rather, they may be considered a form of patron-client relationship, based on mutual or reciprocal assistance and loyalty' (El-Said 1996 p.140). Today, wasta performers expect material gains for their efforts, even when such transactions involve a kin or a 'relative who exchanges useful information in family meetings, but also who pays generously' (Malhas 1993). Under the marketisation of social and economic relations over the past fifteen years, traditionally unacceptable forms of reciprocities, including the request for and obtaining of material reward for *wasta*, have been redefined and revalued, and, along with other activities, such as trade, speculation and profiteering, are no longer unacceptable and are now seen as indicators of enterprise and private initiative.[38]

This phenomenon led to the emergence in Jordan of what Cunningham and Sarayrah (1993 p.14) described as 'contract-based *wasta*,' a process which not only leads to further isolation and exclusion of the poor, but also keeps the doors (and pockets) of officials wide open for bribery and corruption.

Bribery, corruption, and other forms of rent-seeking behaviour have become widespread in the country, and have increased under neo-liberal market reforms promoted since 1989. Some donors have recently cautioned the Jordanian regime against the noticeable increase in the level of corruption in the country. A recent pilot study on bribery in Jordan, conducted by Transparency International (TI) and the Arab Archive Institute, reveals interesting results about the way most Jordanians feel about corruption in their country. According to the study, 93.5 per cent of respondents believe that bribery is a form of corruption, 72.3 per cent do not think the government is serious in combating bribery, 59.6 per cent believe bribery will increase next year, and 50 per cent of those sampled said they had in fact made a bribe in one form or another. In attempting to explain the reasons behind this widespread phenomenon, 52 per cent of Jordanians said they believe those who take bribes do it to feed their families, particularly following the decline in the living standards of public sector employees caused by the rise in the cost of living following the collapse of the dinar in 1989 and freeze on public sector wages. Another 35 per cent of respondents see corruption as caused by greediness; officials 'do it to become rich' (all figures quoted in Hamzeh 2006).

Understandably, these developments have negatively influenced the perceptions of all Jordanian citizens, regardless of their origins, regarding their officials and state institutions. Today Jordanian citizens seem less trusting not only of each other, but also of their deputies and formal institutions. One recent study concluded that the level of 'interpersonal trust' in the country is exceptionally low (Al-Braizat 2002 p.55). Most Jordanians today believe that 'corruption in Jordan is too institutionalised and socially accepted,' and that the government 'can do nothing to eradicate corruption' and nepotism (Al Abed 2005).

Although much less explored and known about, the available empirical evidence suggests that a similar dynamic has been taking place within the Palestinian community in Jordan. In fact, analysts of Jordan get so tied up describing almost 'exclusively' the Jordanian *ashira* (large clan or tribe), as a basis of affiliation and source of prestige and patronage' that they forget the tribal and clan roots and nature of parts of Palestinian society (Brand 1995 p.48).

Under the post-1970 and 1989 environment, bonding SC was also revitalised among Palestinians themselves. Subsidy cuts in basic commodities as well as high unemployment and poverty levels in Jordan in general also 'impoverished the condition of Palestinians in refugee camps' (Singh 2002 p.82). The situation was made worse for these camps by the fact that the PLO's ability to continue to support social networks and sponsor many of the social service provisions there (as it had been doing since the early 1970s) was undermined by the PLO's political stance over the 1990/91 Gulf war, which caused it to lose much of the financial support it used to receive from the Oil Gulf states (Al-Hamarneh 2002 p.176).

The results of a 1997–8 study by al-Hamarneh for four Palestinian refugee camps in the Amman Metropolitan Area (AMA), where more than 85 per cent of the returnees from the Gulf settled,[39] are revealing. The study noticed an important social and economic stratification developing among refugee camps during the 1990s. Although 'social networks' remained very important in the camps' social and political life, their nature has also experienced significant changes that seem to mirror the economic stratification developing inside these camps. This change is reflected in the fact that members of the same groups have also been forced to 'hold together ... to retain social cohesion,' while those who are more 'educated and enjoyed higher incomes than the average in the camps' have, mainly as a result of increased demands and burdens placed on them by the worse-off sections of the camps' residents, been moving out to new areas, thus increasing the 'social isolation' of remaining poorer residents (all quotations from Al-Hamarneh 2002, pp.183 and 185)

One of the main reasons why more than 85 per cent of returnees from the Gulf in the early 1990s settled down in and near the refugee camps in the AMA was due to the fact that 'the majority of them had relatives there' and were hoping to be assisted by them after their forced return to Jordan (Al-Hamarneh 2002 p.179). But under impoverished conditions, the returnees could rely on little assistance from their relatives in the camps: 'Only a minority [of the returnees] were lodged by relatives'[40] (Al-Oudat 1999 p.39). At least 80 per cent of the returnees live in rented apartments inside the camps, costing on average US$170 monthly, a fact which reflects the returnees' modest resources (ESCWA 1991).

Based on a large survey of returnees, Al-Oudat (1999 p.39) noted that 'while the returnees' arrival in Jordan could have been an occasion for strengthening the extended family (taking in returnees, providing various forms of financial support), in fact it was not uncommon for family ties to break under the weight of lifestyles that had diverged too widely, overcrowded housing conditions, and, in a precious economy, fears on the part of the hosts of additional 'burden'. The survey also reported an increase in incidence of divorce related to strains associated with the war uprooting and increased financial strains, and that although 'almost all of the interviewed returnees had relatives in Jordan when they arrived, only about a quarter of them reported having received concrete assistance from them' (ibid. 39 and 50). The survey concluded that observing how social networks, including family ties, are affected by conditions of scarcity challenges traditional notions of the primacy of ties of blood or origin, and shows that ties between those sharing a common lifestyle or residence to be stronger: 'It should not be surprising that friendship or old acquaintances from Kuwait formed the core of the returnees' social circle' (ibid. pp.40 and 41).

Very little is known about the associational life and participatory rates in voluntary civil organisations inside Palestinian refugee camps in Jordan. But the very little that is known also points to a declining trend. For example, while 63 per cent of those registered to vote in the Palestinian refugee camps actually voted in 1993, this declined to only 54 per cent in the 1997 elections (Al-Hamarneh 2002 p.177), and to below 50 per cent in the 2002 elections (Joffe, 2002).

Conclusion

This chapter set itself the difficult and broad task of tracing the evolution of SC in Jordan, particularly bonding SC and bridging SC, evaluating the role of the state policies in affecting various forms of SC, and exploring the ways in which poverty and economic reform affect the nature and extent of SC.

An initially rich society with SC is no guarantee for sustainable growth and development. While SC takes a long time to build and cement, it is easily destroyed. Indeed, this chapter cautions against the assumption that SC, particularly trust and civic cooperative behaviour, is stable over long periods of time. Such behaviour can disintegrate in the face of inappropriate and biased state policies, wars and civil wars, as well as poverty and hardship. All of these factors can undermine various forms of SC, including bridging SC that is so important for social cohesion and political stability. Under such circumstances, group heterogeneity becomes more complex and divisive than under political stability, economic growth and prosperity. The case of Yugoslavia's rapid unravelling of cooperative behaviour under similar circumstances is also supportive of this argument. Such an analysis also carries important policy implications.

SC is not a substitute for a good state. On the contrary, SC and good states complement each other. They also affect and are affected by one another. While wars and civil wars can quickly erode SC and cross-cutting ties, SC itself can play an important role in post-war reconstruction and peace-building. But to achieve this objective, SC needs to be supported by a good governance structure that supports and nourishes associational life. It also requires effective and clean bureaucracy, and just and effectual courts and judicial system. Failing that, social networks, which are characterised by resource and power asymmetry, can lead to further social divisions, isolation, and exclusions. Such divisions and chasms under poverty and scarcity can develop not only between various communities and groups within the same society, but also between them and the state itself. This can be clearly seen in the case of Jordan in the post-1970–1 civil war period.

Rushed and premature economic reform programmes that are not preceded by a sound understanding of a society's social structure, social networks and the resources they command and control, can further increase a society's hardship and poverty by undermining both bridging and bonding SC. This is particularly the case in societies where social networks that are based on mutual exchange and reciprocity, can contract rapidly under poverty and hardship to the detriment of the poor. During hard times, social networks become burdensome for the poor who struggle to meet their more urgent needs like food, shelter, and clothes. In such an environment, the poor are less likely to devote time and resources to costly reciprocal social networks. This short-term strategy undermines their medium- and longer-term access to wider resources and benefits, and contributes to their further isolation and exclusion.

Future policy intervention in Jordan must not repeat its past mistakes and must be careful not to undermine further local and community SC. This requires a complete reversal of the current policies which cause bonding SC to take precedence over bridging SC in Jordan. This policy recommendation is necessary not only to produce more optimal development outcomes, as development based on local initiative, management, and ownership can evidently produce more optimal outcomes than those based on a top-down approach or blindly recommended by foreign agencies with little understanding for local social structure. But it is also necessary to promote social cohesion and political stability, which are also important for investment, growth and development.

Social networks are a wide spread phenomenon not only in Jordan and the Arab World, but also in almost every Moslem society beyond the region, including in Bosnia and Herzegovina, former Soviet Moslem states, and those in Asia and Africa (see Kuehnast, K. and Dudwick 2004, World Bank 2002a). While this chapter focused on SC in Jordan, the latter's case is informative and relevant to observers working on SC issues elsewhere. With regard to the Arab World in particular, and in her work on Arab societies, Singerman (1997 p.xi) noted that because of high demands of every day life in an environment characterised by strong bureaucracy, repression and authoritarianism, people evolved and sustained informal social networks that provide alternative to formal resources of the state. Yet, the literature on SC is largely characterised by absence of any contribution from the Arab World. The hope is that this chapter, which adopted a broad perspective in an attempt to extend our understanding for the role of SC in the region, will raise further questions and provide opportunities to explore many of the specific issues in detail.

This chapter has set the scene for an analysis of faith-based welfare and social capital provision by providing an historical overview of the evolution of social capital in Jordan from a secular point of view. Subsequent chapters will explore the role of faith-based social capital in four economies, including Jordan, which have undergone programmes of economic liberalisation. Each will assesses the effects of liberalisation on different dimensions of social welfare and analyse the growth of faith-based welfare provision and the State's reaction to this.

4

Faith-Based Welfare and Jordan's Muslim Brotherhood Movement

The Jordanian Muslim Brotherhood Movement: the complementary role of religion and politics

The Jordanian Muslim Brotherhood Movement (MBM) was established in 1945 by a group of activists, headed by Haj Abdullatif Abu Qourah, whose roots and origins can be traced to places outside Jordan itself, particularly Syria and Palestine (AUJRC, 1997). Like almost every Arab citizen at the time, Haj Abu Qourah and his colleagues were disappointed with the British policies in Palestine that delivered on a promise to create a Jewish home on Arab land. The ideas of al-Banna, particularly his call for *jihad* to liberate Palestine, appealed to Haj Abu Qourah and his followers, long known for their generosity, charity and voluntary work (Kazem, 1997). Hence, from the very beginning, not only did the men who created the Jordanian MBM's branch have their origins outside Jordan, but the movement itself was linked to a regional, rather than a national context, namely, Palestine. Put another way, while the leadership of, for example, Hizballah, could publicly brag that 'Hizballah is a movement whose members are Lebanese, its leadership is Lebanese, the decision is Lebanese and it is made of a Lebanese leadership' (Quoted in Zisser, 2000, p.3), the Jordanian MBM has been deprived of this significant national context enjoyed by most other Islamic movements in the region. (On Islamist movements in North Africa, see Weitzman, 1997, Enhaili and Adda, 2003, Laskier, 2003.) This has had major implications for the movement's operations and tactics. For example, there is an unwritten constitutional agreement among members that the Brotherhood's overseer general must always be of Jordanian origin to give the movement a Jordanian face and, since 1953, this has been the case. Its image and historical links with Palestine also allowed the regime to use the movement as a political policy instrument, both domestically (against possible local threat) or regionally (to support or undermine certain Arab regimes).[41]

That said, the Jordanian regime itself explicitly encouraged and supported the establishment of the Jordanian MBM in order to counter the rising tide of nationalist Ba'athist, Communist and numerous other leftist movements that dominated the political scene in the 1950s and 1960s. King Abdullah I publicly inaugurated the initiation of the MBM's central quarters in Amman in 1945. The MBM was not the only Islamic charity organisation operating in the country before political independence was obtained in 1946. Numerous small-scale organisations operated fragmentally and in isolation from one another. Haj Abu Qourah himself attended one, where he learnt his letters at a village Koranic school. Following al-Banna's footsteps, and personal advice, Haj Abu Qourah also sought to centralise various charities and Islamic organisations under one organisational structure (Kazem, 1997, pp.15 and 36).

Islamists vigorously opposed leftist ideologies. They also abhorred Nasser's secular regime and blamed him for persecuting their counterparts in Egypt in the 1950s and 1960s. The Jordanian, Hashemite regime, on the other hand, nourished and protected them and their families in addition to hosting many of their Egyptian, and later Syrian, counterparts. This mutual interest was most obvious during the volatile period of the 1950s, when members of the MBM, led by village *mukhtars* and other propertied and status élites, organised mass rallies in support of the King, and clashed violently with radical supporters of Ba'athist, Communist and other leftist movements demanding both redistributive policies and regime change (Singh, 2002, pp.73–78, Dieterich, 2000). Members of the MBM were never considered part of the opposition. On the contrary, historically they represented a core support for the Hashemites, despite the latter's well known close historical ties with the west. As Singh (2002, pp.70–1), while analysing the country's politics in the 1950s and 1960s, observed, 'Jordan's Muslim Brotherhood ... upheld the Islamic legitimacy of the monarchy and respect for private property'. They continuously 'prais[ed] the King and express[ed] appreciation of his commitment to the "Arab and Islamic unity"': the King, in return, drew from his Islamist constituency to appoint successive loyalist governments that cemented his status as the absolute ruler of Jordan, particularly after 1957 (Kazem 1997 p.19).

Following an alleged military coup in 1957, King Hussein dismissed his cabinet, dissolved parliament, banned all political parties, and imposed martial law. Along with the professional associations and trade unions, the MBM was the only organisation permitted to continue its operations in the country, albeit under the umbrella of a charitable, Islamic Society by the name of the Muslim Brotherhood Society (Brand, 1994).

Habits of cooperation and assisting 'others in need is not instinctive but a norm that one acquires through socialisation and observation' (Cnaan et al, 2003, p.29). Islam is Jordan's main religion, according to the constitution, although freedom to practice other religions and rites are also guaranteed. Schools teach Islamic faith, history, values and norms from an early age. Students study in detail the stories of the Prophet and religious virtues of brotherly love, respect for the elderly, maintenance of family and neighbourhood relations, forgiveness, norms of cooperation, care and compassion, and the duty to help the weak and the needy. These values are nurtured by observing the religious habits and behaviour of their families towards family members and others. Although not all children or students remain religious in their maturity, they carry these norms and values through their adulthood.

Habits of cooperation, care and compassion are also reinforced by faith-based organisations in society. Faith-based organisations historically operated freely in Jordan, and not all were necessarily linked to the MBM. Even today, a large number of faith-based organisations operating in Jordan are not linked to the MBM. They take the form of spontaneous associations organised and run by one or two persons at most, in most cases an Imam (clerk) of a mosque, in various areas and are geared to the specific needs of the community in question. All clerks in Jordan are state employees, who get their salaries and in many cases, their accommodation, from the state. There is no need for them to be part of the MBM in order to carry out charity work or be involved in social activities, which is normative for faith-based organisations or religious individuals as indicated earlier. While no accurate, formal statistics are available on the number of faith-based organisations operating in Jordan, local sources put the total number of all civil, non-governmental organisations involved in charity work in Jordan at more than 1400, most of them faith-based associations (interview with a former member of MBM, January 2005).

There is little doubt, however, that the MBM is the most organised, resourceful and widespread faith-based organisation in Jordan. It exploited the new, post-1957 climate to gain ground among the masses. While Ba'athist, Communist and other leftist parties were banned and their members brutally repressed, the MBM profited from its freedom of action and accelerated its processes of social and human capital formation. For example, several new charity organisations were set up by the Brotherhood, the most consequential of which was the Islamic Society Charity Centre (ISCC) and the *sharia* College in Amman in 1965. The key task of the ISCC was to oversee the educational and health-care institutions operated by the Brotherhood in various parts of the country.

Many new Islamic colleges, like the *sharia* College, for example, have become important religious educational centres in the country, playing a key role in fostering human capital and civic culture. Other activities promoted by the *jama* (group) include cleaning up campaigns in poor neighbourhoods, public campaigns to remind people of their faith and values, mosque sermons where members participate in speeches and other presentational tasks, typing and lessons to correct illiteracy, weekly lectures, trips to touristic and historical sites, sports, sewing, and IT skills (AUJRC, 1997).

The Jordanian MBM never called for revolutionary change of regime. All members of the MBM interviewed for the purpose of this study described their social agenda as guided by 'consciously evolutionary, not revolutionary approach to politics'. This is why educational activities are so strongly emphasised by the faith-based organisations in general and by the MBM in particular. It is up to society, they argue, to change its regime if it so wishes one day. The faith-based organisations' primary aim is to alter individual behaviour over time to conform to divine revelation, bringing peaceful change from the bottom up. Their 'commitment to non-violent transformation of society and positive engagement' earned them regime support, which 'allowed the *jama'at* (group) to spread its ideas in mosques, public places, and group offices, and to open branches in all parts of the country' that were run freely by Brotherhood members (Kazem 1997 p.17). It also encouraged them to operate openly and transparently, without the need for covert activities.

All of the above-mentioned activities are carried out voluntarily and freely by members of MBM. Entrusting volunteers with responsibilities to write and deliver public speeches, organise ceremonies, and run campaigns helps to develop a dynamic leadership with various civic skills, including greater participatory tendencies and capabilities. Parents sending their children to learn the Koran feel indebted, even obliged, to reciprocate in whatever way they can. In a traditional society like Jordan's, word of mouth can play a significant role in promoting the MBM's activities and charitable work, leading to 'huge financial support extended to Brotherhood institutions [which] helped them offer services to a great number of beneficiaries from various social strata' (Kazem 1997 p.23).

Islamic-based organisations (or the mosque) have come to be multifunctional, acting as a springboard, bringing people together to discuss community problems, find solutions, foster civic skills, formulate human and social capital, collect funds, and provide social network programmes. They mediate between traditional Islamic values and modern mores, 'show[ing] that Islamic values can be fully implemented in the contemporary world. (Sivan 1998 p.1).

Not only does social capital take a long time to develop, but its effects also 'evolve over time' (Grootaert and Van Bastelaer 2002b p.93). Until the mid-1980s, the MBM failed to achieve any major political successes, apart from their alliance and cohabitation with the regime. For example, candidates from the MBM garnered only four seats in the 1956 parliamentary elections, before their representation deteriorated to just two in 1963. Until the mid-1980s, nationalist and leftist candidates still maintained a strong political influence among the masses, which allowed them to hold decisive influence in professional associations, labour unions, and student movements (Singh 2002, Dieterich 2000, Kazem, 1997, pp. 22 and 39). Despite their expansion, the social network provisions of the MBM were still relatively small, compared to the post-1989 period. During the 1970s, large inflows of financial assistance from Arab, oil rich states enabled the regime to vastly expand public spending and thus to provide a comprehensive subsidy programme, up until the late 1980s. This, along with expanded public sector employment and benefits, traditional family-based social protection networks and various voluntary provisions represented the main 'social protection institutions' in Jordan which reduced poverty from 20 per cent in the late 1970s to only 3 per cent in 1988 (Zakharova 2004 p. 101). The MBM focused in this period on expanding group ranks, preaching the word of God, and forging social and human capital. The MBM assumed far more social responsibilities in the post-1989 financial crisis.

Religion saving public money and supplementing state provisions: the post-1989 period

Large scale and systemic official corruption, macroeconomic mismanagement, an unfavourable shift in the external environment and poor policy advice by the international financial institutions were all key factors in Jordan's 1989 acute twin currency and banking crisis (Harrigan, El-Said and Wang 2006). Immediately following the outbreak of the crisis, the Jordanian government signed its first stabilisation and structural adjustment programmes (SALPs), which marked the beginning of what turned out to be a marathon of stabilisations and SALPs that lasted for more than 15 years up until 2005.

Typical of the IMF and World Bank programmes, severe fiscal austerity measures were immediately imposed on the Jordanian economy, which was already suffering from contracted economic activities, a high level of foreign debt, and spiralling inflation, causing the collapse of the Jordanian Dinar, which lost almost 50 per cent of its value during early 1989. Worse, the IMF in particular insisted on expenditure reduction in a country where 'expenditures were also rigid, leaving little scope for expenditure savings' (Mansur and Field 2004, p. 32).[42] Unable to reduce payments on interest or military expenditures (the largest two expenditure items in the budget), items that affected the poor most became the immediate target of austerity measures. This included food and energy subsidies, freezing public sector wages and employment, and introducing new cost-recovery charges for education and health. Food subsidies alone, which made up 7 per cent of government expenditure (or 3.3 per cent of GDP) in 1989, were slashed to 2.1 per cent and even to 1 per cent of GDP in 1991 and 1994, respectively (IMF 2004 p. 102). This was accompanied by measures that gradually lifted energy subsidies and increased utility prices. A new Sales Tax was introduced in 1994, after four years of delay, at 7 per cent rate, rising to 10 per cent in 1995 and to 13 per cent in 1999 after which it was converted to a General Sales Tax (GST) (for a more detailed study on the IMF policy recommendation and implementation in Jordan, see our companion volume *Aid and Power in the Arab World* (Harrigan and El-Said 2008 IMF, 2004).

Naturally, introducing severe austerity in such circumstances confronted the government with serious poverty and unemployment problems. This situation was made worse by the forced return of more than 300, 000 Jordanians in 1991–2 as a result of the first Gulf war. According to the World Bank, the share of the population living under the poverty line jumped from 3 per cent in 1988 to over 14 per cent in 1992, before declining to under 12 per cent in the late 1990s. Similar upward trends were also observed with regard to unemployment (see Table 2). But these figures remain highly controversial. Other sources estimated the number of Jordanians living under the poverty line to have risen by two-thirds during 1987–91 to 19.8 per cent (Kossaifi 1998 p.6). The government of Jordan itself has been less optimistic than the IMF and World Bank regarding the levels of poverty and unemployment in the country, stating that 'Depending upon the definitions used, anywhere from fifteen to more than thirty percent of the population falls below the poverty threshold'; the same thing applies to unemployment it added (Ministry of Social Development 2003 p. 5).

Table 2: Jordan: Key social indicators 1980-2002

	Poverty Headcount %	**Gini Coefficient**	**Unemployment**
1980	24.0	0.40	4.5 % (1983)
1987	3.0	0.36	8.0 %
1992	14.4	0.40	19.2 %
1997	11.7	0.36	13.7 % (2000)
2002	15.0–30.0$^{\text{ests.}}$	0.36	15.3 %

Sources: MSD 2003 and Poverty Assessment Report Washington World Bank 2004d.

Following a rapid reduction in the level of poverty in the 1980s, the government of Jordan felt confident enough to eliminate all food subsidies in 1985,[43] and to replace them with the National Aid Fund (NAF). The NAF's main task was to distribute direct assistance to the poor and needy, particularly targeting households with heads who were unemployable, either because of age, social status or disability. During the 1990s, as the government removed general subsidies, the NAF emerged as the most 'comprehensive' and 'single state-funded social safety net for the poor and most vulnerable segments of Jordanian society' (Zakharova 2004 p.111). The NAF's new role was consistent with the IMF and World Bank vision, which sought to substitute NAF for the previous general subsidy programme as a mechanism, it was argued, to enhance the quality of public spending. But even the IMF officials acknowledge that 'NAF [has major] coverage limitations' (IMF 2004 p. 100). The government of Jordan itself also admits that the percentage of poor persons receiving NAF recurrent cash assistance to total poor today does not exceed 40 per cent in best circumstances (Ministry of Social Development 2003 p. 20).

Parallel to weak formal safety nets, Jordan's traditional, informal and family-based social protection, largely relied on prior to 1989 to sooth occasional welfare shocks, has also been weakened by a series of financial crises during the 1989–2002 period that reduced the welfare of most segments of Jordanian society. Premature financial liberalisation accompanied by a rapid rise in poverty and unemployment have undermined both the traditional family source or bonding social capital as well as bridging social capital. Reciprocities embedded in social networks have come to be based more on narrow, materialistic tit-for-tat exchanges, to the detriment of the poor: 'Change in the economic situation … has affected social relations … poor families, unable to offer tangible items, prefer not to participate … because the dignity of a man is based on his ability to repay the debt of social events' (a focus group discussion with the poor, UNDP 2004a p.62).

As shown in Chapter 3, poor Jordanian families' ability to participate in social ceremonies and networks (an important mechanism to build social capital) has been weakened because they 'could not afford having a social life or attending social events like wedding parties or exchanging visits with their neighbours …' (DFID 2001 pp. 18 and 22).

The weakening of traditional informal and family social safety nets, along with state policies that reduced subsidies to the poor and vulnerable, raised taxes, reduced public employment and froze civil service wages and salaries without the capacity or resources to provide a transitional safety net or employment-generating opportunities left a vacuum that has naturally been filled by faith-based organisations. In particular, the MBM emerged in the 1990s as by far the largest provider of social services and 'mercy acts', filling a gap left by the diminution of state's role and resources.

The welfare programmes of the MBM are wide, extensive, comprehensive, sophisticated and indeed baffling. They parallel a state within a state, a shadow state, except that the state run by the MBM is far more transparent, efficient and sensitive to the needs of local communities than the Jordanian government had ever been. The MBM divides the services it provides into four main categories: educational and cultural, health, professional, and social. Tables 3, 4 and 5 provide a detailed summary of the financial value of all of these services, which are run and supervised by the Islamic Centre Society, established in 1965 and expanded vastly in the post-1989 period. The Society's organisational structure is relatively modern, consisting of a general management and four major departments: human resources; finance; planning, development and training, and supervision and monitoring. The activities of the Society are monitored by a small number of voluntary committee members, consisting of 9–11 individuals, directly elected by the General Committee whose members amount to 250 voluntary individuals. A total of 500 individuals are directly employed by the Society itself to run all the services provided by its organisational structure; they are simultaneously members and employees of the Society. The first chairman of the Society was Mr. Mohammed Abdul al-Rahman Khalifeh, the second and longest serving Overseer General of the MBM (from 1953 to 1994).

Table 3: Jordan: Educational and health programmes and projects carried out by the Islamic Society Charity Centre (end of 2005)

Type of Institution	**Year Established**	**Nos.**	**No. of Students**	**No. of Employees**
Community College (females only)	1980	1	680 (by 2003, 10,134 already graduated from the CC)	
Universities		1	NA	
Primary and High Schools (males and females)	1980–2005	28	12,065	1,053
Kindergartens (males and females)	1980–2005	23	2,922	151
Total Education		**53**	**15,667**	**1,204**
Health Sector	**Year Established**	**Nos.**	**No. of Patients**	**No. of Employees**
Hospitals*	1982 and 1992	2	331,234 (35,945 of which were in-patients)	1487
Clinics**		15 (down from 18 in 2003)	153,819 (15,635 of which were poor and orphans, thus treated freely)	105 (37 of which are physicians and 13 laboratorians)
Total		**17 Hospital and Clinics**	**485,503 (Health Beneficiaries only)**	**2,796 (All employees)**

Source: Islamic Society Charity Centre, Annual Reports 2003 and 2005, Amman.
* Both hospitals are located in urban areas.
** Only one of these clinics is located in a rural area. The rest are located in urban areas.

Table 4: Jordan: Charity projects carried out by the Islamic Society Charity Centre of the MBM (end of 2005 US$)

Type of Activity*	No. of Beneficiaries	Value
Orphan Adoption	9,801	3,020,338
Poor Families	3,757	1,165,934
School Packs	19,627	143,827
Food Parcels	38,127	952,733
Sundry Hampers	21,470	728,163
Winter Support	8,877	156,192
Eid Support	22,755	389,264
House Renovations	188	122,167
Student Support Packs	895	242,792
Medical Assistance (Medicines only)	22,285	105,120
Total	145,782	7,026,530
Poor Patent Fund**	3,066	375,092
Poor Student Fund***	300	15,000
Total	149,148	7,416,622

Source: Islamic Society Charity Centre, Annual Reports 2003 and 2005, Amman.
* Almost 95 per cent of these activities have been concentrated in urban areas.
** Since the Poor Patient Fund was introduced in 1982 and up until the end of 2005, 56,680 poor patients benefited from it, with a total cost of US$8,010,636.
*** Figures for the Poor Patient Fund are available for 2002 only.

Table 5: Jordan: Professional activities of the Islamic Society Charity Centre (2005)

Type of Activity	No. of Projects	Value (US$ 000)
Microfinance Projects (1)	72	78,038
Vocational Training (2)*	1,788**	24,180
Total	**1,860**	**102,218**

Source: Islamic Society Charity Centre 2005 pp. 22–23.
(1) All but four of these microfinance projects were concentrated in urban areas.
(2) Only one of these vocational courses was delivered in a rural area.
* These include vocational training in sewing, computers, floristry, traditional etching and bead artwork, and electrical skills training.
** Refers to number of students registered in vocational courses run by the Islamic Society's various centres.

There is a division of labour inside the Society. Each category or sector-activity is supervised by a voluntary committee that is directly linked to the chairman of the Society. For example, the educational and cultural activities are supervised by a voluntary Culture, Education and Learning Committee. This committee oversees the operations of all schools, kindergartens, a society college and a university owned by the Society. Education is a core activity in the operations of the Society. Through education, the values and norms of the group are inculcated and incubated. By the end of 2005, the Society owned and ran 53 educational institutions in various parts of the country, one university, one community college, 28 schools and 23 kindergartens (Table 3). Although all of these institutions follow the national curriculum introduced by the state, they are run according to the Islamic *sharia* (emphasising segregation, for example) and place special emphasis on religious teaching, norms and values.

The educational sector of the Society is vibrant with social activities. Parents are regularly invited to meet with staff, an important source of social capital and a key factor behind improving performance of both schools and students (see Colman 1988, Putnam 2000). Regular competitions (in poetry, art, science, oratory skills, writing skills, Koran and faith studies) are organised to motivate students, accompanied by somewhat lavish ceremonies to reward good performers. Not only are parents, friends and relatives invited to such ceremonies, but also high-ranked state officials, thus building linking social capital between members and state officials.

This vast educational network is not without cost – it takes millions to build and operate. But profit is not the primary motive. These institutions provide good quality education but at much lower prices than all other private educational institutions in the country. They also have a Poor Student's Fund, which provides direct and indirect financial (and in kind) assistance to poor students to allow them to access good quality education, build their human capital and empower them for a better future. The Poor Student's Fund was established in 1982 and supports approximately 300 students annually, with a total of US$15,000. This includes a monthly salary of US$70, books, food and transportation. The educational institutions of the MBM attract a good number of like-minded people, people who are interested in teaching their children the Koran, high moral and ethical norms, and values of the Islamic tradition. By the end of 2005, 15,667 students were attending Islamic Centre kindergartens, schools, society college and university.

The contribution of the MBM to Jordan's development and human capital is not confined to the educational sector. In health too, its contribution has been no less impressive. The Islamic society runs 15 clinics in various parts of the country as well as two large hospitals, one in Amman and the other in Aqaba (The Islamic Hospital). These health institutions provide various services to

Jordanians at cheaper prices than all other private or even public hospitals in the country. The clinics provide basic medical services at nominal prices, and include clinics for women, children, dentistry and laboratories all run by highly qualified personnel. Every year, the Islamic Society's clinics serve more than 150,000 Jordanians, at least 10 per cent of whom are very poor or orphans and are thus treated free of charge.

The Amman Islamic Hospital started operations in 1982, while the Aqaba branch started exactly ten years later. Both have since been expanded, modernised and equipped with up-to-date technologies and personnel. The two Islamic hospitals have a capacity of 400 beds, and serve more than 330,000 patients every year, around 36,000 of whom require major in-hospital treatment and operations in various fields. In addition to cheaper services for all patients, a Poor Patient's Fund was also created in 1982 to allow the poorest individuals access to good health services and treatment. It provides partial and sometimes full financial support to the poorest patients, depending on their circumstances. Since its creation in 1982 up to the end of 2005, the Fund served 56,680 of the poorest Jordanian patients, at a total cost of US$80 million. The health sector is supervised by a voluntary Council for Medical Centres, established in 1997, and which holds more than 20 meetings a year, making more than 270 decisions annually pertaining to the operations of the medical and health sector (Islamic Society Charity Centre 2005 p.23).

The social budget and activities of the Islamic Society is equally impressive and widespread. This activity is supervised by another voluntary Social Care Council established in 1998, although social activities of the Society is normative and long predates this time. The Council supervises the operations of more than 45 centres owned and run by the Society, whose primary task is to provide care to orphans and poor individuals. By the end of 2005, almost 10,000 orphans and 3,757 poor people were living in these centres, provided with free education, food and accommodation. The cost of running such institutions amounted to US$4.2 million (Table 4). The social activities of the Society also include distributing food parcels and clothing to the poor, organising 'summer camps, pilgrimage trips, scout camps, music classes and performances, sporting activities and competitions, contests in arts, science, music, and learning the Koran, IT and sewing skills, floristry, hairdressing, glass-etching, training in electrical skills, cooking, and beauty therapy' (Islamic Society Charity Centre 2003 p.9). Around 150,000 poor Jordanians benefit from such social activities and services every year, the total value of which exceeds US$7 million (Table 4). These exclude other professional activities provided by the society, including in particular microfinance projects (72 in 2005) and vocational training (206 courses in 2005), whose total value exceeded US$100,000 in 2006 (Table 5).

The Jordanian Islamic movement obviously saves a great deal of public money because it encourages, and is directly involved in, the provision of numerous services to the poor and needy. The Jordanian MBM does not perceive its role as confined to spreading the word of Allah. Nor does it use the mosque solely for worshipping. The Movement, and the mosque, are today involved in various social, cultural and even political activities. This is part of what Right recently described as the move towards 'modernity', that is, incorporating modern ideas, technologies and management styles in order to show that Islam is compatible with the modern world (cited in Abootalebi 1999 p.1). According to the 2006 Annual Report (p. 5) of the Islamic Society Charity Centre, the primary mission of the Centre is the:

> development of human and financial resources to keep pace with other organisations in the public and private sectors and to keep pace with the globalisation era and economic openness and technological development since the success of charity organisations and their continuity and effectiveness in the societies they function depends to a large extent on their ability to develop their human and financial resources.

This argument flies in the face of the notion that contends that 'modernity and a decline of religion are inexorably linked phenomena', or that more accountable governance requires more secular regimes (Berger 2002 p. 9). Moderate Islamic-based organisations, like Jordan's MBM, unlike the Arab World's dictatorships, see themselves as accountable to their citizens. Providing social and welfare services is important for the survival and dynamic functioning of faith-based organisations. This motivates them to operate transparently, efficiently and arduously to win the 'hearts and minds' of their society, and also to develop, among other things, human capital of their members in order to provide a stream of dynamic leadership that is capable of attracting new recruits and generate new sources of funding (Right 1996 p. 66).

Do social programmes of Islamic-based organisations have any negative distributional effects? Fafchamps (2006 p. 1187) argues that any form of social capital can have negative distributional effects if the benefits and provisions are restricted only to members of a network (religious members, men, white members, etc): in this case, social capital can have 'unequalising effect'. No-one really knows the exact size of the Jordanian MBM's membership. The MBM does not release data on its members in order to protect them from political reprisals, especially after the relationship with the regime deteriorated rapidly after the 1993 elections. Most however agree that, despite their large followings, formal membership of the MBM is no more than 5000 individuals (Interviews with state officials and MBM Amman January 2005). As the analysis cited above demonstrates, hundreds of thousands of Jordanians benefit from the MBM's social and welfare provisions, compared to some 66,000 impoverished Jordanian families receiving small monthly financial assistance from the NAF, whose annual programme assistance to the poor did not exceed US$80 million in 2006 (Dajani, 2007).

Put differently, most beneficiaries of the MBM's social welfare provisions are non-members. Indeed, the available evidence suggests that inequalities have not actually worsened in recent years in Jordan, despite high poverty. Even studies conducted by the World Bank itself show that the Gini Coefficient, the most used measure of equality, has actually declined in the late 1990s and early 21st century, thus reflecting an improvement in, rather than worsening of, equity in the country (Table 2). Not only are most beneficiaries from the MBM's social welfare programmes non-members, but a large number of them are also not very religious or not totally committed to religious practices and traditions. This is confirmed by our observation of, and detailed study of, the way charity and voluntary operations of the MBM operate in Jordan. As one high-ranked official in the MBM stated: 'we give to the poor to let them know about us, we give to the secular to remind them of God's work, and we give to people and women who drink and commit sins to change their behaviour and bring them back to the right path. That's what our profit used to do' (interview with the author, Amman May 2007).

Do Islamic-based social and welfare provisions increase the level of religiosity in a country? That is far too complex a question to be dealt with in this chapter. The available empirical evidence is mixed and insufficient to reach a definitive conclusion on this issue[44] (Al-Braizat 2002, Tessler 2003). What is more certain, however, is the fact that the level of 'sympathy' and support for Islamists 'from the public' has 'increase[ed]' tremendously over the past decade or so (Al-Braizat 2002 p. 12).

Bringing religion back into Jordanian politics

Early signs of increased popularity of the faith-based organisation came in the mid-1980s, when Islamist candidates won one-half of the eight vacant parliamentary seats in the 1984 by-election following a decision by King Hussein to summon the parliament to convene after 17 years of non-parliamentary life (AUJRC 1984). They were also making vast gains in the professional associations, trade unions, students associations, and municipal elections, thus terminating a traditional monopoly by nationalists and leftists movements (Kazem 1997 p. 24).

Following the 1989 financial crisis, the regime restored parliamentary elections after riots erupted in various parts of the country, particularly in rural areas where the heart of Hashemite support traditionally lies. Rioters demanded an end to official corruption, better economic management and a share in the decision-making process (Brand 1994). The regime then understood the popularity of its Islamist movement and that it would achieve a landslide victory in any general and free elections. In addition to their vast gains in the trade union and student movements, Hussein 'quietly' conducted two opinion surveys in urban areas just a few weeks before the 1989 elections; the results of the surveys gave a clear and unambiguous indication on the popularity of the Islamist candidates at the expense of nationalists and leftists (Singh 2002 p. 78).

The first free elections in more than twenty years in 1989 indeed brought a victory for the Islamists. Out of 80 parliamentary seats, a total of 26 were won by Islamist candidates, at least 18 of which were members of the MBM while the rest were independent Islamist candidates. King Hussein's move was carefully calculated. Relations with the US deteriorated rapidly in the second half of the 1980s because of the King's failure to sign an individual peace treaty with Israel. Relations with the PLO simultaneously deteriorated, leading to a 1988 decision to sever administrative ties with the West Bank, which increased tension between Jordanians and their Palestinian counterparts (Satloff 1986 and 1994). A Jordanian parliament dominated by Islamists, albeit temporarily, would give US officials a clear indication of the strength of Islamists alternative and irreplaceability of the Hashemite regime. It would also simultaneously, given the MBM's historical links to Palestine, serve to bolster the regime's position among both Jordanians and Palestinians as the ultimate protector of each party.

Following the 1989 elections, the MBM not only dominated the parliament, but also became part of the cabinet itself. The MBM leadership entered into 'tough and long negotiations'[45] with the regime and ended up with five cabinet positions, despite the regime's initial hesitancy; these were: education, social development, justice, religious affairs and health[46] (interviews with MBM members, Amman, October 2004). The MBM's insistence on these particular ministries was for obvious reasons: these are the things Islamists do best, where they have a comparative advantage. From the point of view of a regime whose main survival political strategies are based on co-optation, corruption, and buying political support (Brand, 1994, and Richards and Waterbury 1996), this, indeed, was an uncomfortable compromise. Six months later, the five cabinet members of the MBM were sacked in early 1991[47] although the MBM continued to dominate the parliament until the 1993 elections.

During their short period in office between late 1990 and early 1991, and during the period when they dominated the parliament in 1989–93, Jordan appeared unique in the region. While Algeria's military regime (supported by the West) entered into its long, bloody and devastating civil war, Egypt's Islamists and state officials were locked in violent reprisals, Sudan was torn apart by its religious civil war, Hamas launched its first *intifadah* against Israeli occupation of Palestine, and Syrian Islamists had been massacred a decade earlier, Jordan looked democratic, reformist, peaceful, stable and in complete harmony with itself (Brand 1994). During 1989-93, the MBM contributed to the enactment or amendment of several laws and regulations that not only responded to the national and popular interest, but also enhanced the Brotherhood's moral standing. These included the following: the ending of martial law; initiation of a new party and elections law that permitted establishment of political parties; the passing of a strong anti-corruption law; the consolidation of the Audit Bureau and Civil Service Bureau roles, surveillance and inspections; and referring nine high- ranked executives to court on charges of corruption, as well as taking part in a seven-member commission set up by the lower house to investigate a number of corruption cases referred to the house by the Prosecutor General for further investigation (Gharaibeh 1997 pp.47–51). A high ranked member of the MBM, the well-respected Dr. Abdul Latif Arabiyat, was elected speaker of lower house for three consecutive elections, thus furthering the influence of the MBM within the legislative.

The legislative pressed for reforms which they felt were necessary and pro-poor but opposed the other legislation. For example, in order to combat administrative and financial corruption and protect public funds, the Brotherhood imposed expenditure-cutting measures, including reductions on luxurious government offices, official trips, benefits for high ranked state officials, and undermined political co-optations and appointments (Gharaibeh, 1997, p. 50). The IMF was quick to claim credit, hailing Jordan as one of the most successful reformers in the Middle East and North Africa (MENA) region; 'a model of successful ... economic reforms' (Khalaf, 2003, p.4), and 'another success story in the making' (Heresh, 2003). But the legislative, dominated by the MBM, also blocked other reforms that they saw as anti-poor, such as privatisation, the complete removal of food subsidies, and the imposition of the new Sales Tax (ST).[48] In fact, the imposition of the ST was delayed by the MBM for at least five years and when it was introduced in 1994, it was introduced at a much lower rate (7 per cent) to that which the IMF wished (13 per cent)[49] (El-Said 1996, 2001 and 2002b).

Jordanian Islamic-based organisations are very suspicious of international financial institutions, particularly the IMF and the World Bank policies and intentions. Not only do they doubt the ability of Washington institutions to reduce unemployment, poverty and inequities, but they see them as an instrument of American policy in the region:

> The IMF/World Bank poverty-reduction programmes are far from reality.. They are commercial institutions whose main aim is profit at the expense of anything else. They are institutions that belong to American policymakers and they execute American policies in the region ... We are closer to peoples'

> hearts. Corruption and bureaucracy distance people from the government. We win hearts and minds.
>
> (Interview Amman January 2005)

This reminded us of an article written recently by America's leading columnist on the Middle East, Thomas Friedman (2004), describing the US foreign policy in the region as basic incubator of 'The ABC's of Hatred'. The Islamic-based movement, on the other hand, became the religious and social conscience of the nation, providing the poor with additional state resources (linking social capital), defending the interests and status of the needy[50], and were, and continue to be, in the forefront of every demonstration and protest against corruption and illegal financial gains, as well as defending social justice, welfare of the society and the rights of the poor. Islamic-based organisations also played a key role in helping relocated returnees from the 1990–1 Gulf War to blend into the Jordanian community and deal with any cultural shocks they faced during and after their traumatic and forced departure from the Gulf (Al-Hamarneh 2002, Bileh 1991).

However, regional and international politics trumped religion and national cohesion. Under pressure from the US government to sign a peace treaty with Israel, King Hussein enacted a new electoral law, just prior to the 1993 elections, which gave a disproportionate share of votes to its traditional, conservative supporters in rural areas at the expense of urban areas where most of the MBM's supporters and activities were actually concentrated. In fact, religious social capital formation in the Arab world, as seems to be the case elsewhere, is an urban phenomenon. Islamist movements in all of our four country case studies of Jordan, Egypt, Morocco and Tunisia are 'urban movements', with supporters and activities concentrated in urban contexts (interview with a Moroccan member of the Justice and Development Party, Rabat December 2006. Also see Tables 3,4 and 5 which clearly show the concentration of the MBM's activities in urban areas). This result is also consistent with the outcome of other studies which suggest that religious-based social capital has proved more successful in urban areas as a result of deterioration of networks in urban settings that generated trust and sustained broad networks like cultural associations, unions, blue-collar workplaces, and families (Wood 1997, Smidt 2003 p. 3, and Cnaan et al 2003).

The evolution of the relationship between the MBM and the Jordanian regime, particularly after the 1993 parliamentary elections and the signing of the 1994 peace treaty with Israel has been discussed extensively elsewhere (AUJRC 1997, International Crisis Group 2003a and 2003b). Suffice it to say here that the post-1993 elections have been marred by increased mutual suspicion, mistrust, occasional violence, arbitrary arrests, increased political repression, and, above all, political instability and repeated 'bread riots' (Harrigan et al, 2006). The unprecedented democratic gains of the late 1980s and early 1990s have been diminished, if not reversed altogether.

Changing the electoral system in 1993 did undermine the domination of the MBM in the parliament, but it did not eliminate it. Brotherhood members won 16 out of 80 seats in the 1993 elections, with independent Islamists winning another six seats. As tension continued to rise between the Brotherhood and the regime through the 1990s, the Movement boycotted the 1997 elections. When it rejoined the political scene in the June 2003 elections, its representation did not seem to have suffered a great deal; its members won 17 parliamentary seats, similar to their 1993 share. As expected, the largest share of the parliamentary seats (52 per cent) went to conservative, rural supporters of the regime.

As democracy has weakened in Jordan, trust in government has also declined rapidly. Jordanians have become disillusioned with their politics. As shown in Chapter 3, their participation in general elections or voluntary associations has declined. For example, while 62 per cent of eligible Jordanians went to the polls in the 1989 parliamentary elections, this declined to 59 per cent in the 2003 elections. A survey by the Centre of Strategic Studies (Centre for Strategic Studies 2003a p.24) found that the overwhelming majority of Jordanians (98.5 per cent) have not joined any political party, while 77.6 percent and 83.2 percent of them, respectively, stated that they could not take part in peaceful political activities or criticise the government publicly because they fear either they or members of their families being tortured by the government's security forces. A more recent survey by the Centre for Strategic Studies (2005 p.15) found that only 15 percent of all Jordanians in 2005 were members of voluntary civil society organisations, such as trade unions, professional associations and clubs. This unequal distribution of political power and resources in Jordan's heterogeneous society has decreased trust between various ethnic groups, undermined bridging social capital and revived narrow, bonding social capital (see also World Bank 2002b p.2).

On the other hand, trust in and 'sympathy' for the Islamic-based organisation does not seem to have suffered. On the contrary, it might indeed have risen. For example, not only do members of MBM continue to dominate professional associations, trade unions, student movements and municipalities, but they have actually increased their hold on them in recent years (Joffe 2002). Second, an increase in the number of donations made to the Movement (Table 6) gives another good indication as to the level of trust in members of an Islamic organisation, as well as its continuously expanding voluntary and charity activities. Finally, and as Tessler (2003) observed an important change in the attitude of Jordanians (and Arabs) towards Islamic values and norms has taken place. While nationalists and leftists commanded large followings in the 1950s and all the way through to the early 1980s, 'popular support for Islamist movements and parties has grown significantly in recent years' and that helped to 'shape the political views of Muslim Arab' (p.9). Most Jordanians today desire a high level of religiosity in their political leaders, bureaucrats and state officials. For example, almost 74 per cent of Jordanians strongly agree that 'politicians who do not believe in God are unfit to be in public office'; 30 per cent strongly agree (while another 31 per cent agree) that 'It would be better if more religious people held public offices'; and 51 per cent strongly agree that 'persons holding public office should be religious' (Table 7).

Table 6: Jordan: Main sources of income of Islamic Society Charity Centre (2004 and 2005) (US$)

Item	**2004**	**2005**
Cash Donations	5,833,879	**8,248,917**
In Kind Donations	1,897,501	3,858,044
Income from Clinical Centres	639,011	655,452
Income from the Education Sector (including all schools, kindergartens and college)	5,380,045	5,903,680
Income from Microfinance Projects	112,527	128,134
From Rents	772,777	765,204
From Hospitals	26,645,193	30,500,137
Other Sources of Income	3,311,119	1,081,666
Total	**44,592,052**	**51,141,234**

Source: Islamic Society Charity Centre, Annual Report 2005, Amman, p. 36.

Table 7: Attitude towards religious leaders in Jordan

Politicians who do not believe in God are unfit in public office:	%
Strongly agree	73.9
Agree	12.3
Neutral	4.2
Disagree	2.4
Strongly disagree	7.2

Table 7 (cont'd): Attitude towards religious leaders in Jordan

Religious leaders should not influence how people vote in elections:	%
Strongly agree	38.5
Agree	33.5
Neutral	7.2
Disagree	8.8
Strongly disagree	11.9
It would be better if more religious people held public offices:	
Strongly agree	30.3
Agree	31.4
Neutral	6.6
Disagree	14.0
Strongly disagree	17.7
Index of attitudes as to whether persons holding public office should be religious:	
Strongly agree	51.0
Agree	16.7
Neutral	21.8
Disagree	7.9
Strongly disagree	2.6

Source: Tessler 2003 p. 15.

Since King Abdullah II ascended to the throne on the death of King Hussein in February 1999, the relationship between the new regime and Islamic-based organisations has deteriorated alarmingly. Tension between the two intensified further following the 9/11 attacks on the US, Washington pressured its conservative Arab allies to hamper the operations of all Islamic-based organisations in their societies and to dismantle their networks in the name of the war on terror. Everything that is Islamic, has now sadly become a 'target', with the US developing an 'obsession with terrorists, terrorists, terrorists' that does not differentiate between moderates and radicals, pragmatists and fundamentalists, peace lovers and warmongers (Fisk 2006 p. 2). Not only do

Islamic charities in Jordan, Morocco, Egypt and Tunisia[51] 'complain they are being unfairly scrutinised and persecuted as part of a broader backlash against Muslims since the September 11 attacks' (Stoddard 2007) but also those in the US too. Six large Islamic charities have been shut in recent years, the last of which (the Holy Land Foundation) was shut in July 2007. The remaining dozen or so believed to be still operating in the US also complain of unfair scrutiny and persecution (ibid.). In Jordan, MBM members have recently been subjected to various forms of harassment. Temporary laws passed in 2003 have been resorted to by the government to bring 'fraud' charges for the Jordan Engineering Association, one of the 'strongest and most influential associations in the country', who also happened to be dominated by members of the Islamic movement (Ben Hussein 2007). In June 2006, the Public Prosecutor was formally asked by the government 'to take the necessary legal action' against the Islamic Centre Charity Society for corruption and financial violations, after accusing it of mismanaging its health, education and other social provisions (*Jordan Times* 2006b). The government is also now threatening to sell all properties of the Islamic Centre or even to appropriate them.

The behaviour of both Jordanian and US governments will only radicalise more individuals and play into the hands of fundamentalist minorities. In addition, Islamic faith organisations not only save public money, but are an important form of social and human capital, the foundation of civil society. Undermining their activities in the Arab world is to undermine an important source of social capital formation.

Conclusion

Islamic-faith organisations represent the most important repository of SC not only in Jordan, but also in the Arab and Muslim worlds. They also save public money in societies where they function. For example, 'In Egypt they provide health and educational services and facilities as alternatives to expensive private outlets and inadequate government institutions. In Turkey, they helped to build housing for the poor and have generally strengthened civil society. In Lebanon, they have established farm cooperatives and provided systematically for the welfare of the children, widows and the poor'. (Right 1996 p.66). In Jordan, Islamic-based organisations' provisions cover almost every aspect of life, including the provision of high quality education, health, housing renovations and even jobs. While carrying out their activities, Islamic-based organisations foster interpersonal exchanges and trust, as well as social capital and human capital, the foundations of civil society.

Although it is normative to be involved in voluntary and charity operations, Islamic-based organisations are also filling an important gap in the Arab World created by the diminution and corruptibility of the state and its formal institutions. Unlike the situation in Western countries, such as the US, where Christian-based organisations are directly promoted by the state's economic policies to play a larger social role, the social welfare provision of Islamic-based organisations in the Arab World close a gap created by the bankruptcy of the state (financial as much as political) and its sudden and premature withdrawal from the social and economic life without first creating effective formal safety nets.

Islamic-faith organisations, like Jordan's MBM, not only save a great deal of public money through social and welfare provisions, but they also provide various benefits to both members and non-members. In fact, the main beneficiaries of such provisions in Jordan are non-members, including secular segments and sectors of the population and society. Their voluntary operations and charities do not discriminate against social classes, and are available to all without prejudice. If anything, they favour the poorest of the poor and the neediest of them all. This is unlike government services and provisions which have come to favour the rich and the connected. Islamic-based organisations, in other words, mediate against both the social (poor vs rich) and ethnic (Palestinian vs Jordanian) discriminations inherent in Jordan's society. They are thus an important source of social and political stability in a society that is otherwise unstable.

Although not discussed here, the Jordanian MBM is not homogenous. Like other associations and organisations, it has its internal divisions and conflicting interests. The joining of government in 1990–1, for example, led to several splits from the movement and there are 'Brotherhood hardliners' within the Movement who continue to criticise the MBM for participating in parliamentary elections and for being a 'positive' and 'loyal' opposition' (Gharaibeh 1997 p.54 and interviews with hard-line members of the MBM Amman January 2005). But the upper echelon and mainstream elements of the Movement represent the overwhelming majority and they are pragmatic, moderate and democratic, calling for a peaceful and just coexistence and evolutionary change through the ballots. Time and again, their high rank officials declare that 'we are pragmatic', 'moderates', and have no intentions of deposing regimes or taking over power by force (AUJRC 1997 pp. 30 and 34).

The greater success recently enjoyed by Islamic-based organisations is due to unhindered access to social networks and trust embedded in Islamic faith and revelations. Jordanians, Palestinians, Egyptians, Moroccans and other Arab societies vote for their Islamic organisations not because they want to turn their countries into isolative, radically religious states but because they want an end to corruption, repression, injustices and daily human rights violations. It is hypocritical of incumbent regimes and their western backers to call for democracy as long as the party that wins favours the regime and the states that support it. In earlier elections, Islamic movements in Jordan, Morocco and Egypt did not actually put forward a large number of candidates. They were not interested in totally dominating their parliaments and risking a bloody conflict with their rulers. But they now feel confident, experienced and 'ready to take over the government in case true democracy was practiced' (Jordan Watch 2006). It is not a question of whether they will win the coming elections. The question is whether they will be allowed to do so through the ballots.

5

Economic Liberalisation, Poverty and Faith-Based Welfare Provision in Egypt 1991–2006

Introduction

This chapter looks at the social welfare effects of Egypt's economic liberalisation programme in the form of the Economic Recovery and Structural Adjustment Programme (ERSAP) that was launched in 1991. It assesses the effect of the programme on Egypt's well established welfare state and looks at trends in poverty and other dimensions of social welfare during the reform period. The hypothesis we wish to explore is whether or not the economic reform programme led to increased poverty and declining social welfare through the retrenchment of state welfare provision. In turn, we wish to explore whether this opened up a space which encouraged greater alternative sources of welfare provision, especially faith-based welfare provision. To the extent that this took place, we also assess the state's response to see whether it was supportive or antagonistic towards such alternative forms of welfare provision.

After a long period of economic growth the Egyptian economy faced crisis by the end of the 1980s. Growth had been based on a rentier economy model with rents in the form of aid, migrant remittances, oil and Suez Canal revenue boosting an otherwise inward looking and interventionist economy. With the collapse in oil prices in the 1980s this model of growth could no longer be sustained and by the late 1980s Egypt faced a major external debt problem, high inflation, a large budget deficit and an unsustainable balance of payments. Her support for the Allies in the first Gulf War brought a huge debt forgiveness package and an IMF and World Bank policy-based lending exercise designed to support a programme of economic liberalisation.

The first phase of the reform programme consisted of a rapid period of stabilisation in which the fiscal deficit was dramatically improved, inflation brought down and the nominal exchange rate stabilised. This attracted a large surge of capital inflows, yet Egypt managed to avoid the financial sector and currency crises so often associated with such inflows. Structural adjustment however was much slower. Although progress was made with trade liberalisation and privatisation, Egypt remained a largely inward looking economy and the growth that materialised in the 1990s was based on domestic demand not export-led growth. By the turn of the century this growth had slowed considerably and in 2004 a more reformist government was appointed by the President to speed up the pace of structural reform.

At the start of the reform period, the World Bank produced a lengthy report on the possible social welfare effects of the programme (World Bank 1991) and in response a Social Fund was set up to alleviate some of these effects. However, during much of the reform period the subject of poverty remained taboo amongst the Egyptian authorities and this, along with lack of data, made it difficult to track the welfare effects of the reform programme. However, by the end of the 1990s the Egyptian government had accepted the need to monitor poverty trends and the household surveys of 1995–6 and 1999–2000 made it possible for the Bank to do its first analytic work on poverty since 1991. This resulted in the 2002 Poverty Reduction Diagnosis and Strategy report (World Bank 2002a) and the 2004 Poverty Reduction Strategy report (World Bank 2004b). Much of the following analysis of poverty during the economic reform period is based on these two reports.

At the same time that growth was slowing in the Egyptian economy in the 1980s, there was resurgence in civic society, including faith-based welfare provision. Egypt has a long tradition of faith-based welfare provision from both Islamic groups and the Coptic Church but this had been suppressed during the socialist Nasserite period. It is extraordinarily difficult to obtain data on the magnitude of this phenomenon in Egypt and it remains an understudied facet of Egyptian society. But the anecdotal evidence and secondary micro level studies we have looked at all suggest that during the period of the ERSAP, this phenomenon increased. As the quality of state welfare provision, especially in health and education declined, faith-based groups along with other civic groups stepped in to fill the gap. In turn, the Mubarak government has felt threatened by this trend and has used legislation to make it increasingly difficult for many of these groups to operate whilst trying to bring them under state control.

The welfare state for the ERSAP

The 1952 military coup that brought Nasser to power also heralded the beginning of an extensive welfare state system in Egypt. Nasser's Arab Socialism involved all encompassing distributive measures such as free education, health insurance, social housing, and guaranteed jobs in the public sector for university and secondary school graduates. The healthcare programme involved a massive expansion of all types of healthcare facilities whilst the education programme consisted of universal free and compulsory education at all levels with a policy of equal access. Thousands of units of public housing were created and the housing market tightly regulated. Although relative price stability under Nasser limited the need for extensive subsidies, housing rents were controlled and ration cards introduced for subsidised sugar, bread and oil. In addition, land reform, an egalitarian wage structure and a moderately progressive tax system all contributed to improvements in income distribution and dimensions of social welfare.

This social welfare system remained in place under Sadat even with the *infitah,* or opening up, policy of economic liberalisation which was launched in 1974. In fact, with growing price instability under the free market the systems of subsidies greatly expanded under Sadat (Waterbury 1983 p.218). The food subsidy was extended to cover almost 20 items and 90 per cent of the population held the ration cards permitting them to benefit from such a system. In addition, the Ministry of Social Affairs instituted programmes for the destitute and chronically poor to offer them a social safety net. Gender equality was also enshrined in the 1956 and 1963 constitutions and women from lower classes were guaranteed educational and employment opportunities (Moghadam 1992 p.41). According to Nassar (1995) the Egyptian state was a welfare state in three respects: the adoption by the state of a human capital approach that improved the productivity of labour through health, education and better employment opportunities; an economic approach which attempted to increase the income earning opportunities especially of the poor through employment and education policies; and a welfare approach that entailed direct transfers to the poor through cash transfers and extensive subsidies.

In terms of the cash transfers system, Egypt had developed a dual system by the start of the ERSAP. The Social Insurance Contributory System was run by the Ministry of Social Insurance and targeted mainly full time workers with old age, disability, death, injury and unemployment insurance whilst the Health Insurance Organisation programme provided medical benefits (Kashef 1987 pp.10–11). The Ministry of Social Affairs provided social aid and cash transfers through its Social Aid and Assistance programme both directly though its offices and indirectly through various NGOs that fall under its jurisdiction. These programmes are tied to lack of adequate household income and cover pensions for widows, divorcees, or deserted women and assistance for the disabled, sick and destitute. They are non-contributory and means tested. According to Bibars (2001) although most of the beneficiaries are women these programmes are patriarchal and inadequate to lift beneficiaries above the poverty line. Likewise Handoussa (1994 pp.5–6), Mansi (1995 pp.4–5) and Sabry (2005) have argued that both the pension scheme and the social assistance schemes leave a huge gap between their benefits and the amount that is needed to survive.[52] The World

Bank (1991 p.63) estimated that at the start of the ERSAP programme the social transfer payments schemes only covered about one in five of those in need. This along with inadequate support led the Bank to conclude that 'the government is clearly failing in its fundamental objective of providing a basic safety net for the poor' (ibid. p.63).

Despite the shortcomings of the schemes offered by the Ministry of Social Insurance and the Ministry of Social Affairs the general welfare state system in place since the Nasserite revolution has meant that Egypt has made tremendous strides in improving different dimensions of social welfare since 1952. The aggressive ration and subsidy programme has been effective in protecting the food security of the majority of the population and the system favours the poor relatively more than the rich (World Bank 1991 p.58, Alderman and von Braun 1984). In addition, although there are methodological problems in measuring poverty in Egypt during this period (World Bank 1991 p.7) approximate measures suggest that poverty increased between 1958 and 1974 but then dropped significantly between 1974 and 1981, especially in rural areas (see Table 8).

Table 8: Poverty trends in Egypt 1958–82

	Proportion of poor households
1958/59 (1)	
rural	35%
urban	30%
1974/75 (1)	
rural	44%
urban	35%
1981/82 (2)	
rural	24% – 30%
urban	23% – 30%

Notes:
(1) Hansen and Radwan 1982.
(2) The lower figures are from World Bank 1989 the higher from Korayem 1987.

Source: World Bank 1991 Table 2.1.

Income distribution remained fairly stable and improved somewhat in the 1980s as a result of both economic growth and distributive policies, including land redistribution, and by 1991 when the ERSAP was launched Egypt had a more egalitarian income distribution than many comparator countries.

The health status of the population also increased dramatically. In the 1970–87 period crude death rates fell from 20 to 10 per thousand, infant and child mortality rates declined from 179 to 60 per thousand and 16 to 7 per thousand respectively and life expectancy increased from 46 to 62 years. Results in education were even more spectacular. Between 1952 and 1989 the number of children in primary education increased from 1 million to nearly 7 million at an average annual growth rate of 5.1 per cent. Secondary enrolments increased from 154,000 to 3.8 million at a 9.1 per cent growth rate and enrolments in higher education increased by 7.1 per cent per year from 37,000 to about half a million.

Despite the large improvements in social welfare indicators, the onset of economic crisis at the end of the 1980s hampered continued improvements. The recession had adverse consequences in terms of employment and standards of living. The rising budget deficit and external debt put pressures on the government budget leading to a marked decline in public sector job creation, wage compression in the civil service, cutbacks in expenditure on the social sectors and cut backs in the food ration and subsidy system. In the private sector open unemployment especially amongst youths rose rapidly and real wages declined. At the same time the rapid growth in population made it difficult to meet the demand for additional schools and health facilities and the quality of social services started to decline. By the end of the 1980s expenditure per student was five times lower than at the beginning of the decade and health expenditure was three times lower per capita. The decline in social service quality was also evidenced by the large share of expenditures on salaries at the expense of drugs and equipment. To overcome this the government introduced cost recovery schemes in secondary and tertiary health centres and modest fees at all levels of education. However, evidence suggested that this led to reduced access by the poorest groups in society (World Bank 1991 p.117). To cope with the poor quality of education such as overcrowded classrooms and lack of books many parents started to send their children for extra private tutoring creating a two tier system. This two tier system had been created by the economic liberalisation of Sadat and amplified by the recession in the late 1980s. To quote Bayat:

> The *infitah* inaugurated the onset of a two-tier social service system. The thriving private healthcare, education and housing systems catered to the expanding wealthy classes, while funding for the poor declined and over-use began to degrade the public services on which the poor depended.
>
> (Bayat 2006 p.139)

Population pressures also meant that there were significant cutbacks in the food subsidy programme with adverse implications for the poor. In order to cut the budgetary cost of subsidies by a half ration and subsidy prices were raised in the late 1980s, the number of items included was reduced as were the quantities subsidised. In particular the price of bread tripled and the increase in food prices disproportionately affected the purchasing power of the lower income groups leading to cut backs in their food consumption (CRS 1989).

In response to economic downturn and recession the government tried to spread the cost of hardship. For example, rather than laying off workers in the public sector, a policy of real wage compression was followed and subsidies continued to be spread across most of the population. While real wages increased in the economy as a whole and reached a peak in 1985, real wages plummeted as inflation surged in the latter part of the 1980s, especially in the public sector. By 1987 real wages of government workers were nearly half their 1973 level. By reducing wages rather than laying off workers, the increase in open unemployment was concentrated amongst the new labour force entrants and the wait for government guaranteed jobs was extended to five years.

By the time the ERSAP was launched in 1991, it was obvious that the economic crisis was exacerbating poverty and that the government's social safety net was inadequate. At the same time there were longer-term declines in the quality of social welfare provision and fears that further cutbacks in budgetary allocation would compromise the coverage and quality of health and education, especially in the rural areas. Poverty persisted and despite the tremendous improvements in educational indicators, illiteracy remained high with the absolute number of illiterates increasing since 1976 and a female illiteracy rate almost double that for men at 62 per cent. In the face of economic crisis doing nothing was not an option, but as the World Bank realised the ERSAP programme, if not properly implemented, threatened to worsen poverty and other dimensions of social welfare.

In acknowledgement of the above the World Bank produced a 242-page document in 1991 entitled *Egypt: Alleviating Poverty during Structural Adjustment* (World Bank 1991). The document acknowledged that the macroeconomic adjustment programme would put further pressure on the government budget while, at the same time, raising the risk of spreading and aggravating deprivation among poorer groups. With 20–25 per cent of the population in poverty and 10–13 per cent classified as ultra poor this was a major concern. The document attempted to identify the poor (women and children, those in Upper Egypt, small landowners and farm labourers and the incapacitated) and how they lived. The Bank also identified three potential social costs associated with the reform programme: employment effects; price increases and delivery of social services. Employment effects included falling real wages and unemployment especially if the reform programme did not generate adequate private sector investment and growth. In particular labour displacement in the public sector and state enterprises was likely to hit the urban poor, significant numbers of who were employed in these sectors. In terms of price increases, the inability of wages to keep pace with inflation and the need to cut back and rationalise the extensive government subsidy programme were seen as potential problems. Those most likely to be adversely affected by increasing food prices were identified as low income urban consumers, landless rural households and small farm households who were net food purchasers. The urban poor were also likely to be hurt by reduced subsidies on water, electricity, transport and energy, especially kerosene. In rural areas small farmers who had previously benefited from subsidised inputs and controlled crop prices were also identified as vulnerable. In terms of the delivery of social services, fears were expressed that further cut backs in government expenditure would undermine services especially in rural areas and would prevent the elimination of regional inequalities with the rural poor particularly at risk.

The World Bank report clearly acknowledged that in the face of the above risks the existing government social safety net was inadequate. The proposed poverty alleviation strategy acknowledged that growth alone was not enough but that the pattern of growth along with government interventions would also be important. Given the heterogeneity of groups in poverty a diversified approach was also necessary and a three pronged approach covering economic interventions, human capital formation and welfare was proposed. The aim was to reduce chronic poverty in the long-run but also to meet the short-term needs of those adversely affected by growing unemployment, falling wages and higher prices, that is, the vulnerable adversely effected by economic hardship and reform. The measures proposed included: structural measures to increase income earning opportunities for the poor through improved access to productive employment and assets; structural measures to improve the equity and cost effectiveness of public expenditures in health and education to increase opportunities for human capital formation for the poor; structural measures to achieve a more equitable and efficient targeting of all secondary income transfers, including consumer subsidies, producer subsidies and direct welfare transfers, and; an emergency Social Fund to protect low-income population groups directly affected during the implementation of the macroeconomic forms.

Much of the emphasis of the proposed poverty alleviation strategy was focused on a better targeting of subsidies and better allocation of social welfare expenditures to both reduce cost and ensure the neediest were prioritised. In terms of social welfare expenditures on health and education, it was clearly stated that the government budget should be protected from cut-backs in real terms. In addition, a Social Fund was created, designed to be a transitory institution set up to provide income generation and human capital formation projects to protect the most vulnerable groups during economic transition using both national and international resources.

Despite a well thought out poverty alleviation strategy as articulated in the Bank's 1991 document, as we shall see not all of the strategy was implemented during the ERSAP and as a result poverty in the first half of the 1990s actually increased whilst in the second half of the 1990s it increased in Upper Egypt and since 2000 the evidence suggests that poverty is again on the increase for Egypt as a whole. Health and education expenditures were protected but the quality of services declined dramatically and little progress was made in improved targeting of the subsidy and welfare programmes. In addition employment generation, although it picked up in the second half of the 1990s, was not sustained due to the fact that despite a successful stabilisation programme in the first half of the 1990s more deep seated structural reforms were slow and partial resulting in a failure to stimulate export-led growth. The Social Fund did help to alleviate poverty especially amongst those laid off in the public sector with significant job creation by the Fund, but this did not tend to benefit the poorest members of society.

Poverty and welfare trend during the ERSAP period

Before analysing trends in poverty and social welfare during ERSAP it is important to note that despite three decades of a welfare state, poverty existed in Egypt when the ERSAP programme commenced. Although the incidence of urban and rural poverty had declined since 1952 (see Table 8) many studies had documented the persistence of serious poverty (Abdel-Khalek and Tignor 1982, Korayem 1987, Hansen 1990). However, lack of reliable and relevant data on poverty at the start of the 1990s makes it extremely difficult to assess the poverty trajectory during the ERSAP period. As the Bank noted 'There are no official surveys or statistics designed specifically to permit the analysis of income, inequality or living standards' (World Bank 1991 p.4). Another point to note in the analysis is that we need to be aware of the counterfactual. Whatever happened to poverty during the ERSAP period it is possible that things would have been even worse had nothing been done to tackle the economic crisis at the end of the 1980s and start of the 1990s. To quote the Bank again:

> At the same time, it is crucial to stress that the social situation is unlikely to improve should the reform programme not be implemented. On the contrary, the negative social consequences of the economic crisis are expected to be even stronger in the absence of any significant structural change ... Thus the

costs of non adjustment, in terms of increased unemployment and falling income, could have severe social consequences.

(World Bank 1991 p.120)

Although, as shown above, the World Bank had done much diagnostic work on the likely effects of the economic reform programme on poverty, the government's initial reluctance to acknowledge a poverty problem in Egypt limited the extent to which this could be taken forward. In the first half of the 1990s, the government refused to use the word 'poverty' and instead referred to 'limited income groups'. However, with the publication of the first UNDP Egypt Human Development Report in the mid-1990s the concept of poverty became more acceptable and the Head of the National Institute of Planning became the government's de facto poverty spokesperson working more closely with the Bank on definitions and indicators of poverty. In addition, tackling poverty was made difficult by the fact that there was no single government entity responsible for planning, monitoring and coordinating the different programmes and activities addressing the poor, although from the mid-1990s the Institute of Planning took a lead in this area.

Two Household Income, Expenditure and Consumption Surveys carried out in 1995–6 and 1999–2000 enabled the World Bank and the Government to present a detailed analysis of poverty trends in the second half of the 1990s (World Bank 2002b). This work estimates poverty lines by accounting for regional differences in relative prices, expenditure patterns and activity levels as well as the size and age composition of poor households which leads to variation in the appropriate poverty line according to location and composition of each particular household. Supplemented with national accounts data, data from secondary sources and government sources it is possible to construct a detailed picture of poverty trends in the first decade of the ERSAP as presented in Table 9.

Table 9 shows that, according to two measures, the National poverty line headcount and the US$2/day poverty worsened between 1990–1 and 1995–6. If so, this is not surprising. The rapid stabilisation programme in the first half of the 1990s took place before the government had sensitised itself to the issue of poverty and it seems that there was a willingness to push for stabilisation and liberalisation with an acceptance of short term negative social consequences in the hope that eventually growth would trickle down. Other studies also confirm this trend (El-Laithy and Osamn 1997, Cardiff 1997, El-Laithy et al 1999). By contrast, all indicators show an unambiguous improvement in poverty in the second half of the 1990s. Again, this is not surprising. By the mid-1990s the difficult phase of rapid stabilisation, including a swift improvement in the government's deficit, had been successfully completed, structural reforms were only slowly implemented and the government embarked upon a more expansionary policy. According to the Bank the moderate poverty improvements of the latter part of the 1990s were the first since the early 1980s and the World Bank report (2002b) indicated that by 1999–2000 poverty in Egypt stood at 16.7 per cent using the lower national poverty line. This amounted to 10.7 million people unable to obtain basic food and non-food needs. At the same time less than 1 per cent of Egyptians spent less than US$1/day evaluated at purchasing power parity. The ultra poor are calculated as those that fall beneath the food poverty line and in 1999/2000 they represented 2.87 per cent of the population.

Table 9: Poverty Trends in Egypt 1990–2000

	1990–91	1995–96	1999–2000
Lower National Poverty Line Headcount	24.32	19.41	16.74
Poverty Gap (Nat. poverty line)	7.08	3.39	2.97
National Poverty Line Headcount	49.27	51.43	42.63
Poverty Gap (Nat. poverty line)	16.98	13.92	10.83
Poverty Line at US$/day PPP Headcount	8.24	2.50	0.68
Poverty Gap	2.27	0.33	0.07
Poverty Line at US$2/day PPP Headcount	39.45	41.52	24.84
Poverty Gap	12.41	9.93	5.00
Food Poverty Line	8.93	3.05	2.87

Source: El-Saharty et al 2005.

The World Bank Report also showed that poverty was very shallow in Egypt with most poor people clustered just below the poverty line. This means, according to El-Saharty et al (2005), that if there were perfect targeting of poverty alleviating transfers it would require only about LE 350 million per year or about 0.1 per cent of GDP to lift everyone out of poverty. At the same time, large numbers were clustered just above the poverty line meaning that small shocks could significantly increase the numbers in poverty.

The 2002 World Bank report also dissected regional trends in poverty. Even though for the nation as a whole poverty improved between 1995–6 and 1999–2000 with the greatest improvement in the Metropolitan area and moderate improvement in Lower Egypt this was not the case for Upper Egypt where the poverty incidence increased substantially from 29.3 per cent to 34.2 per cent in rural areas and from 10.8 per cent to 19.3 per cent in urban areas. The depth and severity of poverty also increased in Upper Egypt, which has traditionally been the poorest region in Egypt. As a result, the previous national urban/rural poverty divide was replaced by a regional poverty divide. The reason for the new regional poverty divide was the regionally biased pattern of growth during the late 1990s. Import substituting manufacturing, the construction sector and trading fuelled by expansionary policies grew rapidly in the second half of the 1990s and these activities were concentrated around the Metropolitan area and Lower Egypt with its proximity to the large Metropolitan area whilst Upper Egypt experienced virtually no growth. This helped create jobs and reduce poverty in Lower and Metropolitan Egypt. Upper Egypt also lost shares in fast growing high value crops such as rice in the second half of the 1990s such that rural incomes stagnated due to low productivity in agriculture whilst lower initial endowments of human capital and infrastructure also meant that Upper Egypt had a lower elasticity of poverty with respect to growth. In contrast to Metropolitan and Lower Egypt, income distribution also got worse in Upper Egypt in the second half of the 1990s and this contributed to increased poverty.[53]

The above indicators of poverty have all used a money metric. We can supplement this with an analysis of broader indicators of social welfare as done in Table 10. One of the strongest correlates with the money metric of poverty is education. Lower levels of education and illiteracy in Egypt are closely correlated with poverty. From the start of the ERSAP to the mid-1990s primary gross enrolments increased but in the second half of the 1990s they fell slightly. Secondary gross enrolments increased between 1990 and 2000. Youth literacy rates also improved somewhat between 1990 and 2000 but by 2000 at 69.8 per cent they were still low.

In terms of health indicators, although the infant and under five mortality rate improved steadily between 1990 and 2003 there was an alarming increase in the percentage of children under 5 who were malnourished and underweight in the first half of the 1990s. This is not surprising given that we have already seen that this was a period in which poverty as a whole increased according to the national poverty line (see Table 9) and stabilisation was aggressively pursued with little concern for social welfare. Malnutrition remains a problem in Egypt with the highest prevalence of malnutrition and stunting in Upper Egypt.

Generally during the decade of the ERSAP Egypt performed well in terms of improved health indicators such as life expectancy, infant and maternal mortality, and immunisation but progress with education and literacy was less spectacular, with slow progress in reducing the youth illiteracy rate and the gender bias in literacy. As a result of the progress in social welfare indicators it seems likely that Egypt will meet the millennium development goals in poverty reduction, infant mortality, under five mortality, contraceptive prevalence, primary and secondary enrolment and access to safe drinking water. But closing the gender gap in literacy, employment and political participation will prove more difficult (El-Saharty et al 2005).

Table 10: Egypt: Health and education indicators 1990–2003

Percentage	**1990**	**1995**	**2000**	**2004**
Children under 5 underweight	10.4	12.4	4.0	8.6
Infant mortality rate per 1,0000	76.0	56.0	38.0	26.4
Under 5 mortality rate per 1,000	104.0	71.0	45.0	36.2
Primary gross enrolment ratio	93.83	99.83	96.64	100.48
Secondary gross enrolment ratio	76.22	76.51	85.34	86.88
Youth literacy rate (% age 15–24)	61.3	65.7	69.8	N/A

Source: World Bank (2006d), World Development Indicators (WDI) online database CD ROM.

Another important non-money metric of social welfare is unemployment. Unemployment rates dropped from 7.8 per cent in 1995–6 to 6 per cent in 1999–2000. Over the same period employment grew by some 2.7 per cent per annum keeping up with the very high labour force growth rate that characterises Egypt. This was due to high growth in the second half of the 1990s which was employment intensive. Employment in services grew at 5 per cent per annum and in industry at 1.7 per cent per annum, mainly focused in construction; however the growing inward looking manufacturing sector created no employment growth. In addition, many of the jobs in the service sector were created by the government with an average of 170,000 workers per year hired into the civil service in an attempt to control unemployment. Such jobs were less likely to benefit the poor. Hence the private sector's share of employment increased only marginally to about two-thirds. In addition, job creation was slow in Upper Egypt where poverty increased during the 1990s.

Despite some success with employment creation in the second half of the ERSAP period real wages declined during 1988–98 in almost every sector of the economy by an average of 3.6 per cent per annum for males and 1.3 per cent for females, although they started to increase in the very latter part of the 1990s especially in the manufacturing sector. But this did not reflect productivity gains. The stagnation of productivity and the associated decline in real wages remains a major problem.

Summarising the above it would seem that during the ERSAP period of the 1990s Egypt experienced mixed results in terms of the social consequences of stabilisation and structural adjustment. In the first half of the 1990s stabilisation was aggressively pursued with little regard for poverty and social welfare. As a result the number below the national poverty line increased and child malnutrition also increased. In the second half of the 1990s poverty for Egypt as a whole fell (although not for Upper Egypt), employment increased and unemployment fell, and continued progress was made with health and education indicators, apart from gross primary enrolments. The only key indicator that deteriorated in this period was real wage levels but this did not result in an overall increase in poverty.

One of the reasons why most health and education indicators of social welfare did not deteriorate during the 1990s was that the government protected expenditure on health and education at a time when the fiscal deficit was being rapidly brought down. This was in accordance with the recommendation made in the 1991 World Bank report on poverty during adjustment:

> It is crucial that human capital formation programs be protected during the transition period of economic reforms despite the planned reductions in government expenditure. This can be achieved through improvements in the pattern of allocation and utilization of available resources...without increasing the government's budget for the social sectors, though it should be maintained at its current level in real terms.
>
> (World Bank 1991 p.xxiii)

During the 1990s when government expenditure was cut back social expenditures were protected. Overall budget spending fell from 32 per cent to 28 per cent of GDP between 1994 and 1999 but the share on education actually rose from 2.9 per cent to 4.2 per cent with recurrent expenditure increasing somewhat faster than investment expenditure. In addition, between 1990 and 2004 Egypt increased the share of the budget devoted to education from 1 per cent to 15 per cent. According to the World Bank 'Although this share is still lower than the 5.1 per cent of GDP spend on education by the average lower middle-income country it represents a substantial fiscal effort during a period of general fiscal austerity' (World Bank 2001a p.66). In addition, the previous trend to focus expenditures on wages and salaries had been reversed with investment expenditure representing 24 per cent of total expenditure. Educational expenditure has also been reprioritised towards the primary level in accordance with the recommendations made by the World Bank in 1991. Between 1990 and 2001 resources were shifted from higher education to basic and secondary education. This has led to a 33 per cent increase in public expenditure per student at the pre-university level and a corresponding 45 per cent decrease in per student expenditure in higher education. Likewise health expenditures as a percentage of GDP increased in the latter half of the 1990s. In addition in the health sector the earlier trend to spend more and more on wages and salaries was reversed with wages and salaries as a percentage of the total budget falling from 90 per cent in 1996 to 83 per cent in 1999. However, the healthcare system remained under funded with only 3.8 per cent of GDP spent on health as opposed to 5.3 per cent in comparator countries.

Between 1992 and 2000 expenditure on the Social Fund, subsidies and the cash transfer payments from the Ministry of Social Affairs also increased by an average of 3 per cent per annum in real terms mainly due to increased government support for the Social Fund, with a 4 per cent per annum increase in the Social Fund, a 0.1 per cent per annum increase in food subsidy, and cash transfer spending remaining roughly constant.

Hence, overall social expenditures were clearly protected as the recurrent budget contracted and the share of investment expenditure in social services was also held constant. In summary, to quote the Bank 'Over the 1990s the Government of Egypt has demonstrated a commitment to its social expenditure program, despite embarking on fiscal austerity' (World Bank 2001a p.65).

In addition to preserving public expenditure on social services the Government also initiated a number of reform programmes in health and education which helped protect social welfare during the ERSAP period. The Education Enhancement Programme (EEP) was launched in the mid-1990s and was designed to: increase the number of schools in poorer areas through a targeted school building programme; increase parental demand, especially for girl's education, through an awareness raising campaign and a stipend programme for qualifying families; improve the quality of education through various initiatives aimed at the teaching and school evaluation process; and improve the efficiency of education spending through changes in the organisation and management of schools. Prior to the EEP, the government had also launched an illiteracy eradication campaign in 1991 through the creation of a new literacy authority. Both initiatives met with success. Illiteracy was reduced from 53 per cent in 1990 to 45 per cent in 2001 whilst enrolments increased in the targeted areas under the EEP. In health a pilot programme of health insurance coverage for primary care was introduced and in 1998 the government embarked upon an ambitious Health Sector Reform programme designed to comprehensively reform the sector over the next two decades by shifting away from traditional vertical healthcare programmes and consolidating the fragmented health financing system to ensure a more equitable distribution of resources and services.

Egypt's social safety nets also helped to protect the poor during the ERSAP period and prevented others falling into poverty. Egypt has three safety net programmes: the food subsidy, the cash transfer programme run by the Ministry of Social Affairs and the Social Fund. Together these three programmes account for about 2 per cent of GDP or 2.9 per cent of total government expenditure. Overall food subsidies account for 85 per cent of safety net expenditure, the Social Fund 13 per cent and the cash transfers programme just over 2 per cent. The Social Fund set up at the start of the ERSAP was an important part of the safety net programme whose funding steadily increased and it played a key role in providing job opportunities through micro credit projects and enhancing technical and vocational skills of unemployed people. Transfers were also an important part of reported income in 1999–2000 accounting for almost 15 per cent of average household income. Most of these transfers were from the government, especially in the form of pensions. The World Bank has estimated that without the poverty-orientated cash transfer system from the government, 350,000 more individuals would have been in poverty (World Bank 2002b p.x). Commodity subsidies also helped lift people out of poverty with the subsidy on baladi bread alone estimated to have raised over 730,000 people out of poverty (ibid.). Overall it is estimated that the three safety net programmes lowered poverty by 3.5 per centage points in Egypt in 1999–2000, that is, without them poverty headcount would have been 20.2 per cent rather than 16.7 per cent. (World Bank 2004b p.46).

Despite the ability of Egypt's welfare state to alleviate some of the adverse effects of economic reform on social welfare, the system itself left much to be desired. According to Waterbury (1983) the welfare state consists of political 'giveaways' rather than a strategically planned system. These populist giveaways at strategic times include pay increases to public workers, extending urban services to poor neighbourhoods, and increased subsidies. This approach intensified after 2000. In the aftermath of 9/11 the 2002–3 budget allocated LE 57.8 billion or 41 per cent of total government expenditure to giveaways (Bayat 2006). This covered direct subsidies to food and transport, indirect subsidies to education, health and pensions, a bonus to state employees and a commitment to hire an additional 170,000 graduates to government posts. Later in 2003 after the Egyptian pound was devalued leading to inflationary pressures a series of subsidised markets were launched across the country and more items were added to the ration card. Some of these giveaways have been explicitly designed to counteract the growing popularity of Islamist groups providing alternative sources of social welfare. For example, the government launched a programme of urban upgrading in the Cairo squatter community of Imbaba which had been taken over by the Islamist group Gama'a al-Islamiya (ibid. p.143). As reflected in the giveaway mentality the Egyptian welfare state has a paternalistic, undemocratic approach to social welfare provision which makes it unsystematic and exclusionary and biased against women (Bibars 2001).

In spite of the rosy gloss put on poverty trends in the second half of the 1990s by the World Bank (2002b), Bank officials acknowledge that poverty is likely to have increased since 2000 and that the poverty and employment gains of the second half of the 1990s are probably unsustainable (personal interviews Cairo August 2005). Using the 2004–5 Household Survey poverty was estimated to have increased to 19.6 per cent compared to 16.74 per cent in 1999–2000 using the national poverty line, whilst for Upper Egypt the figure was around 40 per cent. One of the main reasons for this seems to be rising prices in the face of devaluations of the Egyptian pound and reductions in subsidies. Poverty declined in the second half of the 1990s partly because employment gains were made in the growth period of the late 1990s but these employment gains did not reflect any sustained productivity improvements and real wages declined:

> Overall poverty reduction was mostly due to employment creation and to a lesser extent productivity improvements, which in turn raises questions about the path for further poverty improvements. In 1955–1999, the services sector created most jobs but saw little productivity growth, whiles the sectors with higher productivity growth, especially manufacturing, generated virtually no employment, except in Lower Egypt. Although employment creation may have lowered poverty, the limited level of overall productivity growth suggests that, if growth rates are not sustainable, poverty results may be fragile.
>
> (World Bank 2002b p.39)

Exports did little to help address poverty and unemployment in Egypt as indicated by the stagnant share of labour intensive products in the export basket since 1990 and the growth of capital intensive exports. Growth was concentrated in the non-tradable sectors serving the domestic market – construction, inward-looking manufacturing, services and government employment, which, given the limited size of the domestic market spending on non-tradables were not sustainable sources of income growth as seen by the decline in growth after 2000:

> The trend towards total reliance on domestic demand for economic growth and job creation questions the sustainability of value added and employment growth over the medium term ... The growing trend towards a loss in the competitiveness of labour-intensive exports is also a troubling trend.
>
> (Ibid. p.42)

Table 11: Growth 1990–2004

	1990–1995	1995–2000	2000–2004
GDP growth annual ave %	3.39	5.75	3.45

Source: World Bank, World Development Indicators (WDI) online database.

Growth rates have slumped in Egypt since the last household expenditure survey of 1999–2000 on which the Bank's diagnosis was based (see Table 11). This slow down in growth was due to a slowdown in domestic stimulus especially credit, leading to a slump in the construction industry whilst tourism also fell after 9/11. In 2000 credit to the economy was sharply cut in an attempt to defend the exchange rate peg and growth rates plunged. In addition, growth in services also declined due to tighter macro policy.

Unemployment has also been on the increase since 2000 rising according to official figures (which are most likely an underestimate) to 11 per cent in 2003. In addition, poverty has increased since the devaluation-induced inflation set in during 2003. Although government expenditure on subsidies was increased to try and alleviate the effects much of the increased expenditure simply reflected the higher cost of food imports due to the devaluation rather than lower prices to consumers whilst the quality of subsidised goods also fell. In addition, if the new post-2004 reformist government's intentions to cut back on subsidy expenditure are not accompanied by a well designed new targeting system poverty may well increase.

The associated slowdown in economic growth has led to a decline in average per capita incomes from $1,200 to less than $1,000. Since poverty is very shallow in Egypt with large numbers of the population living just above and just below the poverty line the implications of declining incomes for poverty are severe. Sixty per cent of the population live close to the poverty line. The Bank has calculated that for Egypt as a whole 2.5 per cent of the population was between the poverty line and LE40 above it. This implies that if expenditures of these people fell by just over LE3.3 per month they would drop below the poverty line and the overall poverty incidence would increase to 19.2 per cent. Poverty was most shallow for the poorest regions in Egypt especially rural Upper Egypt. Hence: 'Given that poverty in Egypt is shallow, there is a chance that many of those whom escaped poverty during the 1995–2000 period may have slipped back into poverty again' (World Bank 2002b p.v).

One clear indicator that poverty has increased since 2000 is the rise in child malnutrition, an indicator closely linked to poverty trends. Table 10 shows that between 2000 and 2004 the percentage of under 5s who were underweight more than doubled from 4.0 per cent to 8.6 per cent.

In summary, the high growth, employment creation and low inflation that helped reduce poverty between 1995–2000 was not sustained beyond 2000. It was based on domestic demand and expansionary fiscal and monetary policies with the budget deficit widening from 1 to 4 per cent of GDP and credit to the private sector averaging well over 25 per cent. This could not be sustained and poverty has increased since 2000. Growth based purely on domestic demand will not be the solution to this increased poverty. Rather labour intensive export led growth with significant productivity improvements is the only way to ensure employment growth and improvements in real wages. In 2001 the Bank and the Egyptian Government completed a Social and Structural Review (World Bank 2001a) which provided a systematic evaluation of economic policy and structure to identify the main constraints to poverty reduction and long term development. Five priorities were identified for reform: strengthening economic management to return to the strong performance of the second half of the 1990s; further trade liberalisation; reduced government regulation to reduce transaction costs for business; increased expenditures for the bottom half of the population; and efficiency gains in public services such as health, education, sanitation, clean water and air quality. The review was followed in 2004 by a government and Bank (World Bank 2004b) poverty alleviation strategy which centred on three pillars not dissimilar to those of the 1991 Bank report before ERSAP commenced, namely, growth, education and social safety nets.

It would seem therefore, that in view of the similarities between the 1991 and the 2004 World Bank reports, Egypt has not made a great deal of progress in alleviating poverty during the period of economic liberalisation. Poverty worsened during stabilisation in the first half of the 1990s and improved during the second half of the 1990s – although not for the poorest region, Upper Egypt. But this improvement was based on a fragile inward-looking expansionary strategy, rather than on a genuine structural reform of the economy towards export-led growth and productivity improvements. Consequently, poverty has increased again during the first half of the 2000s. Taking these trends for the period as a whole, many Egyptians feel their living standards have declined since the ERSAP was launched in 1991 and that poverty has got worse and many are now looking to alternative sources of welfare provision.

Alternative avenues of welfare provision and the role of Islamist groups

An hypothesis we wished to explore was whether the World Bank and IMF programmes in Egypt had increased poverty and reduced state welfare provision so opening up a space for increased alternative sources of welfare provision, including faith-based. Poverty may have worsened since 1991 and although shares of public expenditure on health and education were preserved during the ERSAP period, expenditures did not keep pace with population growth and demand or with the needs of basic maintenance. As a result, the quality of state welfare provision has declined significantly. To quote Sullivan:

> The forces of secularism have failed to provide the quality services they have continued to promise: basic educational, nutritional, and health services; employment and job training; housing and transportation. While these services are being provided by the government, many of them are far from being adequate and many more are even further from being of a degree of quality that would make them desired by the Egyptian public.
>
> (Sullivan 1994 p.93)

Bayat likewise details the problem, pointing to overcrowded classrooms, multi-shift schedules, and underpaid teachers. He quotes the 1999 Population Council study which showed that 66 per cent of schools had teacher shortages, 37 per cent of classrooms had more than 45 students so that 45 per cent of students were practically unable to write. In higher education he points to declining infrastructure and classes of 400–500 students. Likewise in the health sector:

> In 1992 the Health Insurance Organisation held only 38 clinics, 41 hospitals, and some 8500 hospital beds for over 30 million beneficiaries ... Hygiene problems, long lines of poor patients in hospital corridors, and doctors treating several patients simultaneously are not uncommon problems. In many public hospitals, patients must provide their own medicine and nursing.
>
> (Bayat 2006 p.141)

Bayat also notes that, since the 1980s, the government has virtually halted the provision of public housing. This has forced many into informal squatter settlements that lack basic services and infrastructure. Government job guarantees have also declined since the 1980s with waits of five years for such jobs now the norm.

In addition to the decline in the quality of state welfare provision, a paternalistic and undemocratic welfare state has meant that many have failed to benefit fully from social safety nets and state provision of social services. Women without identity cards and those unable to afford the high transaction costs of accessing state handouts were excluded from the welfare system (Bibars 2001

Singerman 1997, Sabry 2005). Singerman has shown that although the price of subsidised food is below market cost, people must absorb queuing and networking costs to actually receive both legal and illegal goods.

The poor access to, and declining quality of, state provided welfare services has opened up a space between the state and the family for alternative providers of such services. In Egypt, many of such providers are faith-based, predominantly Islamic but also Coptic. To quote Sullivan:

> These benevolent societies have taken a lead in promoting economic and social development in local communities throughout Egypt. In the absence of effective and well-targeted projects that address the most basic needs of the majority of Egypt's growing population, Islamic private voluntary organisations (PVOs) and other groups are attempting to fill the void left by a government that is increasingly unable to devote its limited resources to a plethora of problem areas: education and training, housing, healthcare, agricultural and industrial productivity, employment and transportation.
>
> (Sullivan 1994 pp.57–8)

Although some of the PVOs are Coptic, the majority are Islamic. The role of charity or welfare provision is central to the Islamic religion, with almsgiving or *zakat* being one of the five pillars of the faith (the others being fasting, pilgrimage, prayer, declaration of faith). It is seen as the responsibility of all able individuals to help alleviate the suffering of others through *zakat*. The Islamic faith sees itself as all-encompassing, covering all things spiritual, material, societal, individual, and political. Hence, in contemporary Egypt Islam is often seen as the solution to the socio-economic ills that both socialism and capitalism have failed to address.

Egypt has a long history of such faith-based welfare activities. Concepts of responsibility towards the needy have long been shared by Copts and Muslims alike in Egypt (Habib 1990 p.89) Egypt's contemporary faith-based social provisioning dates from the 19th century, with the establishment of several Islamic and Coptic Private voluntary organisations (NGOs) which provided material support, education and homes for orphans and the handicapped (Ibrahim 1993 p.53). The first Islamic charity was established in 1878 and the first Coptic one in 1881 (Bibars 2001 p,110). Bibars has argued that there was a significant rise in the number of religious NGOs in the second half of the nineteenth century in response to Western Catholic and Protestant missionaries providing social, medical and economic services. As a result, by the First World War there were 20 Islamic and 11 Coptic NGOs and their activities extended into both social and economic sphere (ibid. p.110). The trend was further institutionalised in 1928 with the foundation of the Society of Muslim Brethren or Muslim Brotherhood under Hasan al-Banna, and the Young Men's Muslim Association. Despite King Farouq's and Nasser's attempts to smash the organisation it has survived (growing rapidly between 1945 and the late 1950s) and is an important source of both welfare and political activity.

From the 1950s on, Nasser successfully dismantled the power of the religious establishment and cracked down on Islamic and other civic groups in the attempt to establish a secular Western socialist state and the activities of religious-based and other NGOs declined dramatically (Ibrahim 1993, Kandil and Nefise-Paris 1994). He failed, however, to destroy the power of either Islam or Coptic Christianity and during the period of Sadat's presidency Islamic groups were initially encouraged in an attempt to overcome the secular socialism of Nasser and the Nasserite opposition (Hatem 1992, Badran 1991). Sadat used Islam to legitimate key government polices while at the same time denouncing extremism. In particular, Islamic student associations (Jama'at Islamiyya) flourished on university campuses and provided much-needed social and community services to students. Despite a crackdown by Sadat, particularly on the student associations, in the years immediately preceding his assassination in 1981, Islamic groups have continued to function under the Mubarak regime, often in conflict with the state. Although Mubarak's security forces have rounded up Islamic extremists, his regime has promoted the image of the Al-Azhar religious establishment and legitimised the Muslim Brotherhood, and, in a somewhat ambivalent manner, tolerated and even encouraged the social activities of Islamic groups. More generally, under Mubarak there has been a marked increase in the activities of all types of voluntary groups and civic organisations, with 'an explosion of Islamic-based NGOs' (personal interview Cairo August 2005). However, since 1992 with the resurfacing of militant Islamic extremist groups specifically targeting the Mubarak regime there has been a suppression of their activities and this has extended to the social welfare activities of benign Islamic groups.

Despite the long history of faith-based welfare provision in Egypt, the subject remains little studied apart from the books by Sullivan (1994) and Sullivan and Abed-Kotob (1999), on which we draw. The role of religion and its impact on both state policies and social welfare has tended to be ignored by both the Marxist and the liberal analysis (Dahlerup 1987, Charlton et al 1989). To quote Bibars:

> Although the existence of this shadow and parallel welfare system is an important phenomenon with a profound ideological impact on society, it has not been studied comprehensively, and the few in-depth and descriptive studies that exist are limited in their scope.
>
> (Bibars 2001 p.107)

Part of the reason the phenomenon remains understudied is data problems. It is notoriously difficult to get data on NGO operations in Egypt and many of the activities of religious groups are informal and surrounded by a degree of secrecy and defensiveness. As Sullivan and Abed-Kotob have argued:

> Whether Egyptians are more or less 'Islamic' today than ten or twenty years ago is perhaps an unanswerable question; given the authoritarian nature of Egypt's government throughout this time frame plus the built-in inadequacies of attempting to conduct survey research in such a setting, the question is not measurable at any rate. What is demonstrable (and measurable) and worthy of attention is the rising popularity of the various Islamic Institutions, political, non-political, violent and non-violent.
>
> (Sullivan and Abed-Kotob 1999 p.125)

Definitional problems also exist in trying to decide what constitutes faith-based welfare provision. In a study of Islamic NGOs in Egypt, Nefise-Paris (Kandil and Nefise-Paris 1994) defines them as those that centre around a religious and Islamic activity such as Koran recital, those that centre around a mosque, and those that have the word Islamic in their name. Bayat defines four kinds of NGOs in contemporary Egypt: classic welfare associations mostly run by aristocratic families; professional NGOs; state sponsored community development associations; and religiously motivated associations. The latter are defined as being organised by mosques and Islamic figures or churches and Christian set-ups and inspired by religious obligations or religio-political factors. The faith-based NGOs range from tiny outfits of just several people to large associations employing scores of educators, healthcare professionals and clerks. As noted by Sullivan and Abed-Kotob:

> As with Islam in general, the plethora of Islamic NGOs is by nature far from monolithic or homogeneous. Some NGOs are GONGOs (government organized NGOs) some amount to Islamic corporations, some are state–supported but privately run CDAs (community development associations), and some eschew any reliance on government support (though they must succumb to government regulation, if not full control) and are the most entrepreneurial. Many of these latter utilize the concept of 'Islamic NGO' more as a cover or a marketing tool.
>
> (Sullivan and Abed-Kotob 1999 p.27)

It is important to note that not all religious NGOs are linked to a mosque or a church, although the government tends to prefer those that are, as they are established in a public space and thus easier to monitor and control than the many private religious organisations.

Anecdotal evidence, the media, interviews and secondary sources all suggest that faith-based welfare provision has increased during the period of the ERSAP as the quality of state provision has declined. All NGOs, including faith-based ones, require official approval and have to register with the Ministry of Social Affairs. Hence it is possible to quantify the increase of NGOs in general over the past decade and a half. At the time when ERSAP was launched there were 14,000 registered, of which about 11,000 were actively working. Of these only 150 were national in scope and registered with the central ministry. The rest are site specific and registered with the governate offices of the ministry and their activities are confined to specific urban areas or villages. These 14,000 NGOs employed about two million people, mostly in a voluntary capacity (World Bank 1991 p.64) had over one million due paying members and 300 had membership in excess of 300 individuals (Sullivan 1994 p.13). These 14,000 NGOs although small by western standards was greater than for all other Arab countries combined (ibid.). Of the 14,000 NGOs about 25 per cent were Community development Associations (CDAs) distinguished from other charitable organisations by the fact they are permitted to carry out a range of activities unlike other charities which are restricted to one or two activities.

By 2000, the number of registered NGOs had increased to 20,000 of which 3,000 were CDAs. This huge increase from 14,000 in 1990 clearly supports the contention that 'Since the 1980s, thousands of new NGOs, mostly specialising in the domain of welfare and development, have mushroomed throughout Egypt, in particular in the poor rural and urban quarters' (Bayat 2006 p.150). Some 35 per cent of these NGOs received some funding from the Ministry of Social Affairs. It is impossible to say how much of the increase in NGO activity has been faith-based but anecdotal and qualitative evidence suggests that this accounts for a significant proportion.

For example, according to interviews with University staff in Cairo, Student Associations, many of them Islamic, have also been increasing rapidly since 1990. At the American University of Cairo for example, such associations have increased from a handful to more than 40.

The nature of poverty since the recession of 2000 also points to indirect evidence of the increased activities of NGOs:

> Despite the recession there is no dire poverty or fight for bread. This is not due to the government or subsidies, or even the private sector. The only explanation is community based-groups, many of which are religiously based.
>
> (Personal interview Cairo November 2004)

One recent trend which is difficult to measure and is not captured in the official figures of registered NGOs is the upsurge in banquets of compassion. These Ramadan banquets provided by mosques, religious figures and prominent business men and women are an informal and unmeasured form of specifically Islamic welfare provision which have developed over the past ten to fifteen years.

Dennis Sullivan's detailed study of Islamic private voluntary organisations in Egypt (Sullivan 1994) likewise supports the contention that the phenomenon is on the rise, although the book was written in the early years of the ERSAP:

> We can conclude from this study that there is substantial evidence to support the contention of the first hypothesis that Islamic, Christian, feminist, capitalist and other PVOs in Egypt are challenging the state's role in promoting socioeconomic development. In addition to the statistical information that demonstrates the impact of individual PVOs on community development, much of the evidence to support the hypothesis is qualitative, based on opinions of interviewees and analysis of the interviewer … Moreover, the government itself has seen this challenge from civil society, especially Islamic forces within civil society, and has sought to control and monitor PVO activity.
>
> (Sullivan 1994 p.154)

Our own interviews carried out in Cairo and Alexandria in November 2004 and August 2005 provide similar qualitative evidence to support Sullivan's hypothesis. Likewise work by Bayat (2006) Ibn-Khaldoun Centre (1995) and Mahfouz (1992) support this thesis. It is clear that faith-based welfare provision is filling a void left by the state:

> Both the positive and negative examples of Islamic and Christian efforts at local development attest to the increasingly assertive societal response to a failing state apparatus.
>
> (Sullivan 1994 p.56)

Islamic groups in particular have developed on a wide scale in both cities and rural areas and provide a variety of services, including education, healthcare services, day care, trade skills centres in activities like carpentry and sewing, youth activities, help finding jobs since government jobs have become harder to find, legal services, orphanages, libraries, and savings schemes. Faith groups also function as charities with welfare handouts in cash and in kind, for examples for widows and orphans. Private charitable transfers are estimated to exceed the handouts from the

Ministry of Social Affairs (Bibars 2001). In addition, World Bank 2004b p,39 estimated that private transfers, including from religious and other charitable organisations made up almost 4.9 per cent of the current income of the poor and 6.7 per cent of the non-poor and that private transfers had a much greater impact on poverty reduction than the two types of public transfers investigated, namely, the two social assistance programmes and food subsidies. Private transfers were most powerful in Metropolitan and Lower Egypt urban regions, where around half the recipients would have been poor without them (ibid.).

Faith-based welfare provision tends to be more active in the area of healthcare than education. Islamic and Coptic healthcare associations often use the same doctors as the government employing them on evening shifts and often paying them more than their government salaries. With the faith-based medical services both doctors and users often point to the higher quality and a strong preference for using Islamic services which are perceived as being more accessible and personal and with more dedicated staff. Doctor's pay in mosque-based hospitals is often determined by their reputation leading to better staff motivation and bed side manner:

> The perception of the public at large is that a patient receives better care from PVO (Private voluntary organization) hospitals. Moreover, many patients come to an Islamic hospital because it is Islamic. They consider Islamic as something between public and private. Islamic has the positive elements of both. It has the concern for the poor that the public sector is supposed to have and has the efficiency and quality that the private sector is supposed to have.
>
> (Sullivan 1994 p.79)

> When comparing the religious programmes to the state's, especially the MOSA (Ministry of Social Affairs) system, people clearly appreciated and respected the efforts of the non-governmental programmes.
>
> (Bibars 2001 p.122)

Patients are often willing to pay for private faith-based medical treatment. This reflects both the higher perceived quality and the fact that the public services are not genuinely free in that patients often have to buy their own medicines and dressings and provide their own nursing care if these are unavailable in the public sector. There are also inequities in access to and quality of different types of state healthcare services and the neediest are not covered by healthcare insurance. Similarly in education, parents are often prepared to pay for private schools and tutoring because of the poor quality of state education. Tawila (2000) estimates from survey work that although most students are enrolled in the state system, 76 per cent of families use private tutoring for their children. Private and group tutoring accounts for almost a third of educational spending by the poor (World Bank 2004b Table 2.6, the rest being spent on books, uniforms, fees and transportation). Singerman argues that private lessons have become much more common in the past decade amongst the poor in urban communities (Singerman 1997 p.161).

The perception among the public is that although faith-based service provision may be costly in both health and education, costs are usually based on an equitable sliding scale, they are less expensive than other private services, and they are provided in an efficient, honest and highly motivated service. It should be noted that it is not just the recipients of such services that benefit. Islamic and Coptic welfare organisations, especially in healthcare, also provide jobs, training and income to young doctors and those who find it hard to get employment, although much of the work is done on a voluntary basis. The popularity of faith-based welfare provision is such that, especially in the poor urban neighbourhoods, demand outstrips supply (Singerman 1997 p.249). One urban area where Islamic services have been in extremely high demand is in the Cairo slum of Imbaba. The squatter settlement of some one million inhabitants was consequently virtually taken over by Islamists in the early 1990s, especially the radical Gamma's al-Islamabad group. In response, the government launched an urban upgrading programme and attempted to eradicate the militants.

Egyptian faith-based welfare organisations receive their funding from a variety of sources. They are all registered with the Ministry of Social Affairs and some of them receive a degree of funding from the Ministry although this is rarely sufficient to cover all their costs (MOSA provides funding to about 35 per cent of registered private voluntary organisations). Other income comes from fees for services, subscription and membership fees, almsgiving at the mosque (*wakf*), and foreign donations. Many mosques have a *lagnit iz-zakaah*, a committee to distribute the alms collected from worshipers. All foreign donations must be reported to the Ministry of Social Affairs, and often consists of donations by Egyptian migrants and returning migrants. According to Singerman, private cash donations are the most important type of income for all types of private voluntary organisation, and this is especially so for those with religious affiliations (Singerman 1997 p.247).

Sullivan (1994) and Sullivan and Abed-Kotob (1999) provide numerous examples and descriptions of faith-based welfare organisations in Egypt. These include nationally-based organisations such as The Young Men's Muslim Association (Jam'iyyat al-Shaban al-Muslimin) which has branches throughout Egypt and runs cultural and social clubs, schools, day care centres, libraries, sports facilities, job training centres, computer and other instruction, day trips, healthcare centres and The Lawful Religious Association for Those Who Behave According to the Book (*Al-Jam'iyya al-Shar'iyya li al-'Amilin bi al-Kitab wa al-Sunna`al-Muhammadiyya*) which has a branch in each of the nation's 26 governates and 123 branches in Cairo providing hospitals, health clinics, day care centres, orphanages, libraries and other types of service craters. Most such organisations however are local and examples include The Community Association of 'Izbat Zayn on the southern edge of Cairo, which provides a nursery school, a vocational training programme, and day care and medical centre on the top floor of the rebuilt mosque to what was previously a squatter community; the Mustafa Mahmud Society, one of the most notable urban Islamic NGOs in the Mohandisin area of Cairo which runs a healthcare centre and a hospital linked to a mosque. Coptic examples include The Coptic-Evangelical Organisation for Social Services (CEOSS) headquartered in al-Minya with offices in Cairo with 1.5 million beneficiaries of its literacy, vocational training, family planning and other services.

The Muslim Brotherhood[54] has gained much popularity due to its welfare work, and consequently has become the main opposition force to Mubarak's National Democratic Party. It is particularly active in the area of healthcare and education, running schools, hospitals, day care centres, job training centres, after school programmes, Koranic instruction and other services. Currently the Brotherhood runs 22 hospitals, numerous small clinics attached to mosques and has schools in every governorate in the country, numbering more than 500. Services offered are much cheaper than other private alternatives. An estimated 20 per cent of registered NGOs in Egypt are Brotherhood run (IRIN 2006). Although banned as a political party the Muslim Brotherhood is able to appeal to its constituencies through this wide range of social programmes. These have earned it the reputation of competence and honesty compared to the Ruling National Democratic party (NDP) which is often perceived as self-serving and corrupt. Muslim Brotherhood candidates run as independents in elections and gain considerable political capital from their social work:

> According to many political observers, the Brotherhood's devotion to social work was the prime driver behind its astounding results in the parliamentary elections, held in late 2005. The group managed to capture 88 seats in the People's Assembly, up from only 15 in the outgoing Assembly…Even though the Muslim Brotherhood lacks an official party license, technically banning it from political activity, the social component of its work has largely offset this disadvantage.[55]
>
> (IRIN 2006 pp.2–3)

The Brotherhood also distributes welfare through the professional syndicates of doctors, engineers, teachers, lawyers and pharmacists, which it dominates and controls. The syndicates provide assistance to their young members and also to the needy in the neighbourhoods where they have branches. In the past, the government has been known to close down some of the Brotherhoods social projects and in recent years the NDP has started to compete with the Brotherhood in this domain by attempting to reach the grass roots with welfare services. For example, the NDP has started handing out food packets during Ramadan but this effort was deemed to have been tainted with corruption and could not match the scale of the Brotherhood's handouts, which amounted to tens of thousands in each constituency. In addition, since the Brotherhood's gains in the 2005 elections the NDP has started to send out groups of physicians to offer services in the constituencies. Recently the regime has also replaced a number of teachers in Brotherhood schools with NDP people but this has been successfully challenged in the courts.

It is the law that both Islamic and Coptic organisations cannot discriminate on the grounds of religious affiliations in terms of who they provide their services to and most girls and women who receive training from Coptic organisations are Muslim. However; in reality in order to benefit from the services of faith-based welfare organisations recipients have to conform to certain norms of behaviour. Often Islamic dress is required of women employees and beneficiaries, or conservative dress for the Coptic organisations. Single and divorced women are often excluded and outreach programmes target those who conform to the religious norms. According to Bibars:

> The Islamic alternative is infused with traditional and patriarchal norms regarding gender relations and consequently impacts heavily on women's status and position.
>
> (Bibars 2001 p.111)

Bibars also notes that the Coptic alternative is similarly gender biased and that both types of welfare system mirror the state's in being undemocratic, non-participatory and focused on paternalistic charity rather than a rights-based system (ibid. p. 151).

The State response to NGO and faith-based welfare provision

Our interview work in Cairo and Alexandria suggested that it is undoubtedly the case that political Islam in Egypt has gained capital from the welfare activities of Islamic organisations and that this is perceived as a threat by the state.

Sullivan (1994) and Sullivan and Abed-Kotob (1999) confirm this view. Sullivan (1994 p.3) suggests that these social organisations, albeit decentralised, disunited and non-conspiratorial, pose an alternative to the national government in Cairo and its subunits across the various governates, cities and villages. He compares the Islamic NGOs with the Christian-based community groups in Latin America, the *Comunidades Eclesiales de Base* (CEBs) in that both pose a challenge to incumbent regimes. Sadat's assassination and the subsequent takeover of police offices by Jihadists and their sympathisers in Assiut, have strengthened the state's perception that the Islamic alternative is a threat. Sullivan also points to the experience of Algeria (ibid. p.151) where, partly in response to the extensive welfare services provided by Islamic groups, the Islamic Salvation Front almost won the aborted 1991–2 elections. More recently, the electoral success of Hamas in Palestine points to the political capital derived from a well organised and effective welfare delivery service. Like-wise Sullivan points to Solidarity of Poland, Charta 77 of Czechoslovakia and Szeta the poor relief fund of Hungary who began life in the 1970s and 1980s as welfare organisations and subsequently went on to play a major role in the downfall of communist regimes. To quote Sullivan:

> This is not to suggest that legally registered PVOs are without political import. ... The association and its leadership generally develop a large following of appreciative clients. There is thus a considerable amount of 'political capital' stored up as a potential resource.
>
> (Sullivan 1994 p.33)

Singerman likewise argues that in the poor areas of Cairo she has studied, faith-based welfare provision often becomes political (Singerman 1997). She notes that while charitable organisations are usually apolitical they nevertheless have complex relationships with powerful figures and institutions in the community and offer politicians, religious groups or other interests a basis of support in the community. Bibars also argues that:

> In its conflict with Islamic groups the Egyptian state is losing ground, especially with increasing dissatisfaction of the people with state performance, and the widening gap between the rich and the poor.
>
> (Bibars 2001 p.15)

It is noteworthy that in parts of Upper Egypt such as Assiut where we have seen that poverty has worsened in the past decade, Islamic groups are at their strongest both in terms of welfare provision and political support. Assiut has also become a major haven of Islamic militants and witness a series of attacks on police officers, banks and tourists' boats and trains passing through the area in 1994. More than half the population of Assiut can be classified as poor with high measures of both the depth and severity of poverty.

The Muslim Brotherhood in particular has gained much political capital from its welfare activities and has become the main effective opposition to Mubarak's regime. This is partly because other political parties in Egypt are weak and ineffective, populated by elderly men or in a state of internal turmoil, and do not offer a credible opposition. At various points in time the government has responded to the political threat of the Muslim Brotherhood with crackdowns. The government has refused to allow the organisation to become a legitimate political party forcing it to put forward its candidates as independents or form alliances with other parties.[56] Before the 1995 elections hundreds of Brotherhood members were arrested.

There was a more general crackdown on Islamic groups in the 1990s. The government was shaken by the prompt Islamist response to the October 1992 earthquake and the extensive criticism of the lack of government assistance to the victims. In addition, the increased Islamic militancy post-1992 and the attempt on Mubarak's life in 1995 in Ethiopia (for which the radical Egyptian group al-Jama'a al-Islamiyya declared responsibility), along with the unrest in Assiut all contributed to the government crackdown, with little discrimination between truly violent and radical groups and groups such as the Brotherhood that had renounced violence. Mubarak seems to have been particularly disturbed by the Islamic response to the earthquake and rapidly passed Military Order Number 4, making it an offence punishable by seven years' imprisonment for any organisation to receive funding or donations in kind or to provide funding or help in the form of charity without state approval.

In addition to its attempts to crack down in an indiscriminate way on Islamists, the Egyptian government attempts to closely monitor and control the activities of all NGOs including faith-based ones. Regulation is enshrined in Law 32 of 1964 which gives the Ministry of Social Affairs (MOSA) sweeping powers to control NGOs. The law was initially passed due to government concerns over Islamic associations in the early 1960s. According to this law, all NGOs must be registered with MOSA, and MOSA has powers of regulation, oversight, management and appointment within the NGOs. MOSA's powers include the ability to prevent money coming from abroad, to prevent the general raising of funds, to appoint a temporary board of directors, and to dissolve or merge an organisation. As a result, NGOs are far from independent of government – indeed many are creations of government itself. In addition to having to register and gain approval from MOSA, most NGOs also require approval from other relevant ministries such that a health-based NGO will need a license from the Ministry of Health and any association tied to a mosque must get permission to operate from the Ministry of Awqaf (Endowments). According to Sullivan, it is easier to register a Community Development Association which can undertake multiple types of activities and is not usually associated with a church or a mosque than a Private Voluntary Organisation, especially a religious one as the government has become more cautious about religious PVOs for fear of an increasing Islamic influence over society. Because the government cannot directly control all NGOs from the MOSA headquarters in Cairo, it also uses the Regional Federation of PVOs and the MOSA directorates in the twenty six governates to help with monitoring and control. A coalition has been formed in Egypt to lobby for the reform of Law 32 and greater freedom from NGOs and international Human Rights groups as well as USAID have joined this campaign. In particular USAID is lobbying for the freedom to provide support direct to NGOs without having to go through government.

Despite Law 32 the government has an ambivalent attitude towards NGOs. On the one hand it often makes their operation difficult, on the other hand it sees them as a vehicle for helping to control local communities and it knows that the state itself no longer has the resources to match the welfare they provide to citizens.

One striking feature of the existence of faith-based welfare organisations is the fact that the donor community in Egypt does not seem to have constructively engaged with them, despite its desire to engage with secular NGOs. This is partly a reflection of the fact that the state makes it difficult for them to engage directly. It also possibly reflects, in the case of the Islamic welfare organisations, a reluctance to be seen to be giving western tax payers money to Islamic groups in the current international political climate post-9/11. Interviews with donor groups in Cairo revealed a reluctance to engage with faith-based organisations and a lack of knowledge about their activities. The World Bank for example, despite employing an outreach person in its Cairo office to work with civic groups stated that 'it is too early for the World Bank to delve into faith-based welfare'. According to another donor representative:

> Donors don't want a dialogue with non-violent religious groups. There are limits to this as we have a different world view. European aid is secular at the institutional level but Islam thinks secularism is wrong and donors don't understand Islamic welfare.
>
> (Personal interview Cairo August 2005)

There is some evidence that more recently the World Bank, despite the above quote, is showing a willingness to work with faith-based groups. Its 2004 Poverty Reduction Strategy Document states:

> Mosques, churches, community groups, and other non-governmental organizations have considerable outreach to the poor and good networks among themselves to identify and help the poor. Supporting their efforts by making it easier to set up and operate private charitable foundations that aim to reduce poverty can be an essential complement to any public safety net.
>
> (World Bank 2004b p.50)

This recent World Bank stance is encouraging since, as Sullivan has stated:

> If, however, the PVOs and NGOs do pose a challenge or threat to the government, there is even greater reason for international leaders as well as Egyptian political and economic leaders to investigate it, to understand it, perhaps to embrace and work with it.
>
> (Sullivan 1994 p.4)

Conclusion

We have shown that although the Bank and the IMF have tended to be upbeat about the poverty and social welfare effects of Egypt's ERSAP, grounds for optimism lie only in the second half of the 1990s. This was a period when, according to the two Household Expenditure Surveys of 1995–6 and 1999–2000, poverty improved. Even then, however, in Egypt's poorest region, Upper Egypt, poverty worsened in the second half of the 1990s. In addition, we cannot say that poverty improved in the second half of the 1990s due to the ERSAP as this was a period of minimal structural reform and expansionary fiscal and monetary policies. In the period of serious reform, namely the first half of the 1990s when Egypt rapidly stabilised her economy, several indicators suggest that poverty worsened. In addition, the improvement in poverty in the second half of the 1990s was based on a weak foundation and it is generally agreed that poverty has got worse since 2000 when growth has slowed and inflation returned.

Overall, due to data limitations, it is impossible to say whether people are worse off now than when the ERSAP was launched in 1991 or whether poverty has worsened. Certainly, the perception of many Egyptians is that this is the case. One area where the Egyptian public expresses particular concern is the decline in the quality of state welfare provision, despite the fact that government expenditure on health, education and social welfare programmes was preserved during the ERSAP period. The decline in the quality of state welfare provision is certainly partly responsible for the explosion in faith-based welfare provision which commenced in the 1980s and has continued since 1991, although this is also due to the general resurgence in the Islamic faith. These organisations, as well as secular NGOs, are filling a space between the state and the family and providing essential welfare services to all sections of society.

It is clear from the government's reaction that the Mubarak regime feels threatened by faith-based welfare provision and the crackdown on Islamists since 1992 has been indiscriminate. In addition, continued use of Law 32, as well as new legislation, is making it increasingly difficult for faith-based and other NGOs to function in Egypt despite the valuable services they provide. This situation is not being helped by the donor community's failure to engage constructively with faith-based welfare provision and to open a dialogue with the government on this issue. A repressive state combined with the state's failure to maintain Egypt's old welfare state system means that Islamists are increasingly gaining political capital from their welfare activities amongst a disaffected electorate such that it now seems that Islamists, in the form of the Muslim Brotherhood, are the only credible opposition to the Mubarak regime.

6

Economic Reform, Social Welfare, Civic Society and Islamists in Morocco

Introduction

Morocco, like many other Middle Eastern and North African states, has a long history of populist state welfare provision in the form of an implicit Social Contract whereby the state provides for its citizens in return for loyalty to the regime. However, although the country has made huge strides since independence in improving social welfare, most of its social welfare indicators remain below those of comparable lower middle-income countries. This is because state welfare provision, although based on a populist model, has been biased towards urban areas and the better off.

Since the early 1980s the government has no longer commanded the resources it needs to sustain the Social Contract. In the midst of the economic crisis of the early 1980s, austerity measures and structural reform measures were introduced under the auspices of the IMF and World Bank. Trends in poverty and social welfare have fluctuated since these programmes were introduced. In the first part of the 1980s both deteriorated. However, with the generation of export-led growth from the mid-1980s to the early 1990s poverty improved significantly. However, this was not sustained and in the economic slowdown of the 1990s poverty crept back up again to levels commensurate with the early 1980s. Since 2000, Morocco has experienced an economic upturn and poverty has again declined. Whether this can be sustained remains uncertain as much of the recent growth has been based on domestic demand rather than on exports.

Unlike countries such as Egypt and Jordan, the provision of social welfare by civic groups, including faith-based welfare provision, is not well developed in Morocco, although it has been increasing in recent years following the political opening up which commenced in the mid-1990s. In addition, the limited amount of faith-based welfare provision has not become politicised in Morocco, with the main opposition party, the Islamic Justice and Development Party, content to leave welfare provision to the state. However, as the regime struggles with the competing needs of preserving a conservative monarchy, which has traditionally dispensed largess to the population, and the pressures for economic and political liberalisation it has become more important for the regime to embrace civic society, including faith-based civic society. Both have the potential to contribute to much needed welfare provision at a time when the state is finding this increasingly difficult.

Social policy in Morocco

Since independence in 1956, social policy and social protection in Morocco have been seen as the domain of the state with the state being synonymous with the monarchy. King Mohammed V emerged as leader of the newly-independent state and immediately set about introducing free education and medical care and guaranteed employment for university and high school graduates. Much of this employment was in the civil service and the parastatal sector. Populist state welfare was strengthened further after the two abortive coup attempts in 1971 and 1972. This involved high levels of public spending, a wide system of consumer subsidies, legislation favouring labour and the introduction of social security. Following numerous droughts, a system of support policies for the main agricultural crops was introduced along with the exemption of the agricultural sector from taxation and redistribution of 400,000 hectares of land. The phosphate boom of 1974–6 provided the state with the resources it needed to further its distributive populist social welfare policies and to forge a new social pact. Irrigation services, infrastructure, social services, food subsidies and public sector employment and wages all expanded rapidly during and after the boom years as the state and the monarchy sought to deepen their support in rural areas and to appease the large numbers of people flocking to the urban areas from the disadvantaged subsistence farm sector – the rain-fed *bour* that made up nine-tenths of Moroccan agriculture in terms of land. Costly subsidies to protect urban consumers were the state's answer to the escalating international price of petroleum, sugar and other commodities. By 1983 the public sector wage and salary bill had reached 11.5 per cent of GDP (the largest item in recurrent expenditure) and subsides and transfers 4 per cent of GDP. Following the second oil price shock of 1979 and the further increase in the international prices of flour, sugar and edible oils the government attempted a price increase in May 1981 but urban riots resulted in the increases being partially rescinded.

King Hassan II, who succeeded his father in 1961, maintained a high profile role as the implicit guarantor of social welfare and provider of services to the poor. Whenever social tension arose over economic decisions, such as subsidy reductions as in 1981, 1984 and 1990, the King stepped in with public announcements to reverse the policies and appease the population. For example, following unrest in 1984, the King announced that there would be no further increases in the price of basic foods, that a slum clearance programme with new low income housing units would be launched in Casablanca and ten million new working days would be financed by the state.

More recently the monarchy has introduced the Mohammed V Fund for Social Welfare Provision. The Fund was established in memory of the present King's grandfather and is headed by the King's personal advisor. It supports social welfare in two ways. First, by calling upon citizens to contribute to the Fund to help the poor, so mobilising societal resources. Second, by directly supporting the poor by, for example, providing food packages (especially during religious occasions such as Ramadan), providing clothing, books and stationary to poor school children, building dormitories for female students, and assisting widows, orphans and the disabled. It is also active during times of natural disaster such as earthquakes and drought. The Hassan II Fund was created in 2001 in memory of the current King's father. This Fund receives half of all privatisation proceeds and donates a percentage of it to roads, low income housing, improved access to drinking water and provision of micro credit.[57] The perception of the Monarchy as a provider is strengthened by the conservative state ideology which is based on traditional principles such as the absolute divine power of the King and the perception that Moroccans are subjects of the monarchy rather than the citizens of the state (Ennaji 2006). In addition, the King is the country's religious leader, known as the Commander of the Faithful (*Emir al-Mouminin*).

The patron state provided strong support for the landed notables, the bedrock of support for the monarchy. Support for the agricultural sector was not seen as an economic issue but as a system whereby the patron state protected farmers and attempted, as part of the Moroccanisation project, to achieve food self-sufficiency. This was administered via a complex system of production and input subsidies along with tariffs on imported agricultural produce in order to protect domestic producers. Despite the attempt to protect the rural poor, the food self-sufficiency policy of protecting wheat, sugar, vegetable oils and dairy mainly benefited the larger irrigated farms, especially sugar producers. Rain-fed producers on the *bour* received little support in the form of extension, protected prices, fertiliser subsidies or irrigation.

Although international prices of phosphates rose in 1974, they collapsed two years later. Unable to rescind subsidies and other price support provided by the regime in the early and mid-1970s, the government resorted to decentralisation in 1976. Responsibility for rural infrastructure and social services was decentralised to regional communes without providing adequate provisions for financing these services. This led to wide disparities in access to basic social and infrastructure services across geographic areas of Morocco, with poorer regions suffering most from lack of adequate resources. There also developed vast differences in the quality of services in rural and urban areas (Walle 2004 p.1). This situation was accentuated during the 1983–93 economic reform under the auspices of the IMF/World Bank that led to large cutbacks in public investment that is so vital for the rural economy. The impoverishment of the latter meant that rural-urban migration, originally stimulated by the colonial policy of land alienation for settlement and concentration of investment in urban centres, continued unabated. While in the pre-colonial period urban population represented only 10–15 per cent of total population, 'This rapidly drifted during the colonial period' and further accelerated 'in the post independence period' (Joffe 1992 p.143).

One of the main consequences of unplanned urban growth has been explosion in squatters and shantytowns in and around urban centres. These represent not only a health hazard since they lack most basic services, but also represent a threat to public order since they also lack rights and privileges of normal working conditions that are usually associated with the formal sector. Indeed, the shantytowns, or the *bidonvilles*, were at the core of riots that swept Morocco in June 1981, January 1984 and December 1990 (ibid. p.143).

It was thus not surprising that the state's social policy as a whole displayed a strong urban bias. The state favoured urban areas due to the threat of unrest in the cities compared to the more passive and conservative rural areas. Despite the fact that more than half the population was dependent on agriculture and the majority of the poor resided in rural areas, state policy favoured urban infrastructure, schools and hospitals. Consequently, most illiterate people lived in rural areas and rural social indicators were below the levels of urban areas. The effects of urban bias can still be seen today. Public expenditure on education still benefits the better-off, health expenditure favours urban-based curative services whilst the urban bias in infrastructure expenditure on services such as water, sewerage and electricity persists. For example, in 2003 not only was health expenditure by the government low by international standards at 1.3 per cent of GDP but more than 75 per cent went to urban hospitals and clinics with an surplus of doctors in urban areas and a shortage of female nurses, midwives and health visitors in rural and peri-urban areas. Although more rural health clinics have been built in recent years they suffer from understaffing and poor access for those in remote areas.

In addition to a marked rural-urban divide, there is also a problem of poorly targeted state welfare. Apart from very specific social assistance programmes, public expenditure in Morocco does not directly target the poor. As a result, in the early 1990s the majority of those below the poverty line did not benefit from public services and for all categories of public expenditure the rich received proportionately more than the poor (World Bank 1994 p.82). In health, for example, in the early 1990s the richest 20 per cent of the population directly and indirectly appropriated 40 per cent of public spending in health while the bottom 40 per cent received less than 20 per cent (World Bank 1994 p.xi). Likewise, in education Morocco spends less on primary education and much more on secondary schooling[58] compared to other countries at similar GDP per capita levels. In general there is a need to refocus public expenditure on preventative health care, primary education and basic infrastructure that benefits the poor including the many poor in rural areas.

The past urban bias and poor targeting of social welfare expenditure led the Bank to conclude in 1994 that:

> In spite of improvements in recent years, access to essential social and economic services is severely restricted in rural areas and among the poorest groups. The analysis of public spending indicates many disparities in the allocation of resources in favour of urban areas and the better off and that most of the benefits from public expenditure accrue to the better off. Thus, there is a strong case for spending more on programmes that benefit the poor, improving the targeting efficiency of existing programmes that are already directed at the vulnerable and moving towards a policy of price discrimination between different users.
>
> (World Bank 1994 p.84)

Another weakness of social policy in Morocco is the inadequacy of social safety nets to protect the most vulnerable such that indicators like child malnutrition are much higher than in comparator countries. Most safety net programmes are ad hoc and fail to catch many of the poor when they are adversely affected by livelihood shocks. The lack of organised social safety nets became particularly evident during the stabilisation policies of the mid to late 1980s when the poor were hit by subsidy reductions and increased living costs.

The ad hoc nature of social safety nets is shown by the fact that various different ministries and government bodies provide handouts. The National Welfare Agency (*Entraide Nationale*) is meant to promote family and social welfare as well as monitor the work of charitable organisations. It runs more than 500 welfare centres for the destitute, elderly, women heads of household and orphans which reach around 46,500 people. It also offers nutrition assistance, pre-school education, vocational training and aid. Although its budget increased from US$25 million at the end of the 1990s to over US$60 million in 2006, it still remains inadequate in terms of providing comprehensive safety net coverage with beneficiaries constituting less than 2 per cent of the poor. The Ministry of Youth and Sports and the Ministry of

Justice run centres for youth in conflict with the law, the Ministry of Health runs centres for children who are victims of violence, the Ministry of the Interior runs centres for vulnerable groups whilst the Ministry of Handicapped families provides handouts to the disabled. The Ministry of Public Health provides nutritious weaning food for children at risk and the Ministry of Education distributes food to school canteens for children in need, particularly in rural areas.[59]All these safety nets are characterised by ad hoc institutional arrangements and a charitable 'handout' mentality. The Compensation Fund supports the poor indirectly through subsidising basic foodstuffs. Again, however, targeting is poor and it was estimated in the early 1990s that only 16 per cent of the value of subsidies reached the poorest 30 per cent of the population (World Bank 1994 p.80 no. 5). By the end of the 1990s, the food subsidy programme was the largest social assistance programme in Morocco with outlays of 1.6 per cent of GDP (compared to 1.08 per cent of GDP spent on health).

These social safety net arrangements forced the Bank to conclude in 2006 that 'Overall, Morocco lacks a comprehensive social safety net programme and support for vulnerable groups is highly precarious.' (World Bank 2006a p.33).

One of the more effective social safety nets in Morocco is the public works scheme known as the *Promotion Nationale* which was established in 1961. It builds infrastructure and projects mainly in the rural areas, such as reforestation, well water capture, dams, roads, schools and rural health centres by employing those without adequate work. Since its creation it has employed around 50,000 people annually and pays salaries at the minimum rural wage or in food equivalent. Unemployment and under-employment is the most serious cause of poverty in rural areas and although the *Promotion Nationale* is well targeted and helps, its coverage is far from adequate (Government of Morocco, Ministère des Affaires Economique et Sociale 1993 p.51).

In addition to ad hoc social safety nets, the Moroccan welfare system includes a formal social security system covering salaried workers in some parts of the private sector and civil servants, local government staff, the military and staff of parastatals. This offers family allowances, health and maternity benefits as well as retirement, invalid and survivors benefits. Around one million private sector workers are covered and most public sector employees. This is only equivalent to 20 per cent of the population, 88 per cent of whom are urban dwellers (Herzenni 2002). The public system of social security is more generous than the private sector schemes. However the Living Standards Measurement Survey of 1991 showed that social security coverage amongst the poor is non-existent while it is limited amongst the middle income expenditure class. Significant coverage was found only amongst the urban upper income groups.

Another important plank of welfare policy has been minimum wage legislation. The government sets minimum rural and urban wages and increases in these during the 1980s helped prevent many households headed by a minimum wage earner from falling into poverty.

Urban bias, poor targeting and inadequate coverage have forced many to conclude that social welfare policy in Morocco is weak despite the strong populist stance of the state and monarchy:

> However, while the nationalists in the 1960s demanded the extension of education, health care and other rights to all Moroccans, Morocco's inability to realise this goal after five decades of independence has become apparent, despite rising per capita GDP and investment.
>
> (Ennaji 2006 pp.117–8)

A 2006 World Bank Report concluded that the Government's approach to dealing with poverty and social exclusion has tended to be centrally driven, with little room for participation, weak coordination among line ministries and inadequate targeting (World Bank 2006a p.1). It concluded that this was due to the fact that most government interventions adopted a top-down approach, were single sector interventions which failed to develop a comprehensive and integrated approach to poverty in both rural and urban areas, had limited autonomy of local decision makers and were poorly targeted both regionally and by social group.

As a result of the failings of social policy, many of Morocco's social indictors are well below those for lower middle income countries and are often below those of poorer sub-Saharan countries, despite high levels of expenditure. Table 12 shows that in terms of births attended by health staff, fertility rates, access to clean water in rural areas, adult literacy rate (especially for females), and malnutrition in terms of weight for age Morocco performs significantly worse than the lower middle income country average. In addition in 2005 Morocco ranked 123 out of 177 in the Human Development Index.

One factor which has prevented even worse social indicators and poverty levels is the role that migrant remittances have played in household expenditures. In 2003 remittances were equivalent to 8.2 per cent of GDP and constituted an important source of income for many poor families. Another mitigating factor has been the growth of the informal sector since the early 1980s. By the late 1990s informal activities employing less than 10 people represented 77.3 per cent of all enterprises and offered a temporary solution to unemployment, slow labour absorption in the formal sector and the decline in public investment and employment growth.

Table 12: Morocco: Comparative social welfare indicators

	Morocco 2004	**Lower Middle Income ave. 2004**
Birth rate (per 1,000)	22.84	16.57
Births attended by health staff (%)	63%	86%
Death rate (per 1,000)	5.73	6.89
Fertility rate (births per woman)	2.52	2.17
GDP per Capita (Constant 2000 US$)	1,349	1,522
Access to clean water (% of population)	81%	82%
Access to clean water urban (% of population)	99%	94%
Access to clean water rural (% of population)	56%	71%
Life expectancy at birth	70.08	70.25
Adult literacy rate	52%	89%
Adult literacy rate female	40%	85%
Adult literacy rate male	66%	93%
Malnutrition weight for age (% under 5)	10.2%	11.76%
Physicians per 1,000	0.51	N/A
Net primary school enrollment rate	86.11%	N/A
Net primary enrollment rate females	83.43%	N/A
Net primary enrollment rate males	88.69%	N/A
Unemployment	10.8%	N/A
Unemployment female	11.4%	N/A
Unemployment male	10.6%	N/A

Source: World Bank (2006d), World Development Indicators (WDI) online database.

Poverty and social welfare under economic reform

An unfavourable external environment and inappropriate internal policy responses led to vast macroeconomic imbalances in Morocco by the late 1970s and early 1980s. Two attempts to stabilise the economy (the 1978–80 Triennial Plan and the 1980–3 Adjustment Programme) were aborted as a result of a weak political coalition whose 'indeterminate economic policy wavered between stabilisation and growth' (Hamdouch 1998 p.13). In 1983, the powerful King Hassan II turned to the IMF and World Bank, leading to a ten-year long stablisation programme promoted by the IMF accompanied by a series of structural adjustment and sectoral loans with the World Bank aimed at addressing Morocco's macroeconomic and structural imbalances.

As in Jordan, Egypt, Tunisia and elsewhere, the Fund and the Bank called for, among other things, fiscal consolidation in return for support. But they disagreed over how best this was to be achieved, leading 'to incoherencies between [their] policies', and even a lack of coordination between the two institutions on the one hand, and the Moroccan government on the other (ibid., p.16). While the Bank felt that too much austerity could jeopardise its own sectoral efforts, the Fund was more concerned with macroeconomic stabilisation and insisted on more expenditure reduction. Eventually, fiscal consolidation was achieved by reducing absorption, as the IMF wanted, mainly by lowering private and public consumptions as well as by cutting public investment.

While capital investment was hit hard, recurrent expenditure was hardly touched for political reasons. Capital expenditure fell by half in real terms between 1983 and 1986, with large, negative consequences for development and operations of both economic infrastructural and social facilities. This was particularly the case in the post-1976 decentralisation policy followed by the regime, which required more, not less, allocations to regional communes. Historically, and up till the early 1980s, public investment always exceeded private investment in Morocco. This trend was reversed after 1983 as a result of expenditure reduction measures, called for by the IMF stabilisation package. In 1986, public investment represented no more than 4 per cent of total investment. In Morocco, 'public investment tends to complement private investment rather than to replace it' (Achy and Hamdouch 2003 p.5). Hence, reducing public investment had serious implications for both growth and employment. It also reduced private investment as several studies have already shown (see ibid. p.5). It was not surprising therefore that cutting public investment, along with raising interest rates (a key condition in the IMF's stabilisation package), drastically reduced private investment, especially in rural areas where large segments of the population lived.

In addition, Morocco's entire rural economy depends heavily on public investment for infrastructure, extension services, fertilisers, and mechanisation. Reducing public investment in rural areas led to delays in the provision of infrastructure (transportation, telecommunication, etc) and social sector services (education, health, training, houses, etc), with severe implication for poor in rural areas (Hamdouch 1998 and Achy and Hamdouch 2003).

The initial years of reforms also involved severe fiscal austerity in the form of a civil service wage freeze from 1981–5, limited public sector recruitment to

10,000 per year for three years, higher taxation, a cut in subsidies with sugar, oil and flour prices up by 30 per cent, 52 per cent and 87 per cent respectively. In addition the prices of about 45 products were decontrolled between 1983 and 1985 and the price of subsidised food, fertilisers, electricity, water and petroleum were increased.

Macroeconomically, the reform measures were considered a success; the budget deficit was reduced from 10.9 per cent of GDP in 1983–4 to 2.6 per cent in 1992–3; inflation was brought under control and declined from 12.5 per cent in 1984 to less than 3 per cent in 1988; and government budget deficit declined from 9.7 per cent in 1982 to as low as 2.2 per cent in 1992 (Achy and Hamdouch, 2003, p.19). The social impact of reform, however, has been dramatic. As in Jordan, figures regarding poverty and unemployment have been contentious and highly debatable. For example, while the official unemployment rate in Morocco was 17 per cent in 1989, 'in reality [unemployment was] probably closer to 20–25 per cent' (Joffe, 1992, p.142). Similarly, the unofficial but generally recognised poverty rates were much higher than publicly published figures. Anecdotal evidence (such as a decline in the primary school enrolment rate, continued high illiteracy rate, rapid rural-urban migration) pointed to higher poverty rates than formally recognised. In fact, the social impact of reform was so traumatising that the Moroccan government terminated its agreement with the IMF in 1993 and since then has not signed any agreements with the Fund, although it continued to collaborate with the World Bank on sectoral basis (Hamdouch 1998 p.17).

The above suggests that the 1980s and early 1990s was a period in which the implicit social contract between the state and the citizens broke down, as Ali (1997 p.207) noted:

> The implicit rules of the game of the previous decade – according to which an interventionist state managed to secure through its own expenditures a satisfactory growth rate as well as a generous policy of clientelism – could no longer be applied in the midst of the crisis of the 1980s. The economy was no longer in a position to sustain previous expenditure levels and continue the economic and social policies adopted in the previous decade.

To be sure, luck and government policies also influenced the performance of the Moroccan economy during the period from the mid-1980s to the early 1990s. Apart from the first few years, the stabilisation programme did not appear to compromise economic growth, although growth rates in the 1980s and even 1990s were much lower than they were in the 1970s. Growth picked up from the mid-1980s through to the early 1990s.[60] But an improved growth rate was caused by exceptionally good weather conditions and growth in the export sector, not by IMF austerity measures.

During this period, official poverty fell (see Table 13) from 21 per cent in 1984 to 13 per cent by 1991.[61] The main reason this might have been the case in the 1984–91 period was not due to income redistribution, as the Gini coefficient hardly changed. The success came from generating labour-intensive economic growth which created considerable employment opportunities for the poor. Poverty reduction in urban areas was driven by government policies to boost industry and exploit its historically close ties with the EU. This led to rapid expansion of employment in the manufacturing sector, especially in export orientated enterprises such as textiles, leather and agro-industries and by a rapid growth in the informal sector. Labour-intensive growth was partly due to the relative decline in labour costs and an increase in capital costs. Profit exemptions were reduced, as were accelerated depreciation allowances while imported capital became more expensive following devaluation. At the same time, employment subsidies were in place to make labour cheaper. Throughout the period real wages fell, particularly in the manufacturing sector where there was a move towards temporary low skilled employment. But employment gains more than made up for this in terms of the impact on poverty and increases in the minimum wage protected the very poor. During 1984 to 1990 the real wage decreased by 1 per cent per annum whilst employment increased by 3 per cent per annum, hence the high elasticity of employment, particularly temporary employment, relative to wages meant that the total wage bill increased and contributed to poverty alleviation. Between 1984 and 1989 temporary employment increased at an annual rate of 11 per cent in the domestically orientated sector and by 25 per cent per annum in the export sector with the latter also increasing its hiring of permanent workers by 19 per cent per annum.

Table 13: Morocco: National poverty headcount

1984	**1991**	**2000**	**2005**
21 per cent	13 per cent	19 per cent	14 per cent (19 per cent)*

* In fact, while official rates of poverty were estimated to be 14 per cent in 2005, just one year earlier the World Bank's Poverty Report (2004c, p.2) estimated poverty in Morocco at 19 per cent. The same Report also added that 'another 25 per cent of the population is considered "economically vulnerable"', and need careful monitoring (ibid.).

Rural poverty declined in the latter part of the 1980s due to good weather and agricultural reforms which created rapid agricultural growth. During the 1980s the agricultural sector grew by an annual average of 8 per cent, twice the rate of overall economic growth. Private sector investment in agriculture increased by about 31 per cent per annum in nominal terms between 1985 and 1991. Although this mainly benefited the irrigated areas, the latter provided a major source of employment for the rural poor, who relied more on wage employment than on land ownership. The rise in the agricultural minimum wage also helped alleviate rural poverty. Hence agriculture made a major contribution to the increase in rural incomes.

Another factor that mitigated against poverty in the first phase of adjustment and stabilisation was the policy of compensated devaluation, whereby increases in consumer prices of imports brought about by devaluation were compensated for by tariff reductions. This minimised the impact on consumer prices and real wages in domestic currency terms yet increased competitiveness expressed in foreign exchange terms. Inflation reduction under the stabilisation also benefited the poor since inflation erodes the real value of both incomes and savings.

Moreover, after an initial sharp reduction in government expenditures in the first phase of stabilisation between 1983–8, these started to rise again in the late 1980s. The government made a firm effort to protect social expenditures with public expenditure on health only falling from 1.1 per cent of GDP to 0.9 per cent of GDP between 1982 and 1991 and expenditure on education only falling from 6.2 per cent GDP to 5.3 per cent. In addition the Government refrained from laying off public sector employees as a way of cutting the budget deficit and thus no new class of urban poor was created during the first eight or so years of the reform programme. Rather, fiscal stringency was obtained by a freeze on public sector wages and by cutting back on public sector investment. Although subsidies during this period fell from 2.2 per cent of GDP to 0.5 per cent, this was mainly due to the fall in the international price of subsidised goods rather than due to domestic price increases. In addition, the subsidies that were eliminated, namely on butter, milk and high quality wheat, were on goods that did not figure heavily in the consumption basket of the poor.

Macroeconomic stabilisation, particularly in the form of inflation reduction, financial sector reform including higher interest rates and exchange rate polices, also contributed to a surge in migrant remittances which by 1991 accounted for 11 per cent of private consumption and 7.5 per cent of GDP. These remittances played an important role in boosting incomes including those of the poor. The World Bank has estimated that about 180,000 or 5 per cent of the estimated poor in 1991 would be added to the number of the poor if it were not for transfers from abroad (World Bank 1994 p.26).

However, although poverty fell from the mid-1980s to the early 1990s, a large number of the population remained close to the poverty line and thus vulnerable to even small deteriorations in economic conditions. This was clearly illustrated during the 1990s when an economic slowdown particularly in the manufacturing sector and droughts reduced growth to an annual average of only 2 per cent and increased poverty from 13 per cent in 1991 to 19 per cent in 2000 (see Table 13). The rise in poverty rates to 19 per cent in the latter part of the 1990s meant that 5.3 million were poor in Morocco. During the 1990s the number of people just above the poverty line also increased such that 12 million were economically vulnerable. The depth and severity of poverty also increased during the 1990s particularly in rural areas. For example, the number of extreme poor, that is, those living beneath the food poverty line (the threshold that distinguishes those with only enough means to maintain minimum calorific intake required for survival) increased in rural areas from 255,000 people in 1990–1 to 844,000 in 1998–9. This increase in poverty occurred despite an increase in government expenditure on social protection[62] from 9 per cent of GDP in the late 1980s to 12.5 per cent in 1998 equivalent to 43 per cent of total government expenditure. In particular, social security outlays increased as did expenditure on drought relief and rural public works schemes but still fell well short of requirements.

The economic slowdown can be partly explained by an appreciation of the real exchange rate (which appreciated by 17 per cent in the 1990s), poor infrastructure, drought (almost one in every two years during the 1990s), a decline in agricultural investment and a general slow down in the economic reform process especially trade liberalisation as the Bank became increasingly complacent. (Our complementary book *Aid and Power in the Arab World* (Harrigan and El-Said 2008) analyses the economic impact of reform in Egypt, Jordan, Morocco and Tunisia in greater depth.) External causes included the economic recession in Europe, a slow down in DFI and deterioration in terms of trade resulting from falling phosphate prices and rising oil prices due to the crisis in the Middle East. Growth turned negative in 1992 and 1993 and remained low for the rest of the decade. During this period unemployment grew and low labour productivity meant that real wages could not be increased without loosing international competitiveness. Hence, increasing labour productivity became essential for further poverty reduction and this did not materialise. Demographic pressures also added to the unemployment and poverty increase. Between 1985 and the end of the 1990s unemployment rose from 11.5 per cent to 15 per cent with most of the increase concentrated in urban areas. The growth of urban unemployment during the 1990s was fuelled by rural to urban migration and to a lesser extent by growth in the population and rising labour force participation rates. The appreciation of the real exchange rate during this period also had adverse effects on unemployment by encouraging a return to more capital intensive production methods. Urban unemployment peaked in 1995 at 23 per cent.[63] One marked feature of the increase in unemployment has been the extent to which it has hit the young and the educated. The rate of unemployment amongst university graduates increased from 6.5 per cent in 1984 to 26.2 per cent in 1995 whilst for high school graduates it more than doubled rising from 14.6 per cent in 1984 to 31.2 per cent in 1993. More than 90 per cent of unemployment is in the urban areas compared to 50 per cent in 1985.

Growing urban unemployment has been accompanied by an increase in urban slums. During the past two decades informal housing has developed at a faster pace than formal housing and the presence of informal settlements in urban areas has steadily increased due to population growth, rural to urban migration and a dysfunctional urban land and housing market. Since the early 1990s slums have continued to increase at a rate of 4 per cent per annum (World Bank 2006b). Although poverty remains predominantly rural in Morocco the 2004 Census on Population and Housing showed a clear increase in the incidence of urban poverty.

Other non-income indicators of poverty also deteriorated in the early 1990s. For example between 1987 and 1992 the nutritional status of children declined. Non-income measures of poverty were adversely affected by the fact that not enough income was channelled into categories of public spending which help the poor such as primary health and education and essential infrastructure services. In addition, the quality of health care and education deteriorated as expenditures failed to keep pace with population growth. The growth of poverty during the 1990s has led the Bank to conclude that although Morocco was successful in the mid to late 1980s in terms of growth and poverty reduction this had fallen short in the 1990s (World Bank 1997). In the Bank's 2001 review of the Country Assistance Strategy the report opens with the statement: 'Economic and Social indicators show little improvement.' (World Bank 2001b p.i). The importance of growth for poverty reduction has been stressed by the Bank. The Bank has ascribed 85 per cent of the poverty increase as being directly due to low growth as opposed to deterioration in income distribution (World Bank 2005 p.2).

As growth has picked up again since 2000, official sources believe that poverty has fallen to 14 per cent in 2005. However, no accurate figures for poverty rates exist, and the current figures are highly contentious. The World Bank believes that poverty remains at the same level as it was in 2000 (see Table 13). It is true that between 2000 and 2004 GDP growth increased to 4.5 per cent per annum with strong growth in agriculture due to favourable weather (agricultural growth accelerated from -1.3 per cent in the 1990s to an annual average of 8.2 per cent in the early years of the 2000s) and in manufacturing, services, tourism and IT. But the employment opportunities as a result of this growth have not been sufficiently high enough to achieve a big dent in poverty or even unemployment. According to World Bank officials, Morocco needs an annual average growth rate of 7–8 per cent in order to cause a real dent in poverty and unemployment. A 5 per cent growth rate, they add, will only prevent the current levels of poverty and unemployment from deteriorating (cited in Achy and Hamdouch 2003 p.25).

To achieve above 5 per cent annual growth rates, Morocco's Gross Fixed Capital Formation to GDP must exceed 27 per cent. It reached only 24 per cent and 25 per cent in 1999 and 2000 respectively. During 1995–2000, average investment was only 21 per cent of GDP. After it dipped following the IMF stabilisation programme in 1983, it never really recovered. Indeed, during the 1980s the average investment rate was still higher than in the 1990s (Achy and Hamdouch 2003 p.4). Hence, it is doubtful whether the official unemployment rate which points to a decline from a national average of 13.6 per cent in 2000 to 10.8 per cent in 2004 can be taken for granted (see Table 12).

Even if one accepts the argument that rural poverty and unemployment have actually improved since the mid-1990s, anecdotal evidence suggests that they have been worsening in urban areas. As the World Bank (2004c p.10) recently wrote: '...poverty and presumably inequality, and urban unemployment has continued to climb. The increase is disproportionately among the young and educated which register employment rates of 32 percent and 27 percent respectively'.

It remains to be seen whether the growth upturn of the early 2000s translates into sustainable long-term growth and poverty reduction. Much of this growth is based on remittances and tourism receipts along with growth of domestic demand and agriculture as opposed to being export driven. Since the mid-1990s, however, the government has woken up to the severe challenge posed by poverty and unemployment and has introduced a new, ambitious national programme to alleviate poverty and unemployment in poor areas (Walle 2004 p.1). The next section sheds more light on Morocco's national programme. Suffice it to say here that the national programme has commanded the full support of the World Bank and the international community, and seems to have already improved social conditions in rural areas, albeit not without challenges.

World Bank and government focus on poverty 1994–2006

Morocco has undertaken World Bank structural adjustment programmes since 1983. The Bank paid little attention to social welfare effects during the 1980s.[64] However, from the early 1990s onwards the Bank has taken an increasing interest in Morocco's social welfare policies. This followed from the Bank's own acknowledgement that its policies in the past had failed in respect of reduction in income inequality and the provision of services to the poor:

> The fundamental aims of the Bank's assistance strategy since 1983 have been threefold: to help stabilise the economy; to raise the rate of economic growth;

> and to reduce income inequality and extend social services to the poor. The first of these objectives has been achieved to a much larger extent than the other two.
>
> (World Bank 1997 p.8)

It was also accepted that past reforms in the agricultural sector had focused excessively on subsidy removal to improve the fiscal deficit with little in the way of increased expenditures and government support and services to help poor rain-fed farmers and small scale irrigated farms. Education reform was also judged to have been a failure in the 1997 report (ibid. p.39).

In the early 1990s the Bank carried out a poverty assessment which resulted in the Report 'Poverty, Adjustment and Growth' (World Bank 1994). The report reviewed the dimensions of poverty in Morocco and current government policies and made policy recommendations for improvements. The findings were to be incorporated into the government's strategy for poverty alleviation which was under preparation at the time. The report concluded that labour intensive economic growth, particularly in rural areas, was fundamental to achieve improvement in poverty indicators, that the policy of food self sufficiency should be abandoned and farmers encouraged to grow profitable crops and public expenditure should be re-orientated towards rural areas. The poverty report was followed in 1994 by a Bank review of public expenditure which concluded amongst other things that public expenditure on basic human capital formation should be increased with priorities given to primary education, basic health care, and water supply especially in rural areas. This was echoed in the Bank's 1997 Country Assistance Strategy which placed added emphasis on education for rural girls in light of the high female illiteracy rate. The Bank's 2001 Country Assistance Evaluation (World Bank 2001b) concluded that poverty had been increasing and:

> We also agree that that the lack of tangible results in terms of living standards are now becoming more pressing than ever, calling for renewed efforts and increased action. This discussion is at the centre of our dialogue with the country as we prepare our new CAS'
>
> (World Bank 2001b p.55)

Poverty reduction in Morocco has remained firmly on the Bank's agenda in the new millennium. In the 2005–9 Country Assistance Strategy (World Bank 2005) the 'overarching objective' of the strategy was poverty reduction in response to lacklustre economic growth, inadequate social indicators relative to the country's income levels and high unemployment. The Bank argued that unless there was accelerated growth with job creation, poverty and social exclusion were likely to spark unmanageable social tensions. Again the Bank placed emphasis on increasing the access to basic services by the poor and marginalised, with Bank support to reduce slums, create low cost housing and to foster greater access to basic services, social programmes and economic opportunity, including increases in the quality and quantity of basic education. The CAS focus was backed up by the Bank's 2004 Poverty Report which included communal poverty maps and other innovations to measure and locate poverty.[65] The report (World Bank 1994) had shown that poverty was predominantly a rural phenomenon in Morocco with 72 per cent of the poor in rural areas with the poor consisting of wage earners and small scale farmers with less than a hectare of land. The main cause of rural poverty was identified as the historically low level of public spending on essential services such as water, electricity, roads, schools and health clinics. In isolated areas this was compounded by lack of social and agricultural infrastructure such as roads, flood protection and irrigation.

The Bank also acknowledged that agricultural reform remained a key item on the agenda and that any such reform would require strong social safety nets to protect those whose livelihoods might be threatened by the removal of protection and subsidies. In addition to safety nets it was hoped that employment creation in tourism and other emerging sectors would absorb those who lost their living due to the restructuring of the economy away from protected agriculture. The Bank's emphasis on poverty and social welfare was also facilitated by the opening of a Bank office in Rabat in 1998 which initially focused its work on social and rural development.

Coinciding with a greater Bank emphasis on poverty and social exclusion was a major re-orientation of government policy in the same direction. Shocked by the vast disparities between rural and urban areas, as well as by rapid rise in the level of poverty and unemployment, the government introduced in 1997 the Social Priority Programme, which includes several programmes such as a wider provision of electricity (PERG), water (PAGER), and rural roads (PNCRR), along with a poor area development programme (BAJI). The latter aims at better targeting both education and health expenditure as well as infrastructure and employment interventions in the country's poorest 16 provinces. In particular, it aims at boosting school construction and enrolment in rural areas, partly through school feeding programmes, and has placed new priority on primary health services in rural areas with expansion of primary health care facilities, the establishment of itinerant teams in rural areas, improving the staff quality, stepping up maternal and child health care to tackle diseases and malnutrition and enhancing immunisation coverage. This improved targeting has paid dividends. Net primary enrolments for rural females have increased from 28 per cent in 1990–1 to 47 per cent in 1998–9.

The World Bank 2004 Poverty Report (World Bank 2004c) was able to conclude that the social programmes were generally well targeted in poor zones of rural areas but not so in urban areas. Walle (2004 pp.X, 15 and 16) provides the most comprehensive evaluation for the performance of these national programmes up to date. He concluded that the national:

> programmes covered here appear well targeted to the rural poor but not to the urban poor. Indeed, the findings point to substantial benefits accruing to urban non-poor, while bypassing the urban poor altogether … There is impressive progress in primary and secondary school enrolments for the poor as well as for poor girls since 1994. However, here too, the gains are concentrated on the rural poor while the urban poor appear not to have particularly benefited … However, BAJ is implemented in provinces that cover at most only half of the country's rural poor and under 40 per cent of its total poor.

The accession to the throne of King Mohammed VI in 1999 marked a major turning point in political and social policy in Morocco. Under the new King not only was economic reform sped up, but considerable political liberalisation took place under a policy of democratisation and modernisation and greater emphasis was placed on social policy. Democratisation was signalled by legislative elections in 2002 and municipal elections in 2003, the creation of a national institute for Berber culture and a reform of the personal status and family law (*mudawana*) in 2003 which made polygamy illegal, raised the age of marriage for girls from 15 to 18 and gave wives joint responsibility with their husband for family matters. In addition, there was legislation to protect press freedom and the freedom of civil society groupings. The King repeatedly articulated the need for employment generating growth, education, low income housing, responsive local decision making and women's rights. Social policies were also strengthened with new legislation making life insurance, social security and health care compulsory for all workers. The King's early speeches focused on poverty eradication and social development. One of his earliest initiatives was the Royal Commission on Education Reform. The new King also initiated the mobilisation of funds and the creation of new institutions such as the Social Development Agency in 1999 which was charged with creating and supporting social development projects with target population participation to promote community development at grass roots rural and peri-urban levels. The Social Development Agency also gives NGOs a prominent role on its Board and funds projects executed by NGOs.

In normal Moroccan fashion, several new bodies were created and linked to the monarch, such as the Hassan II Fund for Social and Economic Development created in 2000 and the Mohammed V Foundation for Solidarity created in 1998. These Funds and Foundations are large in terms of their resources. For example, in 1998 the Mohammed V Foundation raised US$8.3 million and in 1999 it raised US$43 million (compared to the annual budget for the country's main social assistance programme the Entraide Nationale which is just under US$20 million). The Hassan II Fund started out with US$700 million and devoted US$40 million to adult literacy training compared to a government budget of US$3.4 million and US$110 million to social housing compared to a government allocation of US$15.5 million. These Funds and Foundations also had strong local and NGO representation. The King has challenged the government, civil society and the private sector to face up to and tackle the problems of poverty and social exclusion. He has also encouraged the strong Ministry of the Interior and the provincial governors to become actively involved in community development beyond their traditional security role (World Bank 2002c).

The new King's approach coincided with a new coalition government led by the socialist party (*Union Nationale des Forces Populaires*) which was in power from 1998–2002 followed by an amended coalition government in which the socialists were also in a majority. The coalition government's commitment to social welfare policies was signalled by the renaming of the Ministry of Social Affairs to Ministry of Social Development, Family and Solidarity in 2005 which was mandated to address issues of persistent poverty, social exclusion and their negative effects on social cohesion. The government also initially increased the budget allocated to social development from 41 per cent of the budget in 1997–8 to 47 per cent in 2000. The budget for the newly-named Ministry of Social Development increased fivefold (Ammor 2003). The government was assisted in its new strategy for social development by UNDP and the first report on Human Development was published in 1998. The government's strategy was similar to the Bank strategy outlined above, namely to reduce poverty, facilitate access to proper housing; reinforce social protection of the most vulnerable and poor, increase the participation of the poor in economic activities, for example via micro credit (Ennaji 2006, p.131). In order to implement this strategy the government placed more emphasis on decentralisation and the role of NGOs in service delivery.

More specific government initiatives to reduce poverty and social exclusion included the creation in September 2005 of an Employment Initiative costing US$200 million. This targeted first-time job seekers, with a focus on micro incentives to create 200,000 jobs, especially among the young unemployed, via incentives to set up their own businesses. Likewise the Cities without Slums programme, supported by Bank policy-based lending in the form of a US$150 million Bank Development Policy Loan, was an initiative launched by the government in 2004 to clear all slums by offering better housing to slum communities.[66] Like so much social welfare provision in Morocco, the slum clearance project was fronted by the King who had elevated the eradication of slum dwellings to priority status in 2001 in a royal speech. His personal involvement included visits to slum settlements, opening of building sites and ceremonies handing housing units over to the poor.

In September 2005 the government launched the National Initiative for Human Development (INDH). This was a highly visible programme promoted by the King, led by the Prime Minister and implemented by the Ministry of the Interior. INDH has now become the government's primary programme for poverty reduction. Six hundred and fifty targeted communities were chosen to benefit from the programme. Poverty maps were used to choose the poorest rural communities and urban neighbourhoods. Each rural and urban neighbourhood gets a block grant irrespective of size with US$900,000 for urban and US$600,000 for rural. Local committees identify projects to be financed by INDH and activities to be funded from other sources such as line ministry budgets. INDH has US$1.2 billion of funding consisting of 60 per cent from Central Government, 20 per cent from local government and 20 per cent from international donors. The World Bank is a major sponsor with a loan of US$100 million over four years 2007–10. According to the Bank:

> The project will assist the Government in improving inclusiveness, accountability and transparency of decision making and implementation processes at the local level in order to enhance use of social and economic infrastructure and services by the poor and vulnerable groups.
>
> (World Bank 2006a p.5)

INDH complements the government's other programmes to tackle poverty and social exclusion such as the Social Development Agency and the *Entraide Nationale.* However, it promotes a new culture of participation and supports the government's efforts at deconcentration and local governance with a greater role for civil society in identifying, planning and executing local development projects.[67] The INDH has four components: i) alleviate poverty in rural areas by targeting 400 rural communities with poverty rates over 30 per cent, ii) alleviate social exclusion in urban areas by targeting 250 urban neighbourhoods, iii) alleviate extreme vulnerability by working with NGOs and other centres providing services to the vulnerable and iv) mainstream INDH governance mechanisms and strengthen institutional capacity. It does so through increasing access to basic services, enhancing the economic infrastructure, supporting income generation, and promoting cultural, social and sports activities and strengthening local governance and capacity.

To support the INDH and other initiatives a National Observatory of Human Development was established in 2006 as an autonomous institution reporting directly to the Prime Minister. Its mandate is to carry out studies and surveys relating to human development, monitor and evaluate the implementation of INDH, and document good practice.

The expenditures of the INDH are small when compared to the total social sector budget of the government but the aim is to create a new participatory culture to community development, make line ministries more responsive to local needs, and strengthen the role of NGOs, other civil society groups and municipalities in identifying and implementing projects. In addition, the King closely monitors the INDH and all Ministries have been given orders to align and support the initiative.

The INDH offers the opportunity to change the approach to social policy in Morocco from a very top-down, ad hoc and paternalistic approach, which has characterised policy since independence, to a much more participatory and inclusive approach. This fits well with other recent developments under the new King including greater openness and transparency, a strengthening of civil society and greater democratisation.

In response to the new King and government's reorientation towards poverty reduction and democratisation the Bank has stated that:

> Morocco was in the vanguard of the Middle East and North Africa in terms of open civil society, democratisation, promotion of the rule of law, decentralisation, and community participation.
>
> (World Bank 2005 p.33)

Civic society and Islamic welfare provision

Although the INDH aims to promote civil society participation in poverty reduction, historically civil society and faith-based welfare provision have not been well developed in Morocco in contrast to countries such as Egypt and Jordan. In this respect Morocco is similar to Tunisia (see Chapter 7). Civil society in Morocco dates from the 18th century when tribes developed social systems called twiza and agadir to render assistance to the poorest members of society (Ennaji 2006 p.128). During the colonial period Moroccans were not permitted to create associations. After independence a number of associations emerged such as trade unions (L'Union Marocaine du Travail and L'Union Générale des Travailleurs) and professional syndicates. However, in the period since independence prior to the accession of King Mohammed VI the development of civil society was not encouraged. According to Ennaji in the 1970s and early 1980s: 'Associations interested in development were scarce in number, because at that time most Moroccans were more interested in political parties than in associative action and social development' (Ennaji 2006 p.113).

During the period of economic reform under the auspices of the IMF and World Bank, civil society was largely hostile to the state's reform efforts and until recently tended to be marginalised. Trade Unions and civic groups argued that privatisation and economic liberalisation were leading to unemployment and recession (as was the case in the first part of the 1980s and most of the 1990s as shown earlier in this chapter). Opposition parties, Trade Unions and civic groups mobilised several national strikes as well as street demonstrations, for example in protest to the reduction in food subsidies such as the 1982 and 1990 food riots. Not only did the state keep a close watch on such organisations they also created their own parallel state structures to counter the effect of civic groups, trade unions and opposition parties. For example, the regime created regional associations such as the Fes-Saiss Association, Association du Grand Atlas and Association Oujda-Angad to help develop different provinces. In addition, as shown above, the monarchy, assisted by the state, tried to retain a monopoly over welfare provision presenting itself as both the defender of the faith and the provider of welfare through organisations such as Hassan II Fund, the Compensation Fund, and the Mohammed V Fund.

More recently, civic society has grown in Morocco. Since 1999 the new Monarch and the new coalition government, partly in response to external pressures, have introduced a process of democratisation and political liberalisation. Even before this, in the early 1990s, civil society had started to increase its activities. In the mid-1990s the late King Hassan II encouraged village associations and other NGOs to undertake community level actions to improve their living conditions. This included the introduction in 1997 of non-formal schools run by village level NGOs and targeted at children who had never been enrolled in the formal system. The schools teach basic literacy and ongoing training-education. In 1999, for the first time the Adult Literacy Directorate formed partnerships with over 50 NGOs for the provision of training. In response to such initiatives a large number of NGOs and voluntary groups started to develop, many of them funded and supported by the international NGO movement. Village level NGOs have also used migrant remittances for community development projects. As poverty and a decline in the quantity and quality of state welfare services emerged in the 1990s these NGOs became more active in providing the services that the state was failing to adequately provide, such as humanitarian assistance to communities afflicted by drought and sever poverty, provision of basic social services in health and education. Many were also involved in advocacy work campaigning for women's rights and human rights.

Ennaji has estimated that by 2006 there were over 30,000 NGOs across the country (Ennaji 2006)[68] while the World Bank estimates that there are between 17,000 and 30,000 (World Bank 2002c p.47). In 2002 the government prepared a report regarding the measures necessary to promote partnerships between the government and NGOs (Government of Morocco 2002). Ennaji argues that the rapid growth in NGOs can be attributed to external pressures and financial support to help develop democracy and civil society, the high rate of unemployment amongst the young, the increase in the urban population and a growing lack of confidence and hope for the future (Ennaji 2006 p.130).

Ennaji has identified three types of NGOs. First the Regional Associations created in the 1980s by those close to the Monarchy to provide economic, social and cultural activities which are complementary to those of the state and local government. Secondly, advocacy associations that tackle sensitive political issues such as human rights, the rights of women and the promotion of Berber culture. And finally those NGOs that are socio-economic organisations attempting to improve the social welfare of the poor and vulnerable. Some of these NGOs have been created by affluent business people, most of who are closely aligned with the state. In addition, many are dependent on support from international organisations or from the state itself whilst all have to obtain legal recognition by registering with the state as well as obtaining state permission for all of their activities.[69] This has led Ennaji to conclude:

> A fair description of civil society is that it is still incipient, poorly institutionalised, and marked by the characteristic divisions of class, gender, religion and region... The lack of economic autonomy means that civil society groups and their organisations continue to be vulnerable to political pressure from the ruling elite.
>
> (Ennaji 2006 p.129)

The Bank concurs with this view:

> The voluntary sector is relatively underdeveloped in Morocco, even though it has been growing significantly over the past ten years, a period of political opening.
>
> (World Bank 2006b p.26)

However, the Bank has also acknowledged that NGOs in Morocco are:

> ... a small but credible force for development and a major source of innovative ideas and approaches for the delivery of social services (schools, literacy, human rights, environmental management and social assistance). For the more severe types of social exclusion (unwed mothers, battered women, those with HIV, street children) the NGOs have been the only place where these people can turn for help. Demand for their services far surpasses

what they are able to provide. The bilateral donors are all increasing their contacts, training and direct financial support.

(World Bank 2002c p.52)

Although the government still remains the main provider of social welfare, NGOs respond to the demands of the population and provide services to those that the government will not or cannot reach. In response to the recent growth of NGOs the World Bank and other donors have attempted to work in partnership with the NGO community. Donors are trying to integrate their assistance with modest support for non-governmental actors such as local communities, professional associations and NGOs. In 2002 the Bank office appointed an NGO coordinator to develop stronger ties with NGOs and to help NGOs cooperate with one another whilst NGO partnerships have become more common in World Bank projects.

It is clear from the preceding analysis that the Moroccan state, despite paying increasing attention to the social consequences of reform, currently commands both insufficient organisational capacity and financial resources to eradicate poverty and considerably reduce unemployment rates. It has also been shown earlier (see Chapter 4 on Jordan) that, under similar circumstances, social capital is essential for public good delivery, and that in Muslim or religious societies it is common for faith-based organisations to be involved in charity and voluntary activities that saves public sector money and fills a social gap left by the diminution of the state's welfare provisions. In this case, social capital, in particular religious social capital, can provide either an alternative for or a complement to public provisions when the state is weak or undefended.

More recent work (Tessler 2003) also suggests that faith congregations remain significant in Morocco's public life, as elsewhere in the region. Table 1 (Chapter 2) sheds some light on Moroccan's religious orientations and congregations. For example, almost 24 per cent of all people from Egypt, Jordan, Morocco and Tunisia meet with other people in mosque on a weekly basis, while over 10 per cent meet other like-minded people on a monthly basis; more than 32 per cent attend religious ceremonies (apart from funerals, weddings and christenings) more than once a week, while another 12 per cent attend once a week; almost 30 per cent are highly involved in Mosque's charity and voluntary activities, while another 5 per cent are highly involved. The point here is that faith-based organisations have enormous capacity to mobilise members for the provisions of public goods, which require voluntary involvement in societies with weak, undefended or corrupt states. 'Here, sharing a common religious fervour is the basis for trust and the religious hierarchy provides the necessary leaders' for mobilisation (Fafchamps, 2006, 1187–8).

However, just as the development of civil society in general has been limited in Morocco until recently, so too has the provision of faith-based welfare provision from Islamic groups. There is no data to estimate how many of the current 17,000–30,000 NGOs operating in Morocco have religious affiliations but faith-based welfare provision has not developed in the manner witnessed in Egypt and Jordan. This is partly because of the Monarchy and State's attempt to monopolise such activities. However, according to the World Bank (2002c) these Islamic charities are very active in social programmes such as basic health, education, adult literacy, sanitation, child care, summer camps and food distribution and their activities have been growing steadily over the years. In particular, they are very active in cities and peri-urban slums.

Table 14: Politics and religion in Egypt, Jordan, Morocco and Algeria

Politicians who do not believe in God are unfit in public office:	%
Strongly agree	66.5
Agree	15.3
Neutral	8.1
Disagree	4.2
Strongly disagree	5.9
Religious leaders should not influence how people vote in elections:	%
Strongly agree	41.3
Agree	23.6
Neutral	22.2
Disagree	6.8
Strongly disagree	6.1
It would be better if more religious people held public offices:	%
Strongly agree	30.6
Agree	22.8
Neutral	18.7
Disagree	17.0
Strongly disagree	10.9
Index of attitudes about whether persons holding public office should be religious:	%
Strongly agree	40.7
Agree	30.3
Neutral	17.4
Disagree	7.5
Strongly disagree	4.0

Source: Tessler 2003 p.15.

Islamic politics in Morocco

The development of faith-based welfare mirrors that of Islamic political parties in Morocco. Both have been suppressed by the state but in recent years have grown in importance with the opening up of the political process and the development of civic society. Currently the main opposition party to the coalition government, which is dominated by socialists and nationalists, is the Justice and Development Party which is an Islamic party.[70] Unlike the Islamic political movement in Egypt and Jordan, particularly the Muslim Brotherhood, the Justice and Development Party is relatively young and does not have strong linkages to regional parties and movements. According to one of the current Parliamentary members of the Justice and Development Party:

> The Islamic movement in Morocco is not regional or international. It has no links to the Muslim Brotherhood. The Moroccan context and reality is different from other countries, such as Jordan. There are several factors that played an important role here. First, was the role of the monarchy which rules with an iron fist and did not allow the Islamic movement to have any external links outside Morocco. Second, the regime did not allow the establishment of a wide spread social network that can be found to be run by some Islamist movements in other states, like Jordan. Therefore our social role remained limited to helping the poor during special religious ceremonies such as providing food during the Eid period or distributing clothing. These social projects did not rise to the level of those found in Jordan and Egypt.
>
> (Personal interview Rabat December 2006)

Traditionally, the Islamic movement in Morocco has been more radical than that of Jordan's or Tunisia's similarly faith-based organisations. The parent Islamic movement in Morocco, known as the Adjustment and Unity Islamic Movement (*al-tawheed welislah)* was established in 1958 but did not commence overtly political activities until 1970. In 1974 it sent a powerful letter to the King denouncing corruption and calling for an end to what it perceived to be the absolute power of the constitutional monarchy. As a result, the movement was banned and many of its leaders imprisoned. Although initially a revolutionary movement it denounced armed struggle in 1975 in favour of democracy and pluralism. However, confrontation with the regime meant that the movement was not permitted to form a political party and in 1991 it joined with an existing party, the Popular Democratic Constitutional Movement, which was headed by Abdual Kareem al-Khateeb who had a strong Islamic orientation but was also pro the constitutional monarchy. It was not until 1996 that the Islamic

Movement had its own legitimate party in the form of the Justice and Development Party. The political party developed an independent organisational structure and hierarchy from the Islamic movement from which it had originated, with the latter continuing to focus on Islamic teachings, education and charity work. The party is quick to point out that is not a religious party in the sense of delivering religious interpretations (*fatwat*) but rather is a political party which is proud of its religious roots and its ethical content, akin to the Western Christian Democratic parties. Its interpretation of Islam does not involve isolation, radicalism, fundamentalism or a rejection of democracy.

To combat the role of opposition parties, including the Islamic opposition, the Monarchy has encouraged the development of a large number of small political parties loyal to the crown such that at present there are over 30 political parties active in Morocco. This has helped to diffuse the strength and power of major opposition parties and has resulted in a current coalition government led by an independent technocratic Prime Minister appointed by the King. In addition three important ministries are beyond the reach of political parties with the King appointing the Minster of Religious Affairs, the Minister for the Interior and the Minister for Exterior Affairs. Hence, four of the most important political positions are held by regime loyalists. There remains a clear limit or ceiling at which democracy stops in Morocco and even the supposedly free elections of 2003 were deemed to be rigged by a number of political parties.

Despite restrictions imposed on their activities by the state, and although their role in social provisions is far more limited than Islamic movements in Jordan and Egypt, Morocco's faith-based organisations have managed to attract large followings and have also achieved important political strides. Table 14 suggests that political Islam commands vast sympathisers in Morocco, as it does in our other case studies of Jordan, Egypt and, to a much lesser extent, in Tunisia. For example, almost 67 per cent of people from Egypt, Jordan, Morocco and Tunisia 'strongly agree' that 'politicians who do not believe in God are unfit in public office'; almost 31 per cent 'strongly agree' that 'It would be better if more religious people held public offices', while another 23 per cent 'agree' with the same statement.

The Islamic Justice and Development Party participated in elections for the first time in 1997 and won only 9 seats. But it successfully challenged the election as being rigged and the Court deemed that re-elections were needed in many areas such that the party eventually obtained 14 seats. However, it fared much better in the 2003 elections when it won 42 seats to become the third biggest party and the main opposition. Even in this election, the party was forced by legislation passed by the regime not to enter candidates in a large number of electoral areas and was restricted to nominating candidates in only 60 per cent of the *daw'aer*. Restrictions were also placed on the number of candidates the party could put up in the six major cities where its support was strongest. This restriction made it impossible for the party to win more than 91 out of the total 325 seats in parliament ensuring that it could not dominate. The party reluctantly agreed to these restrictions to avoid conflict with the regime and as part of its gradualist approach to winning power. It is widely believed that had such restrictions not been applied the party would have gained an unprecedented victory.[71] In the forthcoming 2007 elections the Justice and Development Party has declared that it will campaign to enter the maximum number of candidates and is confident of becoming the dominant party in Parliament. Whether this will prompt a conflict with the regime, as in Algeria, remains to be seen. The Party does not believe that this will be the case, citing the considerable work it has done to present itself as a moderate democratic party both to Western governments and the Moroccan regime.

The Justice and Development Party has clearly benefited from the Islamic revival that Morocco has experienced over the past decade. In addition to the Afghan War, the Iraq wars and the Palestinian crisis, Morocco's Islamic revival has also been partly prompted by the failure of domestic policies and ideologies in the form of both populist state welfarism and the more recent economic liberalisation. To quote one Justice and Development MP:

> The Islamic alternative today is the only genuinely alternative solution because all other alternatives have failed, including Arab socialism and the neo-liberal alternative. Despite all this we do not carry the slogan that 'Islam is the solution' as in Jordan and Egypt. What we say is that Islam is part of the solution.
>
> (Personal interview Rabat December 2006)

In addition to the Justice and Development Party, which grew out of the Adjustment and Unity Movement, a number of more radical groups have also evolved from the original movement. These include the Justice and Charity Movement (Adalah and Ihassan) which calls for a completely Islamic state, a termination of the monarchy and a republic based on Islamic *Khalifat*. It refuses to participate in the democratic political process.

Just as the support for political Islam has been growing in Morocco, so too has the Islamic provision of welfare services. However, this provision is not overtly politicised. Ennaji (2006 p.114) has argued that in the 1982–97 period Islamist groups began to appear and expand in the poorest districts providing help and social services. The radical Justice and Charity movement for example, provided services and developed a well-organised women's movement. The growth in faith-based welfare provision in recent years mirrors the more general growth in NGOs, particularly in areas of education, rural development and poverty alleviation. Commenting on the social fabric of Morocco's slums the Bank noted:

> Longer term residents perceive a rise in asocial behaviour displayed by the younger generation, and experience a weakening of social ties and a decline in community activities (except from religious groups).
>
> (World Bank 2006b p.31)

More generally, in urban areas a weakening of family and kinship ties means that the poor and vulnerable have nowhere to turn to and welcome the limited welfare provision from Islamic NGO groups. Such NGOs provide help to widows, orphans, the divorced, and disabled.

Despite the growth in both NGO and faith-based welfare provision and social capital formation, the mainstream Justice and Development Party does not have a large network of welfare provision, unlike the Muslim Brotherhood in Egypt and Jordan. Most of the party's outreach work consists of education and the teaching of Islamic principles as extra curricula activities to the mainstream education system. To quote a Justice and Development Party MP:

> Parties in Morocco are outside the system of charity work and are more focused on political activity. Instead we encourage people to give to other charitable organisations that help the poor. The King does not want charitable activities to become politicised. We do have a small number of charity associations, but they are open for everybody and anyone can become a member.
>
> (Personal interview Rabat December 2006)

> We don't compete with the state in the area of social welfare. We are happy to leave this to the state. Unlike Egypt, the Party does not focus on welfare activities.
>
> (Personal interview Rabat December 2006)

One of the reasons for the limited amount of formal social welfare provided directly by political Islamists is the tight control the state exerts over welfare work. Charity work first requires permission from the government and all such work must be registered with the authorities. Permission must also be sought to access any financial resource both from within and without the country. As a result, the Justice and Development Party tends to act more as a mediator in the provision of welfare. For example, a large number of people often come to the party offices at the beginning of the academic year seeking help with such things as stationary, clothes, and books. Party officials record the details and then pass them onto prominent businessmen or others in the community who might be able to help. Hence, the role of the party is as a mediator or a provider of *wasta*. Members of Parliament do not see this as part of their job as parliamentarians, which is to legislate, but see it as their duty as a good Muslim. Thus the process is not overtly politicised. Indeed most Islamic MPs take the view that welfare provision is the duty of the government not politicians and are happy to leave this to the state or to individuals operating in a non-political context. Many party members are members of charitable organisations but see this as a religious rather than a political role. However, more recently some richer party members, operating essentially as individuals, have started to establish private schools but the curriculum is tightly controlled by the state. In response to the growth of private Islamic schools the government in the form of the Ministry of Islamic Affairs, the Ministry of Education and Local Governors have been trying to reform and control the schools by tightly specifying the curriculum and monitoring religious teachings. This is part of a more general crackdown on Islamists which started under the socialist Prime Minister appointed by the King in 1998 and included an attempt to marginalise Islamic education and reduce the number of Islamic programmes on the main television channels.

The limited role of Islamic and other civic society welfare provision is illustrated by the fact that about 95 per cent of all enrolled students are in state schools which are under the responsibility of the Ministry of Education and more than 80 per cent of the population depend on health services provided by the state (World Bank 1994). The Bank has also commented that social organisation and private welfare activities in the slums of Morocco are both weak and ad hoc (World Bank 2006b, p.4). In addition, the Bank considered one of the main risks for the recently launched National Initiative for Human Development (INDH) to be the weakness of NGOs in Morocco (World Bank 2006a p.14).

Islamists' view of the IMF and World Bank

The Justice and Development Party reaches its supporters less via charity work and more via political campaigning and political outreach work in the urban areas and amongst the educated and professionals, which is the basis of its support. As in Jordan and Egypt, 'The Islamic movement in Morocco is an urban-based organisation, with most supporters concentrated in urban centres' (Personal interview with an Islamist MP, Rabat December 2006). Outreach work is assisted by over 70 branches throughout the country and by the Party newspaper and the electronic media, which is free to criticise domestic policies as long as the criticism is not directed towards the Monarchy. This criticism however, does not generally extend to criticising the role of the IMF and World Bank in Morocco. The Party has criticised the harsh recessionary policies of the early 1980s and the high social costs associated with the IMF and World Bank programmes, for example through the freezing of civil service salaries, but this criticism was directed more against the government that was implementing IMF and World Bank recommendations rather than against these institutions *per se*. Indeed, it was the left wing democratic and socialist parties that made most capital out of the riots in 1985, 1986, 1990 and 1991. The Islamic Party, although acknowledging the high social costs of reform has praised the achievement of macroeconomic stability and low inflation under World Bank and IMF guidance.

However, Islamists disagree with the argument that growth alone can solve Morocco's social plights. They recognise the significance of high growth for poverty reduction, but do not accept the mantra that growth alone will lead to an equitable outcome. They therefore criticise the Fund's and World Bank's previous emphasis on growth in Morocco, particularly during the 1983–93 decade, and have played an important role in pushing the social agenda to the front in the 1990s. The World Bank's recent support for Morocco's social agenda is seen by Islamists as a concession on behalf of the Bank who eventually came to recognise the soundness of Islamic movement's call for more pro-poor growth policies in Morocco. To quote one Justice and Development MP:

> These international organisations have their own role to play and we understand this fact. Therefore we have no problem sitting down with them and talking to them. They themselves are now applying the policies we were calling for, for a very long time.
>
> (Personal interview Rabat December 2006)

The Party has a mercantilist economic philosophy derived from the fact that the Prophet himself was a merchant. Hence there is no strong opposition to policies such as privatisation, the encouragement of private enterprise and economic liberalisation so long as key strategic sectors remain under some state control and so long as the poor are protected during the process. Indeed the party has long been pushing for reform of the agricultural sector in order to improve competition. On this issue, as well as the issue of tackling corruption, the party is strongly aligned with the position of the World Bank. The Party's main concern with privatisation, for example, has been the fact that it has not been a transparent process and those close to the regime have benefited most.

Likewise, the Party was in favour of the Association Agreement with the EU and the bilateral trade agreement with the USA and voted for both in Parliament.

Although faith-based welfare provision is limited in Morocco, the government has nevertheless become acutely aware of its growth and in recent years has launched a high profile slum clearance programme and the INDH in a big bang approach to counter the growing influence of Islamists in poor urban areas.[72] The government and Monarchy were shocked into action by Morocco's low ranking in the Human Development Index and by the Casablanca bombings of May 2003. Atypically, the suicide bombers were from poor slum backgrounds where they had become radicalised. To quote Ennaji:

> The 16 May 2003 attacks in Casablanca revealed that terrorism and extremism can exploit the poverty and ignorance of young marginalised people to spread violence. Many, though not most, violent Islamists live in appalling socio economic conditions and have a low level of education…and many of them are either unemployed or have small low paid jobs.
>
> (Ennaji 2006 p.132)

The Bank also stated that its 2004 Poverty Report was timely given the government's renewed efforts after the bombings to identify policies and programmes to reduce poverty, including urban poverty (World Bank 2005 p.37).

Given excessively high levels of unemployment among youth it is little surprise that Ennaji notes that:

> The young were disappointed with the conventional political parties, and showed greater interest in Islamist organisations.
>
> (Ennaji 2006 p.117)

With the new and more open political environment which has developed in Morocco since the mid-1990s as well as the declining quality of state welfare provision, it seems that NGO activity will strengthen, including the activities of faith-based welfare providers. This has the potential to fill a growing gap in state welfare provision. However, at the same time fault lines are appearing in the regime as a result of the tensions between economic liberalisation and a regime based on patronage and clientelism:

> The structural adjustment programme has placed Morocco before two kinds

> of logic which appear to be mutually exclusive: a 'makhzenian' logic, founded to a large extent on the administrative allocation of resources and a discretionary power, and a liberal logic based on allocation through the market and a democratic power.
>
> (Ali 1997 p.206)

> The ever-increasing pace of economic and social transformations has often produced ruptures that are likely to give rise to new political structures and practices … The generalisation of state clientelism invariably leads – in a context of paucity of resources, as in the case of Morocco – to an overabundance of demands and a crisis of legitimacy, and the increasing exclusion of youth may well constitute a breeding ground for radical and violent protests. Furthermore, the existence of a growing middle class leaves no room for a political game restricted to notables and tame elites.
>
> (Ibid. p.213)

This fluid situation has led the Bank to conclude that the greatest risk to its 2005–9 Country Assistance Strategy is:

> that insufficient growth, high unemployment and social disparities, will lead to socio-economic tensions which hinder further economic and social reforms.
>
> (World Bank 2005 p.19)

Furthermore the Bank's May 2001 Country Assistance Evaluation pointed out that many NGOs expressed anger at both the government and the Bank:

> NGOs see the Bank and the Government as close partners whose interactions are totally non-transparent to society at large. While the specifics of the Bank's activities are unknown to civil society, it is apparent to them that there has been no economic or social progress, least of all for the poor.
>
> (World Bank 2001b p.12)

In response, the Bank has declared a need to spend more effort on consensus building and new ways to tap the emerging civil society.

Conclusion

For much of the period since independence the provision of social welfare has been the domain of the state and the monarchy. Both have used it as a way of garnering political support and legitimacy. However, much of this welfare was biased towards the urban population and the better-off. As a result, social indicators in Morocco are poor for a lower middle income country. In addition, since the early 1980s the social contract, whereby the regime provided welfare and other perks in return for loyalty, has started to unravel under the pressure of economic liberalisation and a retrenchment of the state. At the same time, following a political opening up which commenced in the mid-1990s, there has been a significant growth of NGOs and civic society, including faith-based civic society. These new groupings are starting to play a growing role in welfare provision, especially in urban areas.

Clearly, the challenge ahead is for both the state and the Bank to harness the potential of both secular and religious-based social welfare provision which is beginning to emerge. At the same time, the regime needs to ensure that the rapid process of both economic and political liberalisation does not lead to a political crisis. It is essential therefore, that civic society, including faith-based civic society, is embraced by the regime and appreciated for the positive role it plays in welfare provision and the formation of social capital at a time when the old social contract of populist state welfare provision is unravelling. So far, Morocco has avoided the overt politicisation of faith-based welfare provision, but if this is not embraced by the regime and its donors, it is likely to be hijacked by more extremist political groups.

7

Structural Reform and the Political Economy of Poverty Reduction in Tunisia: What Role for Civil Society?[73]

Myriam Blin

Introduction

Despite the inclusion of poverty concerns in World Bank and IMF stabilisation and structural reform analytical reports, these reforms continue to be perceived as leading to a stagnation or even worsening of social conditions in countries where they are implemented. Indeed, the priority given to reduction in government budget deficits often implies a disengagement of the state from social provisioning. In such a situation, the space left is likely to be filled by non-governmental organisations (NGOs) that provide social welfare support to the losers of the reforms. In countries with a strong religious tradition, the space is likely to be filled to a large extent by faith-based organisations. There is evidence that this has been the case in the Middle East and North Africa (MENA) region, for example in Egypt, Jordan and Palestine (Lubeck 1998, Roy 2000, Wiktorowicz and Farouki 2000). This is clearly a positive development, as it allows cushioning the social impact of economic reforms by providing valuable services to the most vulnerable. Furthermore, faith-based social provisioning has often been found to increase faith-based political influence, particularly in Muslim countries, thereby contributing to political pluralism.[74] In the MENA region, the extensive provision of social welfare by Islamic charity organisations (for example, in Egypt and Jordan), has led to an increased influence of political Islam as a force of opposition to authoritarian rulers[75] (Benthall and Bellion-Jourdan 2003, Wiktorowicz and Farouki 2000). Yet, this trend reflects an interesting irony: while governments in power often use violent repressive policies aiming at eradicating political Islam, the economic reforms they implement, on the other hand, increase the influence of political Islam through the work of Islamic based NGOs. The irony can be pushed even further since IMF and World Bank board members are as much (if not more) interested in eradicating the 'Islamic threat' as they are in implementing economic reform (Hibou 2006).

While a link has been found between structural reforms, increased faith-based social provisioning and rise in popular support for political Islam in countries such as Egypt and Jordan, this chapter shows that it has not been the case in Tunisia. Indeed, the implementation of Bretton Woods and EU policy packages have not led to an increase in poverty or the disengagement of the state in social provisioning in Tunisia. On the contrary, throughout the 20 years of structural adjustment started in 1986, the Tunisian government has reformed, but preserved its strong role in social provisioning. As a result, poverty has been reduced considerably, while inequality has remained stable. Admittedly, there remain some pockets of poverty especially in rural areas, and social problems such as unemployment have persisted, but on aggregate, it can be argued that Tunisia was successful in implementing structural reforms while simultaneously reducing poverty. This chapter asks why the Tunisian government has been able to preserve social provisioning throughout its structural reform. We show that the capacity of the Tunisian State, but more importantly the need for social policy as a source of legitimacy and as a tool for control have been determinant in preserving social provisioning throughout the structural adjustment period.

The massive reduction in poverty and the nature and form of social provisioning in Tunisia, implies that no space (legally or operationally) is left for independent NGO activities. Furthermore, the repressive nature of the Tunisian state has made independent forms of civil society almost impossible, while Islamic based non-governmental organisations are, in practice, banned. As a result, political Islam has not become more influential in Tunisia through faith-based social provisioning, not only because poverty had been reduced and state social provisioning preserved, but also because independent civil organisations are controlled and/or repressed.

Yet Tunisia is witnessing an 'Islamic revival', in other words, an increasing proportion of Tunisians are manifesting their Islamic identity, whether politically, religiously or culturally (or all of those). In effect, the next question we ask is whether the Islamic revival reflects a growing influence for political Islam in Tunisia and whether the potential rise in political Islam is rooted in the Bretton Woods- EU sponsored economic reforms.

We review herein the impact and role of structural reforms on poverty reduction in Tunisia. We show that on aggregate most poverty indicators improved substantially. Nevertheless, despite strong poverty reduction in rural areas and in the west of the country, these regions still suffer from greater poverty than the rest of the country. Furthermore, strong unemployment especially for young graduates raises serious questions in terms of the sustainability of Tunisia's social fabric. We then show that poverty reduction during structural adjustment was achieved in Tunisia because the Tunisian government did not reduce (and in fact expanded) social provisioning during that period. We further argue that social policies were successfully maintained during structural reforms for three main reasons: first the Tunisian administration had the capacity to negotiate with Bretton Woods institutions, second, social policy had always been part of the social contract in Tunisia, and finally, social policy has been used by the Ben Ali regime as a source of legitimacy and control, and therefore was politically necessary. We show that the Tunisian Government has successfully prevented any form of independent civil organisation and has literally eradicated any form of Islamic-based organisation. Finally, we review the history of faith-based organisations in Tunisia, their source of influence and their relationship with the State. We show that today their presence has been almost eradicated by the Ben Ali regime. All the same, there has been an Islamic revival in Tunisia since the early years 2000, and we explore whether there is a link between the Islamic revival, political Islam and economic reform. From the analysis of in depth interviews with Tunisian political Islamists, we argue that while the extent to which the Islamic revival implies a rise in the influence of political Islam is unclear, there seems to be evidence that the support for political Islam (whatever its size) is largely rooted in international geopolitics (in particular the war on terror and the Israelo-Palestinian conflict) and as a reaction to the pro-western corrupt Tunisian government and its repressive policies against Islam. Globalisation and economic reforms are also put forward as sources of Islamic revivalism, but more because they are perceived as part of western hegemony than because of the socio-economic impact of the reforms as such.

Social policy and poverty prior to structural reform in Tunisia

The commitment to social development has always been part of the Tunisian government's priorities. Since independence, social spending had remained high, making it one of Tunisia's key characteristics. In 2004, social spending represented 16 to 20 per cent of GDP depending on the measure (Ben Romdhane, 2006), and in 2003 social transfers were equal to 258.4 Tunisian Dinars (TD) per household per month, that is 1.2 times the guaranteed minimum wage. In fact, Tunisia is the highest social spender in the region as can be seen in Table 15.

Table 15: Tunisia: Social spending as a percentage of GDP, 2001

	Egypt	Morocco	Jordan	Tunisia	Syria	Korea
Social spending/GDP	8.5	10.1	15.1	16.3/20.1*	4.5	6.1

Source: IMF (2006); Ben Romdhane (2006).
* 16.3 according to the IMF; 20.1 according to the World Bank.

When Bourguiba took power in 1956, there was an immediate commitment to social policy; most symbolic was the implementation of the *Code du Statut* Personal (CSP) which abolished polygamy, gave women the right to divorce and increased the legal age of marriage for both sexes, among other things. Despite some relatively austere wage policies in the 1960s and 1970s, these were largely compensated by generous social spending: there was particularly large spending in education, health, and diverse social welfare programmes such as maternity benefits, food subsidies, and aid for poor families[76]. Between 1961 and 1980, social spending as a percentage of GDP was around 13 per cent on average each year, with an average annual increase around 2 per cent per year (Ben Romdhane 2006, INS various years).

Table 16: Tunisia: Government spending as a % of total spending by sector, 1961–80

Years	Education/total	Health/total	Social spending/total	Education, health and social/total
1961	18.9	9.7	0.7	29.3
1962	19.7	9.7	1.0	30.4
1963	19.1	7.8	1.2	28.1
1964	21.2	7.8	3.5	32.6
1965	22.6	6.9	4.0	33.5
1966	23.1	6.8	5.2	35.1
1967	23.1	7.3	5.6	36.0
1968	23.8	7.9	5.5	37.2
1969	26.2	8.2	5.2	39.6
1970	25.9	7.7	7.1	40.7
1971	27.4	7.9	7.3	42.5
1972	25.7	8.0	6.1	39.8
1973	23.1	7.7	5.5	36.3
1974	22.7	8.2	5.2	36.1
1975	21.1	8.0	5.2	34.3
1976	20.4	7.9	5.0	33.3
1977	22.8	8.0	5.6	36.3
1978	22.8	8.3	5.4	36.5
1979	22.4	8.9	5.4	36.6
1980	21.1	8.6	5.1	34.9
1981	18.2	8.3	4.6	31.1
1982	19.5	9.0	4.7	33.2
1983	21.2	9.3	4.9	35.4
1984	20.5	9.5	4.7	34.7
1985	20.7	8.5	5.0	34.1
1986	28.3	10.7	6.0	45.1

Source: INS, statistical yearbook (1990), calculation from author.

While in the 1960s a larger proportion of the government budget was devoted to education (both infrastructure, staff and training), in the 1970s, spending shifted to the health sector (increase in hospital beds, improved and increased staff and training); but overall commitment to education and health was sustained throughout the two decades[77] (Table 16). These large social transfers translated into impressive social achievements throughout the two decades.

As can be seen in Table 17, GDP per capita increased from US$730 in 1965 to US$1,460 in 1985, while the Human Development Index (HDI) increased from 0.516 to 0.623 in the 1975–85 period, and inequality was reduced slightly from a Gini of 0.459 in 1961 to 0.430 in 1985. Most impressive has been the reduction in poverty; according to the INS, in 1975, 22 per cent of the population lived under the national poverty line; by 1985 this rate was reduced to 7.7 per cent. Using the World Bank measure of poverty,[78] the drop is even more impressive with poverty headcount reduced from 20 per cent in 1980 to 9.6 per cent in 1985, in other words a decrease of almost 11 percentage points in five years. The largest share of reduction took place in rural areas (mainly due to rural-urban migration), but by 1985 rural poverty remained significantly higher than urban poverty according to World Bank data (Table 17).

Improvements in human indicators were equally impressive, in particular for women. Life expectancy at birth increased from 50 years old for women and 49 years old for men in 1962 to 66 and 64 years old for women and men respectively in 1985. The percentage of children under five years of age suffering from malnutrition (height measure) decreased from 39.5 per cent in 1974 to 17.9 per cent in 1988 (using the weight measure; the drop was from 20.2 per cent to 10.3 per cent from 1974 to 1988). Enrolment in primary education was universal by 1980 (100 per cent for both boys and girls), while secondary education enrolment saw the most dramatic increase for girls from 13 per cent in 1962 to 35 per cent in 1985. Overall, the commitment to social policies prior to structural reform implied a dramatic improvement in the well-being of a majority of Tunisians.

Table 17: Tunisia: Social indicators, 1961–85, selected years

	1962	**1965**	**1970**	**1975**	**1980**	**1985**
GDP p.c. $US constant 2000	--	730	900	1132	1352	1460
HDI	--	--	--	0.516	0.572	0.623
Unemployment	--	15.2[1]	--	15.8	--	16.4[2]
- male	--	15.3[1]	--	16.1	--	16.9[2]
- female	--	13.4[1]	--	14.1	--	14.8[2]

Table 17 (con't): Tunisia: Social indicators 1961–85, selected years

	1962	1965	1970	1975	1980	1985
INS poverty headcount (%)	--	--	--	22	12.9	7.7
- rural	--	--	--	26.5	14.1	7.0
- urban	--	--	--	18	11.8	8.4
World Bank poverty headcount	--	--	--	--	20.1	9.6
- rural	--	--	--	--	30.1	17.2
- urban	--	--	--	--	7.7	4.0
GINI total[3]	0.419	0.423	0.488	0.440	0.430	0.430
GINI urban	--	--	--	0.440	0.418	0.432
GINI rural	--	--	--	--	0.412	0.379
Life expectancy at birth, total	49.6	52.1[4]	54.1	60.5[5]	62.4	65.2
Life expectancy at birth, female	50.0	52.6[4]	54.7	61.5[5]	63.5	66.4
Life expectancy at birth, male	49.1	51.6[4]	53.7	59.6[5]	61.4	64.0
Under 5 malnutrition, height for age, %	--	--	--	39.5[6]	--	17.9[7]
Under 5 malnutrition, weight for age,%	--	--	--	20.2[6]	--	10.3[7]
Under 5 child mortality rate (per 1000 live births)	228					
Primary school enrolment[8]	100	--	--	112	118	132
- male	121	--	--	133	136	143
- female	80	--	--	89	100	120
- students/teacher	57.3	55.8	47.6	39.7	38.7	31.6
Secondary school enrolment[8]	23	--	--	20	25	42
- male	33	--	--	26	31	48
- female	13	--	--	18	37	35
- students/teacher	--	--	--	17.0	16.7	16.6

Notes: [1] year 1966; [2] year 1984; [3] Data from several sources, 1961 and 1970 are based on income measures, while the other years are based on consumption measures. Note that quality of data is poor for that period (WIDER 2006). Disaggregated data between urban and rural are taken from Ayadi et al (2001). [4] year 1967; [5] year 1977; [6] year 1974; [7] year 1988; [8] No data on enrolments are available prior to 1990 from WDI and the INS, the data above were calculated by the author using population data assuming population age 5–9 for primary education and

10–14 for secondary. Such assumption is likely to underestimate enrolment in primary and secondary education.

Source: Authors's own calculation for education enrolment using INS data (various years), poverty data come from Ayadi et al (2001), GINI data come from WIDER (2006) and Ayadi et al ((2001), unemployment data come from INS (various years) the remaining data come from World Bank, World Development Indicators (2006d).

In 1986, Tunisia implemented stabilisation and structural reforms in association with the World Bank and the IMF. The reforms were a relative success, with key macro indicators stabilised and continued economic growth during the stabilisation phase. The structural adjustment phase was very gradual and implemented through a twenty year period,[79] and consisted of the traditional structural reform policies: trade liberalisation, financial liberalisation, price liberalisation and privatisation. The reforms were relatively successful in diversifying the economy, maintaining a relatively high level of growth rates, but little improvements were made in private investment levels and employment creation.

The implementation of structural reforms in 1986 could, in theory, have jeopardised the commitment to social provision in Tunisia and led to an increase in poverty. In fact, just before the reform, there were signs that the World Bank and IMF might push for a reduction in the social spending, since in 1983 these organisations were quite influential in pushing for a reform of the food subsidy system which at the time cost almost 4 per cent of GDP, sucking out fragile government finance. The price of wheat, flour, and semolina were increased by 70 per cent and the price of bread by 100 per cent (Ben Romdhane 2006). The reform inevitably led to street riots which spread across the country, and after a month of protests and riots the price increase was abolished and calm restored. The Tunisian government learned from the failure of the drastic subsidy reform and subsequently succeeded in preserving social policy throughout the structural reform.

Social policy and structural reform in Tunisia[80] (1987–2007)

During the two phases of structural reforms (1987–94 and 1995–2005), social spending as a proportion of GDP has been maintained at around 19 per cent, representing a two-fold increase in social spending in constant terms. Social transfer per habitant increased by 55 per cent, from 386 TD in 1987 (representing 0.8 times the minimum wage) to 599.3TD in 2002 (representing 1.2 times the minimum wage) (Ben Romdhane 2006). Table 18 shows that all sectors apart from the General Compensation Fund saw an increase in spending in constant terms: spending on education and health both doubled during that period, while social welfare spending increased by 214 per cent, that is an average annual increase of 13.4 per cent. The real wage increased on average by 0.8 per cent per year between 1987 and 2001 (Ben Romdhane 2006).

Table 18: Tunisia: Social transfers, 1986–2002 (millions of constant 2002 dinars)

	Education	**Health**	**GCF**	**Special funds**	**Social welfare**	**Others**	**Total**	**Social spending p.c.**	**Social spending % GDP**
1986	1024.0	353.5	472.5	141.1	554.5	336.2	3218.0	386.0	18.9
1987	994.9	351.5	393.9	280.0	574.2	358.1	3310.7	386.5	18.4
1988	1006.2	365.2	515.3	195.3	620.6	475.1	3652.8	409.0	19.5
1989	1085.5	380.1	683.0	219.9	647.7	462.3	3940.8	439.8	20.8
1990	1162.8	390.2	517.2	259.3	683.9	481.8	3977.0	428.6	19.5
1991	1180.6	406.3	408.0	218.3	734.4	437.0	3821.6	406.9	18.3
1992	1237.3	435.0	416.8	266.7	815.3	431.9	4034.9	424.4	18.0
1993	1293.4	446.6	432.3	332.2	896.2	412.6	4225.9	440.5	18.2
1994	1391.8	489.7	426.9	368.0	950.1	408.7	4443.9	457.7	19.4
1995	1477.0	504.2	444.3	389.8	1021.4	412.1	4660.9	474.3	20.0
1996	1578.5	519.3	517.2	399.9	1081.7	383.6	4863.8	492.9	19.8
1997	1666.5	544.6	426.8	352.7	1163.4	485.2	5124.4	503.4	19.2
1998	1700.9	558.6	388.2	436.0	1251.4	532.2	5399.5	521.5	19.3
1999	1831.2	574.1	223.2	626.9	1379.5	541.0	5716.9	547.4	19.3
2000	1929.6	592.6	237.8	607.3	1485.7	581.8	6016.6	568.3	19.3
2001	2090.6	614.0	255.7	606.8	1598.6	537.9	6241.5	589.0	19.2
2002	2185.1	612.7	227.0	568.6	1744.6	522.8	6383.6	599.3	19.5

Source: Ben Romdhane (2006) p.64.

During the 1986–2002 period, the government was under pressure from the World Bank to reform it social protection system (see for example World Bank 1996, Dimitri 1993), and to some extent the Tunisian government has responded to many of those pressures (for example, the government reformed the food subsidy system and the health compensation system). But we will see that the government has also created new institutions that would systematically compensate the losers of these reforms. Furthermore, the period was characterised by an expansion of the social security system, which, however, is not financed by the government budget.

With the support/pressure of the World Bank, three key social policy reforms were undertaken or negotiated during the structural adjustment period. First, education underwent a massive reform in 1989 and benefited from a number of investment loans from the World Bank (in 1989 and 2000 for primary education, in 1994 and 2004 for secondary education, and 1990, 1992, 1998 and 2000 for tertiary education, www.worldbank.org, accessed April 2007). These reforms actually translated into an increase rather than a cut in government education spending as shown in Table 18. The objective of these reforms had been to improve the overall quality of the education system and its relevance to the changing economic realities of Tunisia.

The second reform concerned the health compensation scheme. The medical care system in Tunisia consists of two parallel systems: the social security scheme (representing around two-thirds of the population), and the free medical care regime which covers families enrolled in the National Programme for Aid to Needy Families created in 1986 (NPANF) (Achouri 2005). There is evidence that the latter is suffering from extensive inefficiencies where a large proportion of beneficiaries are not entitled to the programme, while some are excluded (Ben Romdhane 2006). The number of cards distributed under the scheme in 2002 implies that almost 40 per cent of the population had access to this service (Ben Romdhane 2006). On the other hand, the social security system is under pressure as the expansion of health care supply and its increased costs imply that, as the government decreased its contribution, an ever larger proportion is being financed by the social security scheme and households (Achouri 2005). As a result of these inefficiencies, in 1996, and under the advice of the WHO and the World Bank, the government has started consultation on a reform of the health insurance system (Achouri 2005). It is as yet too early to know whether such reform will actually improve or worsen health provisioning for the poor.

The third reform concerns the General Compensation Fund (food subsidy system), which led to the most drastic drop in spending by the government. After the bread riots of 1984, the government opted for a self-targeted system with a gradual reduction in prices. In effect, government spending on GCF decreased by almost 52 per cent (see Table 18). Ben Romdhane (2006) however, highlights that each increase in basic food prices tended to be followed by an increase in the minimum wage. Furthermore, in order to compensate the poor for the increase in basic food price the National Programme for Aid to Needy Families (NAPNF) was created in 1986. Under this scheme, households receive on average 478 TD per annum, on top of free medical care.

During the Structural Adjustment period, there has been great expansion of the social security system with two-fold increase in membership and a large increase in amount spent in contributions, with pension and health capturing the largest share in expenditure (Ben Romdhane 2006). The World Bank has put increasing pressure on the Tunisian Government to reform the social security system in its totality (as opposed to simply the health compensation scheme), but there has yet to be a confirmed agreement.

The most significant change in social provisioning during that period, or, rather, the most original one, has been the set up of Presidential programmes by Ben Ali. These are partly financed by the government, but mostly, funding comes from the private sector (Hibou 2006, Ben Romdhane 2006). The two most important programmes are the National Solidarity Fund (NSF or project 26:26) and the National Job Fund (NJF or project 21:21). The NSF funds (created in 1993) offers a series of programme directed at low-income groups and covers needs and activities not provided by existing public schemes (see Table 19 for details of programmes covered). The National Job Fund was set up in 2000 to promote job creation and provides support for micro investment projects and training. Other Presidential programmes such as the 'Back to School' Programme and the Religious Festival Programme are also in place.

While these programmes are likely to have contributed to some improvements in social conditions and to some extent cushioned the impact of the second phase of the reform, the funds' functioning raises some serious questions: the programmes have a special treasury, and working units function outside ministries' jurisdiction as they act directly under the President. Furthermore, the extent to which the different schemes are socially desirable is unclear, and there is opacity as to how much money the funds actually receive and where the money goes as no data are available.

More research is required to establish the efficiency of these programmes, but interestingly the Presidential programmes cost little to the government since a majority of the funding comes from the private sector through the form of supposedly voluntary contribution by employers.[81] As a result, a whole proportion of social provisioning in Tunisia is directly financed by the private sector, allowing the government to increase social provisioning while keeping its budget under control (simultaneously satisfying the IMF and World Bank budget deficit targets).

Overall, despite some reduction in social spending in the GCF for example, the structural adjustment period in Tunisia has been one of social provisioning expansion with increased spending per capita in education, health and social welfare throughout the period. As a result, that period also translated into impressive improvement in the social conditions of most Tunisians, with a significant decrease in poverty between 1986 and 2002, therefore continuing the trend of the 1960s to 1980s.

Table 19: Tunisia: National Solidarity Fund, main achievements 1993–2006

Main achievements	Number	Costs (MD)
Housing (number of houses)	64,520	212.729
Roads and tracks (in kilometres)	4,492.6	222.981
Electrification (number of families)	72,500	145.447
Drinking water (number of families)	82,400	106.737
Healthcare centres	139	6.147
Education	132	3.968
Other projects*	864	17.939
Maintenance of residential areas and leisure centres		2.200
Maintenance of schools and other educational institutions		4.000
Total		722.148
Income-source projects ** (number of beneficiaries)	61,471	87.890
Contribution to the World Solidarity Fund		2.500
Contribution to the capital of the bank for the financing of small- and medium-sized enterprises		5.000
Contribution to digital solidarity for low-income families		1.000

* Purification, fight against sand encroachment, creation of youth clubs, public showers, and environmental spaces.
** These projects concern the period between 1994 and 2000. The Fund's tasks were then taken over by the Tunisian Solidarity Bank, micro-credit associations and the National Employment Fund (21–21).

Source: www.26-26.org, National Solidarity Fund, accessed April 2007.

Structural reform and poverty in Tunisia, 1986–2007

After the reduction in poverty from 22 to 9.6 per cent in the 1975–85 period, poverty continued to decrease, and in 2000 reached 4.1 per cent; a drop in the number of people from half a million in 1985 to 400 000 in 2000 (Table 20). During that period, poverty increased between 1990 and 1995 (from 6.7 per cent to 8.1 per cent), mainly because of droughts between 1993 and 1995, impacting agricultural production and increasing inequality (Ghali and Mohnen 2004).

The second half of the 1990s largely compensated for that increase, and poverty was halved between 1995 and 2000 (ironically this drop occurred in the most intensive liberalisation phase in Tunisia).

Geographical desegregation of poverty suggests that poverty is mostly a rural phenomenon, with 8.3 per cent of poverty in rural areas as compared to only 1.7 per cent in urban areas (upper bounds are 16.1 per cent and 6.2 per cent respectively).[82] Table 20 also shows that there are strong regional disparities, and poverty is particularly concentrated in the west of the country. The North, North West and Centre East, which have benefited from particularly strong growth rates through tourism and offshore activities, are the regions that saw the most impressive drops in poverty (North West poverty rate decreased from 30 per cent in 1980 to 3.7 per cent in 2000, the North East saw a drop from 15.6 per cent to 3.5 per cent, and the East a drop from 16.5 per cent to 1.9 per cent, in the same years). On the other hand the South and Centre/West of the country, poverty reduction was much slower. For example in the Centre West poverty rates decreased by 8 percentage points between 1985 and 2000, but 10.8 per cent still lived in poverty in that region in 2000 (see Table 20). Also, the South West of the country has experienced almost no change in poverty with a rate of 6.4 per cent in 2000 as compared to 6.7 per cent in 1985.

Table 20: Poverty incidence in Tunisia (Regional Headcount, 1980–2000)

Region	**1980**	**1985**	**1990**	**1995**	**2000**
Greater Tunis	4.3	2.3	2.1	2.4	1
North East	15.6	8.9	5.9	6.3	3.5
North West	30.1	17.9	14.3	11.1	3.7
Centre West	33.8	18	12.5	20	10.8
Centre East	16.5	6.2	3.9	3.5	1.9
South West	13	6.7	8.8	8.2	6.4
South East	15.7	12.1	3.1	10.5	6
All Tunisia	20.1	9.6	6.7	8.1	4.1

Sources: Ayadi et al (2001).

Nevertheless, on aggregate, reduction in poverty was accompanied by a reduction in inequality with the most drastic drop in the 1985–90 period. Inequality was on the increase in the early 1990s but dropped back in the late 1990s. In 2000, inequality was higher in urban than rural areas, and overall inequality had decreased during the structural adjustment period from a GINI coefficient of 0.430 in 1985 to 0.406 in 2000. It remains an open question whether inequality has increased in the last seven years, in particular rural/urban inequality.

On aggregate, consumption poverty reduction is matched by a drop in capability poverty, and, as for consumption poverty, rural areas seem to fair worse than urban areas.[83] We look at capabilities in three core areas: education, health and social infrastructure (see Table 21).

Education has seen the most improvement; in 2004 primary education had almost universal coverage in net terms and equal enrolment rates between boys and girls. The increase in quantity was matched by an increase in quality: according to World Bank data, drop out rates have decreased, so did the rate of repetitions, and there was a drop in the ratio of students per teacher. There remain, however, stark differences between rural and urban areas. In 1994, while net enrolment in primary education was 97.2 per cent in urban areas, in rural areas it was only 77.8 per cent (most recent data, World Bank 2000). The implication is that it will be even harder for the rural poor to grow out of poverty as job creation in the agricultural sector is low and the human capital level of the poor is likely to be too low for most non-agriculture employment given Tunisia's development level.

Evidence from Tunisia suggests that secondary education is particularly important for moving out of poverty (Ghali and Mohnen 2004). Here too improvements are substantial: gross enrolment increased from 39 per cent in 1985 to 97 per cent in 2000, the increase was particularly steep for girls whose gross enrolment rate increased from 29.3 per cent in 1985 to 80 per cent in 2000 (Table 21). Note that Ben Romdhane (2006) argues that the quality of secondary education has not necessarily increased, since the student/teacher ratio has almost doubled since the late 1980s, and, while pass rates are on the increase a study by Dimassi (2000 in Ben Romdhane 2006) suggests that this is more a reflection of poor standards than real improvement in the quality of education.

While no rural/urban disaggregated data is available for secondary education, the sharp increase in girls' primary and secondary education is likely to have a particularly positive impact on poverty reduction, since female education improvement increases women's chance to enter the labour market, therefore contributing to family welfare (everything else remaining equal[84]). Furthermore, female education is positively correlated with the probability of child survival and health status, and tends to be negatively correlated with fertility rates. Adult literacy rate has also increased dramatically from 53 per cent in 1984 to 86 per cent in 2000. Again, women remained behind with 17 per cent of adult women still illiterate.

Reduction in consumption poverty has also been accompanied by an improvement in health status. Tunisian women and men lived, respectively, 9 and 7 years longer in 2004 as compared to 1985, while under five child mortality rate was reduced from 70 per thousand live births in 1985 to 25.4 per thousand live births. There was some fluctuation in malnutrition data when measured by height (stunting), with a sharp increase between 1985 and 1990 and again between 1995 and 2000. However, the weight malnutrition measure has shown a regular decline from 10.3 per cent in 1984 to 4 per cent in 2000 (as compared to 12.3 per cent of stunted children). It is difficult to judge these contradictory data given the important methodological problems associated with malnutrition measures, but both measures suggest some improvement overall.

While there has been an increase in the number of physician per habitant between 1985 and 2000, there is also evidence that the health system is being stretched as the number of hospital beds per habitant has been decreasing regularly throughout the period, reaching 1.7 beds per habitant in 1999 (Table 21). Government spending on health has not increased as fast as the need of the health sector, with an increasing cost burden on the social security system and households. Nevertheless, Tunisia has achieved better health indicators than the average for lower-middle income and middle-income countries (World Bank 2000). Unfortunately, no disaggregated data are available, so there is no indication as to whether there are geographical or gender differences. Evidence on health infrastructure suggests that while health facilities are well established in both urban and rural areas, there remains some disparity in capacity to access these facilities as well as in health status between the East and the West of the country (World Bank 2000).

Infrastructure data are scarce, but by combining World Bank data with National Household Survey data it can be shown that there has been a large improvement in access to basic infrastructure by the poor in both urban and rural areas, but with rural population still lagging behind urban population.

While there was almost universal access to water in urban areas, only 82 per cent of the rural households had access to water in 2004 (an improvement however from 62 per cent in 1990). Similarly while 96 per cent of urban households had access to sanitation facilities in 2004, only 65 per cent of rural households did (with little improvement since 1990 when 62 per cent of households had access to sanitation facilities). However, data from the National Household Survey suggest that the infrastructure gap between urban and rural might be much larger: in 1999, 90 per cent of urban households had access to drinking water in their home, compared to only 29 per cent in rural areas (and only 35 per cent had access to drinking water inside or outside their home).

Rural/urban disparities were less acute regarding housing. In 2000, 86.6 per cent of the poor owned their house (compared to 87.4 per cent for the non-poor), and rudimentary housing has decreased from 24 per cent of total housing in 1975 to 8.8 per cent in 1985 and was only 1.2 per cent in 1999 (1.9 per cent in rural areas and 0.9 per cent in urban areas) (UNDP 2004b).

Table 21: Tunisia: Human development indicators, 1980–2004, selected years.

	1980	1985	1990	1995	2000	2004
GDP p.c. $US constant 2000	1353	1460	1503	1655	2036	2336
Population (million)	6.4	7.3	8.1	8.9	9.5	9.9
- rural (%)	48	46	42	38	37	36
Labour Force						
Unemployment	--	16.4[2]	15.9	15.8	15.7	14.2
- male	--	16.9[2]	14.3	15.3	15.3	13.2
- female	--	14.8[2]	21.8	17.5	16.9	17.1
Pverty/Inequality						
INS poverty headcount (%)	12.9	7.7	6.7	7.1	4.2	--
- rural	14.1	7.0	5.8	4.9	2.9	--
- urban	11.8	8.4	7.3	7.3	4.9	--
World Bank poverty headcount	20.1	11.3	7.4	7.7	4.1	--
- rural	30.1	19.2	13.0	14.0	8.3	--
- urban	7.7	4.6	3.5	3.6	1.6	--
GINI total	0.430	0.430	0.401	0.417	0.406	--
GINI urban	0.418	0.432	0.374	0.389	0.391	--
GINI rural	0.412	0.379	0.354	0.353	0.358	--
Health						
Life expectancy at birth, total	62	65	70	71	72	73
Life expectancy at birth, female	63	66	72	73	74	75
Life expectancy at birth, male	61	64	68	69	70	71
Under 5 malnutrition, height for age, %	--	17.9[1]	22.5[2]	8.3[3]	12.3	--
Under 5 malnutrition, weight for age,%	--	10.3[1]	9.0[2]	3.8[3]	4.0	--
Under 5 child mortality rate (per 1000 live births)	100	70	52	40	31	25.4
Population per physician	3,694	2,170	--	1,754	1,284	--
Hospital bed per habitant	2.1	--	1.9	1.7[4]	1.7[5]	--

Table 21 (cont'd): Tunisia: Human development indicators, 1980–2004, selected years

	1980	1985	1990	1995	2000	2004
Education						
Literacy rate	45	53	64	70	63	86
- female	31	39	52	59	52	83
Primary school enrolment	102	115	113[6]	117[4]	114[7]	110[8]
- male	121	--	--	120	117	112
- female	80	--	--	107	111	108
- students/teacher	38.7	31.6	27.8	24.6	--	29[7]
Secondary school enrolment	27	39	44	57	93	97
- male	--	--	49	--	94	97
- female	--	--	39	--	73	80
- students/teacher	16.7	16.6	19.9	24.1	--	--
Infrastructure						
% household with electricity	--	--	73	87[4]	94[7]	--
% household with water access	--	--	81	--	--	93
- urban	--	--	95	--	--	99
- rural			62	--	--	82
% household sanitation facility access			75	--	--	85
- urban			95	--	--	96
- rural			62	--	--	65

Note: [1] year 1988; [2] year 1995; [3] year 1997; [4] year 1994; [5] year 2002; [6] year 1991; [7] year 1999; [8] year 2003; [9] data from Ben Romdhane, 2006.
Source: Poverty data come from UNDP (2000), Ayadi et al (2001) and World Bank (1995), GINI data come from WIDER (2006) and Ayadi et al (2001), unemployment data and teacher/pupil ratio come from INS (various years), household with electricity data come from Ghali and Mohnen (2004), the remaining data come from World Bank, World Development Indicators (2006d) and IMF (2002).

Several studies have looked at the determinants and characteristics of poverty in Tunisia; see for example UNDP 2004b, Ghazouni and Goaied 2001, Ghali and Mohnen 2004, and Ayadi et al 2001. These studies, based on the diverse National Household Surveys, reveal that poverty in both urban and rural areas is positively correlated with low levels of education (especially secondary education and if it is the head of the household), size of the household (for example, the poverty rate was 9.5 per cent for households of eight or more people, but only 3.6 per cent for households with five to seven people), (Ghali and Mohnen 2004)), and number of young children in the household. In urban areas, the head of poor households is more likely to be unemployed,[85] or a construction worker, while in rural areas, the head of poor households is more likely to be a landless farmer/agricultural worker, construction worker or unemployed. Ghazouani and Goaied (2001) find that a greater ratio of male to female employees in the household and an increase in the number of children enrolled in secondary education decreases the probability of being poor (even though for the latter there might be an endogeneity bias). Poor households also tend to spend a larger proportion of their income on wheat-based products, suggesting that the food subsidy programme is likely to have a particular strong poverty reducing impact. Finally, female headship seems to be associated with a greater probability of being poor in urban areas, but not in rural areas.

Wage policy and agricultural conditions seems to have a direct impact on the poverty trend. For example poverty reduction was particularly strong in the period 1980 to 1985 when there was a significant increase in wages and government salaries. Similarly favourable agricultural conditions especially in 1985 contributed to poverty alleviation while it was detrimental during the prolonged drought of the early 1990s.

While we do not wish to diminish the incredible achievements in poverty reduction in Tunisia, the above analysis suggests that there are four interwoven factors that have contributed in creating pockets of poverty in Tunisia: living in rural areas, unemployment, low education level, and gender biases.

During the structural reform, reduction in poverty has been stronger in urban as compared to rural areas; between 1985 and 2000, poverty decreased by 65 per cent in urban areas, but only decreased by 56 per cent in rural areas. The structural reforms as such, are unlikely to have helped poverty reduction in rural areas, since the reforms have mostly benefited middle and large private farmers (King 2003, World Bank 2000). Similarly, further liberalisation of agricultural markets under the EU agreement and World Bank pressure is unlikely to work in favour of the rural poor. Agricultural activities are likely to struggle to compete internationally, affecting mostly those who already constitute a large proportion of the rural poor: small farmers and landless agricultural workers. Ayadi et al (2001) point out that the rural population has been using livestock as a source of livelihood thanks to high protectionist measures on meat and dairy products. Chemingu and Chokri (2001), using a general equilibrium model, similarly find that trade reforms and subsidy reduction will most likely decrease the average welfare of the rural poor. Unless alternative sources of revenues are made available in rural areas, the urban/rural divide may grow wider in Tunisia. There are further questions regarding the food subsidy reform, since the 'neutralising' policies adopted by Ben Ali through increases in minimum wages and alternative social provisioning are unlikely to reach rural areas to the same extent as urban areas. First, because farmers depend less on wage employment and therefore will not benefit as much as the urban poor from the minimum wage increase. Second, official poverty data used by the government grossly underestimate the extent of rural poverty, risking poor targeting of poverty policies in rural areas. For example, while in 1995 the proportion of poor was almost four times higher in rural areas as compared to urban areas, in 1997 the number of NPANF beneficiaries in rural areas was only 1.5 times higher than in urban areas (UNDP 2004b). In effect, the reform of the subsidy programme and the geographical spread of social spending may slow down rural poverty reduction in Tunisia.

Structural reforms in Tunisia failed to redress the high unemployment rate the country has been experiencing for more than twenty years. At a probably underestimated 14 per cent[86] at the national level, the unemployment rate is relatively high amongst the poor (22 per cent of the unemployed are poor). One of the reasons for high unemployment rates is likely to be the extremely rigid labour market legislation making it almost impossible to lay off workers. Ironically, these legislations are there to protect workers and make them less vulnerable to poverty, but they also prevent potential new entrants entering the labour market and therefore growing out of poverty. High unemployment rates are also related to low investment levels and the wide gap between employment creation in urban as compared to rural areas. Furthermore, the small size of businesses, most of which are family run, means that job creation remains limited. As far as the poor are concerned, such a trend is aggravated by their low human capital stock, in particular, the absence of secondary education puts the poor at a disadvantage in the labour market. Unemployment is also particularly high for young graduates and first-time job seekers. While young graduates might not be those most vulnerable to poverty, such a trend can have serious implications in terms of marginalisation and exclusion thereby threatening social stability. Unemployment is likely to become a growing problem as liberalisation strengthens with the end of the MFA and the Euro-med agreement. The labour-intensive sectors such as textile and clothing will be the most hard hit; yet these are the sectors which have benefited the poor the most. As a result, we would expect further liberalisation to increase inequality and either freeze poverty trends or worsen poverty rates.

The achievements in Tunisia regarding gendered poverty are commendable, especially if compared to other countries in the region. Nevertheless, female labour force participation rate remains significantly lower than male labour force participation (24.4 per cent for women and 68.6 per cent for men in 2005), their unemployment rate has been rising and, at 17.3 per cent, is much higher than male unemployment (13.1 per cent), and there remains an important human capital stock gap between men and women. Given the strong role female education has on poverty alleviation, it becomes imperative to bridge that gap.

The above discussion suggests three main trends: first, despite undergoing a stabilisation and structural adjustment programme between 1985 and 2000, that period was characterised by a dramatic reduction in income and capability poverty, with a simultaneous drop in inequality. Second, the drop in vertical inequality was not matched by a drop in horizontal inequality between the poor. While women seem to have benefited on aggregate as much as men in terms of many indicators, they still lag behind in terms of employment and education. Furthermore, rural areas and the West of the country seem to exhibit strong pockets of poverty both in terms of income and capability poverty. The rural/urban difference in Tunisia is largely explained by the fact the economic development has concentrated in the north and east of the country (mostly urban). While the urban/rural poverty gap has been narrowed thanks to extensive social programmes in rural areas (see UNDP 2004b, for a detail mapping of government social programme and spending by regions), these have remained short of fully bridging the gap. Finally, the Tunisian government's commitment to social policy, despite its limitations and inefficiencies, is likely to have played a crucial role in the impressive poverty reduction the country has experienced. Nonetheless, it is possible that some of the structural reform policies, in particular the food subsidy reform and the agricultural reform have slowed down poverty reduction in rural areas and that poverty has been disguised by biased national poverty measures.

Political economy of poverty reduction and impact on civil society

Two questions remain: Why has the Tunisian government been so committed to social development, and how did it manage to implement these policies despite pressures from the World Bank and IMF to reduced government spending? We argue that three phenomena can explain this trend: first, social policy is an integral part of the Tunisian social contract; second, the Tunisian State had the capacity to negotiate with the Bretton Woods Institutions, and finally, social policy has been a key source of legitimacy as well as a tool of control for the government.

Social provisioning has always been part of the social contract between the Tunisian government and the population. As argued earlier, right from independence, social development was considered at the core of the development objective set by the state. Thanks to stability in leadership, this commitment never faltered. The social contract or the 'culture of social provisioning' in Tunisia (interview with government high ranking civil servant, February 2006) was brought out as a reason for the continuity of social provisioning by all the international organisations and government officials interviewed.[87] Ben Ali constantly refers to the Tunisian specificity in making social policy an integral part of its development programme:

> Besides, we have given particular attention to social aspects in our development approach. We have conceived a coherent social policy, in harmony with [consistent with] the other aspects [of our development approach]. In effect, we have transcended the conventional approach of international financial organisations, as well as the purely liberal approach, which simply perceives the social and human dimensions of development as complementary to the economic dimension. Such is the specificity of the Tunisian model, who has been the first in opting for such an approach.
>
> (Ben Ali, RCD Congress Speech, Le Kram 1998 in Cavallo 2002; translated from French by the author)

However, such commitment could not have been preserved without the government's capacity to negotiate with the IMF and World Bank. As argued in our companion volume (Harrigan and El-Said 2008) the Tunisian government was equipped with highly skilled technocrats who have been able to negotiate the terms of the different policy packages. For example, the government was highly involved in the conceptual phase of both the reform of the health system and that of the food subsidy system. Furthermore, as seen in the previous section, the government managed to compensate or neutralise to some extent the drop in social spending in one area by creating new schemes such as the NPNF or the NSF with the latter costing little to the government budget. The latter actually suited international donors quite well, given that it allows Tunisia to be not only an economic success story but also a social success story. Here, international donors were quite happy to 'ignore' the repressive nature of social policy in Tunisia as we will see next.

The need for social policy as a source of legitimacy and a tool for control meant that it was politically impossible for the Tunisian government to abandon social provisioning. Indeed, while Bourguiba had nation state building (ideology), personal charisma and his modernist development programme as sources of legitimacy, these started to fizzle out as nation state building was complete. This was particularly the case when Ben Ali came to power: the party had no political or religious ideology that could gather support, and he did not have the personal legitimacy Bourguiba had gained through his role as a nation state builder. As a result, Ben Ali needed to create an alternative source of legitimacy: that is, social provisioning. Ben Romdhane (2006) argues:

> [T]he party is considered, and presents itself, as a 'pragmatic' entity. The power that the party still enjoys derives from its handling of social policy – that is, from clientelisme. By distributing favours and transforming citizens into clients – into human beings who are obliged to it – the party gains grateful citizenry, plays a practical role and maintains power. (p.33)

Thanks to social provisioning, Ben Ali and the party have until recently been able to maintain important support from the population as a whole. The 'Presidential programmes' such as FNS and the FNE are particularly representative of the clientelist nature of social provisioning. The institutional structure of the programmes is such that any benefits that poorer families receive is directly related to the President or his immediate family. Most social and human rights activists we met supported the idea that the Tunisian people have, overall, been supportive of President Ben Ali despite his repressive and security obsessed policies.[88] The director of a microcredit NGO, whose organisation worked particularly closely with both urban and rural poor argued that the support for Ben Ali remained extremely strong amongst the poor (interview, September, 2006). However, this support is starting to diminish amongst the business and intellectual class in particular, as there seem to be increasing evidence of the privatisation of the state; that is, economic rents (for example, major investment contracts, privatisation proceeds) are increasingly being distributed to Ben Ali's family and those surrounding him (Garçon 2007). More research is required, but the lack of social uprising or limited protests against the regime could suggest that social policy remains a successful source of legitimacy in Tunisia despite the oppressive nature of the State.

Social policy is not simply a source of legitimacy; it is also a source of control. Control is undertaken through two channels: the institutional structure of social provisioning in Tunisia, and the impact of social policy on civil society.

In the name of a grassroots approach to social welfare, the Tunisian government has set up 6,000 neighbourhood committees across the country, whose mission is to improve the living conditions of Tunisians, mostly through infrastructure development. However, during our interviews with NGO activists (whether political opposition parties, human rights NGOs or charity based NGOs), neighbourhood committees were systematically singled out as a government tool to exert its control over the population. Similarly, Chekir (2001 in Ben Romdhane 2006) argues that these committees:

> [...]aim to achieve submission of the citizens to central decision-making authorities and to contain them in their respective neighbourhood.
>
> (Chekir 2001 p.8 in Ben Romdhane 2006 p.74)

In a way these neighbourhood committees, which depend on the Interior Ministry (the same that manages the police and security services), complement the 8,362 party cells spread throughout the country, providing the government with alternative sources of information (Ben Romdhane 2006).

Social provisioning has also become a source of control through the

Presidential programmes, in particular the NSF. Hibou (2006) highlights that the different sources of 'voluntary' contribution financing the NSF, are in fact forced contributions: all firms contribute 2TD per employee per year and provide further substantial donations on special days (such as the National Solidarity day or on the anniversary of Ben Ali's accession to power). The donations are necessary if businessmen want to avoid tax control, bureaucratic delays or red tape. In fact, all Tunisians receive some form of pressure to contribute to the NSF. The programme is also disproportionably visible[89] if one compares its level of funding to other social programmes in Tunisia (see Table 18). This is largely explained by the fact that the programme is as much a tool for political control as it is a social programme: first, it provides propaganda concerning government social awareness to the middle class, second, it is a means of control of the business class through the monitoring of 'voluntary' contributions to Presidential programmes, finally, it is a means to control the poor, eradicating any chances of social uprising or chances for Islamists to gain terrain in poorer areas. In that line, Hibou (2006) argues:

> Above all else, the 26.26 [NSF] is a mechanism for enforcing order, a tool, which, by eliminating the 'shaded zones', claims to anticipate the inevitable social and economic dangers of poverty. It is likewise a technique of discipline and control that renders manifest the subjection of those who are perceived as its 'objects' and the objectivisation of those who are subjected to its control. In its exercise of power, the 26.26 makes visible those subjects that require surveillance; it turns each individual into a 'case' to be gauged, classified, listed, exemplified, corrected, excluded, or normalised.
>
> (Hibou 2006 p.201)

Social provisioning has also been a means of state control through the state's relationship with civil society. The Tunisian government is very much aware that civil society is often at the root of political opposition. Political opposition groups have therefore either been banned (such as Al Nahda, the Islamist political organisation), or tightly controlled and repressed, making room for manoeuvre almost impossible. But charity NGOs are also seen by the government as potential sources of political opposition. In effect, the Tunisian government went out of its way to ensure that it had complete control over charity based civil society by colonising the NGO world. In the last ten years, the Tunisian government has created numerous 'governmental' NGOs: in other words NGOs which are infiltrated by party members or that work under government control and influence. For example, the Tunisian government created Jeune Médecine sans Frontière and various other 'sans frontière' organisations, while at the same time limiting freedom of movement and action of legitimate NGOs (Pitner 2000). An interview with the director of a theoretically independent charity NGO (that is, they had their own sources of funding), suggested that the government still ensured that it had some indirect means of controlling the more independent organisations as well. It was explained that until the organisation received an official blessing from the President, the organisation faced numerous (mostly administrative) barriers in implementing their projects. The director pointed out:

> To be able to act in the NGO world in Tunisia, you need recognition from the President.
>
> (Interview September 2006)[90]

The control is also exerted through the use of amendments of associations laws; for example NGOs now require government authorisation to receive any external funding (Ligue Tunisienne des Droits de l'Homme, www.fidh.org accessed April 2007), and recently amendments were made to allow the government some indirect control on association membership (Marshy 2005). Effectively, the government gives the appearance of further commitment to social issues through its 'support' of NGO charities, while in fact such support is justified mostly by the government's desire to control NGO activities, perceived as a potential source of political activism.

The above discussion suggests that the Tunisian government has remained committed to social policy mostly because it would have been political suicide to abandon it. The discussion also clearly implies three things: first, because of repression and control,[91] civil society in Tunisia is very limited: politically based civil societies even when legal are very weak, while charity based civil societies are controlled if not infiltrated by the government. Second, very little space is left for independent charity based activities in Tunisia as the government has literally colonised social provisioning activities across the country. This means that very little space has been left for NGOs to provide for the poor. Finally, while faith-based NGOs are legal in theory, in practice they are almost non-existent in Tunisia, apart from a couple of Christian based charity organisations. In effect, in the Tunisia context, no such link can be made between structural reform, drop in Government social provisioning, and the rise of political Islam through the rise of faith-based social provisioning.

Nevertheless, Tunisia is experiencing what one might call an Islamic revival. The question we ask is whether such a revival is in any way related to the structural reform, and whether it implies greater support for political Islam in Tunisia.

Islamic revival, structural reform and political Islam

We have established above that social provisioning is not a channel used by the opposition, in particular Islamic opposition, to gather support. That is not to say, however, that political opposition is inconsequent, even though the extent of its influence is largely limited by the repressive nature of the Tunisian regime. The authoritarian power structure in Tunisia implies that any form of legal effective opposition has been extremely difficult to achieve. More recently, there seem to be a revival of opposition groups; mostly secular left groups and the main Islamist group: Hizb'Al Nahda (the Renaissance Party, hereafter Al Nahda). Such revival has taken the form of a greater number of legal or illegal opposition parties, exchanges of ideas, group protests (such as a hunger strike in 2006) and even negotiations between secular and the Islamist opposition (Khiari 2002, Kéfi 2006).

Recently also, Tunisia, like many other countries in the MENA region, has been witnessing an Islamic revival: that is, an increasing number of Tunisians manifests publicly their Islamic identity. Could such a revival be linked to the recent economic reform? And does it imply greater support for Islamists in opposition? These are questions we attempt to answer in this section. To do so, we propose to review the history of Al Nahda, its source of support, and its relation with the state and the other opposition groups. We then explore the links between Islamic revival, economic reform and political Islam, mostly through the analysis of secondary literature, media articles and interviews undertaken by the author in London and Tunis with leaders of the Islamist opposition and a human rights NGO which has been particularly involved in collecting data on the repression Al Nahda has suffered throughout the 1990s.

Al Nahda, the opposition and the State

In Tunisia, the Islamist political opposition was born under, and is, in fact, a direct product of the Bourguiba regime. The Bourguiba regime exploited protests and contestations as a means to control leadership of organisations.[92] As a result, the 1970s and 1980s were characterised by relatively active civil society in the form of labour unions, student movements and other political opposition groups, with labour unions being the most influential at the time. In the early 1970s, as the economic liberalisation of the time raised hopes for political liberalisation, the left/centre left secular political opposition flourished. To counter these critics, Bourguiba gave a green card for the creation of the Association for the Preservation of the Koran under the auspices of the Ministry of Religious Affairs (Alexander 2000), hoping a religious organisation would deter attention from opposition groups. The organisation, which later became the Jamma Islamiyya, was composed mostly of religious scholars, teachers and writers, who limited their reflection to religious issues, so that when criticism emanated from that organisation, it was mostly around issues of morality and faith (Harmassi 1996). There were no attempts at the time to explore social and economic issues (interview with R. Ghanoushi, London, May, 2006) or to seek popular support (Alexander, 2000).

However, by the late 1970s, cracks in the Tunisian development model started to show, a workers' revolt in 1978 was heavily repressed and followed by several years of conflict between the government and the worker's union (UGTT, Union Générale des Travailleurs Tunisiens). According to Alexander (2000) and Harmassi (1996) this is when the Islamists started to develop a more populist message including socio-economic concerns and opened themselves to the workers' and unions' movement. R. Ghanoushi (interview with author, London, May 2006) argued that two events have been crucial in the shift from purely religious concerns to more socio-economic concerns. First, he explains that the movement and protests of the worker's union played an important role in raising their awareness and concern for social issues. Second, he argued that the Iranian revolution helped the movement situate their socio-economic concerns within an Islamist discourse. Alexander (2000) also argues that in the early 1980s, a younger generation of Islamist joined the organisation. These were mostly students bringing with them a more militant approach. Until then, the Islamists were not an official political organisation, they had, however, a written manifesto, and became increasingly political from the late 1970s. They came out officially as a political organisation in 1980, under the name 'Mouvement de la Tendance Islamique' (Islamic Tendency Movement, MTI) asking for recognition from the government. The request was refused, and from the moment it declared its political intentions, the Islamist movement has been marked by waves of repression, which grew stronger with time.

Despite the movement's social and workers' discourse, and despite some limited involvement in the union movement, the MTI had very limited grassroots activities. In fact, the movement was very much elitist, made up of middle class intellectuals, and did not organise mass social movement such as in Egypt or Algeria[93] (Alexander 2000).

The change of regime in 1987 opened up new opportunities for the MTI, as Ben Ali freed thousands of Islamists including their leader R. Ghanoushi and started a phase of political liberalisation. By then the MTI had a clear pro-democratic discourse and to accommodate and enable their political participation, changed its name the Hizb'Al Nahda (the Renaissance Party) to comply with a law banning parties with a religious reference. Nevertheless, the party was never recognised by the Ben Ali regime, so when opposition parties were allowed to participate in the legislative elections, Islamists ran as independent candidates. The Islamists independent list won 14 per cent of the vote (30 per cent in urban areas) as opposed to 5 per cent for all other opposition groups combined. In other words, despite their limited grassroots activities, the Islamist movement gained substantial popularity at the time. This success in the poll, however, was to mark the end of visible Islamist activism in Tunisia, as the most violent and extreme wave of repression was launched by Ben Ali against the Al Nahda movement, successfully dismantling the organisation forcing its leaders into exile (including R. Ghanoushi) while imprisoning and torturing the rest. During the next ten years, often with the support of left opposition groups, and 'silent acceptance' from the general population, the movement was violently repressed.

Ben Ali, however, feared other forms of opposition as much as the Islamists, and that period of repression also meant that other forms of political opposition or any form of independent civil society activity was frozen. It is only in the last 5 years that Tunisian civil society has reawakened, being given some legality (even though they remained controlled and repressed) and some limited space for manoeuvre. Al Nahda remains an illegal party, and therefore is still at a 'survival' stage, suffering from continuous, though more subtle, forms of repression from the state. Nevertheless, in the last couple of years, many of its leaders have been freed, and the party has been increasingly vocal, calling for talks with the government as well as starting dialogue and even signing agreements with other secular opposition groups (interview Al-Nahda leader Tunis September 2006). The main objectives of the party at this stage are to be recognised as an opposition party, push for a democratic reform and bring in political liberties in Tunisia[94] (interview R. Ghanoushi London May 2006).

The Tunisian Islamist movement has quite unique specificities. Indeed, Islamic activism in Tunisia was not only united under a single organisation, that organisation was also elitist with little grassroots movements or social activities. While it had a socio-economic discourse that could have appealed to popular masses, it did not interact with them whether through social uprising or social welfare provisioning. In effect, the reasons Al Nahda did not benefit from social welfare provisioning as a source of support is not only explained by the government's control over civil society and its successful social policy as we saw earlier in this chapter, but it is also due to the organisation's institutional structure and its poor links with the popular masses. These three factors are of course interrelated.

Economic reform, political Islam and Islamisation

The question is, How much support does Al Nahda have from the population, and if the support does not come from Islamic organisations' grassroots activities, where does it come from? Through our analysis of open-ended interviews with the head of Al Nahda, Rashid Ghanoushi in London, one of the Tunis-based leaders of the organisation (X hereafter), and a human rights activist highly involved in the defence of the Islamists repressed in the 1990s[95] (Y hereafter), three points can be made:

First, the leaders of the organisation are unsure as to the extent of support they have from the population, but believe it is on the rise. Second, international geo-politics and internal factors are key to the Islamic revival in Tunisia. Finally, economic reforms and the intervention of international donors in Tunisia only have an ambiguous link with the Islamic revival in Tunisia.

As a result of the many years of repression and the dismantlement of Al Nahda, it is difficult to know the extent of support the organisation receives from the population. Both Rashid Ghanoushi and Al Nahda's local leader pointed out that their only referential until recently was the proportion of votes they received in the 1991 election. However Ghanoushi speculated that they might have greater support now given the Islamic revivalism Tunisia is experiencing:

> Now in Tunisia, there is a sort of Islamic revivalism, Mosques are now full of young people, they are a new generation that comes to the Islamic movement and we think that our movement [today] is among the most popular in Tunisia.
>
> (Interview with R. Ghanoushi London May 2006)

Similarly X speculated that if there were free elections today, Al Nahda might indeed turn out to be one of the most popular parties.

The Islamic revivalism is also put forward by the media and Tunisian specialists who refer to the 'Islamisation' of Tunisian society (Kéfi 2006 p.1). The Islamisation trend, while never clearly defined, has generally referred to an increased incidence of visible Islamic signs in the public sphere. More specifically the media has commented on the increasing number of women wearing the Islamic headscarf (*hijab*) and the increasing number of men wearing beards in the streets of Tunisian cities. These are, of course, only external signs of Islamisation. Such growth in the visibility of Islamic signs in the public sphere is in itself a reflection that a growing number of Tunisians are returning to more traditional expressions of their Islamic faith.[96]

Ghanoushi, X and Y all discussed the Islamic revival, its source and political implications. What comes out of these discussions is the complexity of that trend, which is understood by all as being, among other things, a reaction to both internal and external factors. Internal factors include the repressive religious policies and the rise of corruption around the Ben Ali family, which translates itself into Tunisians taking refuge in Islamic values.

Indeed, the Tunisian government has not only violently repressed the

Islamists, it has also effectively controlled all Islamic institutions (mosques, *maddrassahs*, and so on.) and repressed public religious expression under an extreme form of secularism.[97] Such control of religious institutions has removed the credibility of the mosques, so that Tunisians look elsewhere in their spiritual search, often turning to the foreign media from the Middle East which push Muslims to more traditional practices and to claim their Islamic identity.

The return to Islamic values, however, is also perceived as being influenced by international events such as the war in Iraq, the Israelo-Palestinian conflict and the war on terror in general. The strong Arabo-Islamic identity in Tunisia and in the MENA region more generally means that the war on terror tends to be perceived as an attack on the Muslim community (the *ummah*), reinforcing this Islamic identity and pushing Tunisian back to their faith:

> [...]The Iraqi question, the Palestinian question, the Bosnian question, people have been influenced by these catastrophes and they seek in Islam a form of protection; to defend themselves, because the foreign campaigns are very strong and [Arab] governments did not respond to them.
>
> (Interview R. Ghanoushi London May 2006)

> These wars in the Middle East are taking place in Muslim, or Arabo-Muslim countries. [...]Unfortunately, we have seen very serious wars, and we have witnessed changes which have influenced everyone, especially with the mass media extensively covering these events. So the international context is an important factor in pushing [people] to join the movement.
>
> (Interview with local Al Nahda leader (X) Tunis September 2006 translated from French by the author)

Recent economic changes and globalisation have also been put forward for the Islamic revival. The rapid economic changes Tunisia has been experiencing, and their socio-cultural implications, are perceived as outcomes of Western imperialism:

> You know, the international context is a major factor. There is this globalisation, where people fear loosing their identity, their authenticity, they are afraid of loosing everything, not only their religion. There is this question of modernisation where one finds oneself with televisions, new technologies and a certain hegemony of Western civilisation, especially American

[civilisation]. And there are some people who find security and serenity only by getting closer to their faith, to their values, whatever they may be. It is this effect that sometimes generates extreme positions. So you'll find people who sympathise with the Al Nahda movement, but others who see it as too open, too soft.'

(Interview with local Al Nahda leader (X.) Tunis September 2006 translated from French by the author)

The world Bank/IMF reforms have contributed to these economic changes, and in a way are symbols of the change to a market economy and globalisation in the developing world. Nevertheless, the differing positions between the two leaders interviewed suggest that the position of the organisation towards the reforms in Tunisia is far from uniform. While R. Ghanoushi seemed to use the traditional rhetoric of the movement by condemning the World Bank and the EU reforms for marginalising the most vulnerable while favouring the most powerful; X on the other hand recognised that reforms had been quite successful on economic and social grounds, but not on political or cultural grounds. Such contradiction in views is likely to reflect the organisation's dilemma that, faced with reforms that have not been detrimental to the poor on aggregate, the organisation's leaders cannot convincingly use their traditional socio-economic discourse to oppose the reforms. However, what was highlighted by both Al Nahda leaders was the double discourse of international organisations, in particular how they have continued to sign agreements with Tunisia, even when the repressive nature of the Ben Ali regime had been made clearly apparent. The latter suggests a shift in discourse by the organisation:

Both liberalisation and corruption are a problem. International bodies know what is going on and they protect their collaborators, so they are responsible for what happened [in Tunisia].

(Interview R. Ghanoushi London May 2006)

There is a duality; they [international donors] close their eyes here and open them over there. Each time they have a problem with a country, they bring out the political question, while with the good students they act with complaisance.

(Interview with local Al Nahda leader (X.) Tunis, September 2006 translated from French by the author)

Can we argue that Word Bank/EU reforms have contributed to the Islamic revival in Tunisia? While the rapid socio-economic transformations generated by globalisation and economic reforms have certainly contributed to an identity crisis, the reasons international donors are blamed by Islamists are more related to what international donors' reforms are perceived to represent (Western imperialism) and to the organisation's perceived double-standards, than to the nature and impact of the reforms as such.

Islamic revival however, does not necessarily imply greater support for political Islam. Such social phenomenon, however, necessarily has political implications. It is reasonable to think that the Islamisation trend is an indication that support for political Islam is on the rise in Tunisia, an argument that the Islamists leaders and Y have all put forward (see quotes above). Another indication that political Islam is on the rise, but also that it is taking new forms, is the appearance of a small number of Islamist seeking refuge in more radical forms of political Islam and distancing themselves from the moderate stance of Al Nahda. There was recent evidence of such a trend, when in December/January 2006/07 clashes erupted between the police and political Islamists which ended with 30 deaths (*Jeune Afrique* 2007). While the radicalisation still concerns a small minority of Tunisians, it is also understood as a reaction to the pro-Western and repressive Ben Ali regime as well as to the international context such as the war on terror and the Israelo-Palestinian conflict (interviews R. Ghanoushi X. and Y.).

The above discussion suggests that the Islamic revival in Tunisia is perceived as a reaction to complex social, political and economic changes at the national and international levels. The structural reforms are part of that complexity, but more because of the fact that they are perceived as a symbol of western hegemony and because of international donors' double standards, rather than because of the reforms' socio-economic impact *per se*. In fact, it is very likely that the Islamic revivalism in Tunisia would have happened irrespective of the reforms.

Conclusion

We have showed that structural reform in Tunisia did not lead to a withdrawal from the state in social provisioning. As a result, the reforms were accompanied by a formidable drop in aggregate consumption and capability poverty in Tunisia. We highlight that the drop has been somehow unequal with rural areas and women still lagging behind, but that the results remain impressive. We argue that the reasons Tunisia was able to preserve social provisioning throughout the reform are not only rooted in the government's capacity to negotiate with international donors, and its historical commitment to social concerns, but also because social policy has become an essential source of legitimacy for the Ben Ali regime, as well as a source of control. One implication of the nature of government social provisioning in Tunisia, in particular its use as a source of control, has been the eradication of independent civil society movement whether political or charity based.

In effect, we argue that unlike countries such as Egypt and Jordan, the economic reform did not generate greater popular support for political Islam through faith-based social provisioning. We showed that in Tunisia the main Islamist group is at a survival stage with an unclear level of popularity given the strong repression it suffered in the 1990s. Nevertheless, Tunisia has been experiencing an Islamic revival, and we were interested in exploring whether the structural reforms might have contributed to that revival through other channels. Through the analysis of interviews with Al Nahda leaders, it surfaces that the Islamic revival in Tunisia is a complex reaction to both the internal state of affairs in Tunisia such as government repression, and to the international context, in particular the war on terror. While the economic reforms implemented with the international donors are mentioned as part of the reasons for the Islamic revival, this is more because of what Islamists perceive they represent, that is, western hegemony and the donors' double standards, than because of their impact on the Tunisian economy.

What is interesting about the Tunisian case is that the form taken by Political Islam in Tunisia is such that it has positively contributed to political opposition and pluralism in Tunisia by entering into a democratic dialogue with the Tunisian secular opposition. It is possible that one reason political Islam has taken more 'moderate' forms in Tunisia could be that social provisioning was preserved and poverty reduced. On the other hand, it is also very likely to be part of some Tunisian historical specificity and the elitist structure of Al Nahda.

8

Conclusion and Synthesis: What Can be Learnt from our Four Country Studies?

Introduction

We set out to explore three themes centred around the Islamic provision of social welfare services and social capital. First, we wished to assess the extent to which economic liberalisation programmes, implemented under the auspices of the IMF and World Bank, were associated with a decline in state welfare provision and an increase in poverty. Second, to the extent that this was the case we wanted to examine whether Islamic groups had moved in to provide social welfare and fill the welfare gap created by the gradual withdrawal of the state from economic affairs. Finally, to the extent that economic reform had restricted the ability of the state to protect the poor, we wished to examine whether this had strengthened the hand of political Islam and undermined the political legitimacy of the incumbent regimes the Washington institutions such as the IMF and World Bank sought to support, forcing these regimes to become increasingly authoritarian.

In order to investigate these hypotheses we chose four countries to study in-depth: Egypt, Jordan, Tunisia and Morocco. These were chosen as they have been put forward by both the IMF and the World Bank as successful reformers, who, for prolonged periods carried out World Bank and IMF guided economic reform programmes. What we discovered was that the analysis is more nuanced than our three themes would suggest but that nevertheless they contained elements of truth.

In terms of trends in poverty and social welfare, the country experience was diverse and variable with periods of improvement and periods of deterioration under the economic liberalisation programme. We found that during the economic liberalisation period Islamic welfare provision had been growing, especially in Egypt and Jordan and that Islamists often gained political capital from this. In all four countries the donor community, including the Bank, had not fully appreciated the scale of faith-based welfare provision or engaged fully with it.

Social welfare during the reform period

All our four country studies showed that in the period between independence and the economic collapse of the 1980s there was a strong implicit social contract. Under this contract the state provided various forms of social welfare, including free health and education, subsidised food and utilities and guaranteed jobs in an overextended public sector. In return, this provisioning garnered loyalty from the population for the political regimes in power. One of the hypotheses we wished to explore was whether the period of economic reform under the IMF and World Bank led to a breakdown in this social contract with a retrenchment of the state in terms of social welfare provision and a worsening of poverty and social welfare. IMF austerity programmes as part of the stabilisation process are often associated with fiscal austerity and a decline in public expenditure, including that on social welfare.

We found that in the case of our four countries the picture was much more complex. We found that in Tunisia the state did not disengage from social provisioning, rather there was an expansion of state provisioning and, as a result, an unambiguous improvement in poverty and social welfare during her reform period contrary to our hypothesis. We argue that this can be explained by three factors. First, the state did not want to violate the social contract. Second, the Tunisian state had the capacity to negotiate with the IMF and World Bank in order to prevent any cut back in social expenditures and third, social policy has been a source of legitimacy as well as a tool of control for the government. Although the strongest gains in poverty alleviation in Tunisia were made before the period of IMF and World Bank reforms, with poverty falling from 22 per cent of the population in 1975 to 7.7 per cent in 1985, gains continued during the reform period with poverty falling to 4.1 per cent in 2000. Throughout the reform period social spending by the government remained at around 19 per cent of GDP which amounted to a doubling in real terms and an increase in per capita spending, whilst the minimum wage also increased. At the same time inequality improved with the Gini coefficient decreasing from 0.430 to 0.406. Although Tunisia, like our other three countries, was under pressure from the IMF and World Bank to reform elements of the social contract, especially food subsidies, the strong Tunisian state and bureaucracy was able to argue against this. Reforms that were made, such as a reduction in food subsidies, were counterbalanced by other measures such as an increase in the minimum wage and the creation in 1986 of the National Programme for Aid to Needy Families. However, despite Tunisia's impressive gains in poverty reduction and social welfare improvement, there was a much greater improvement in urban poverty than in rural poverty with agricultural reforms mainly benefiting the larger farmers and further agricultural liberalisation is likely to worsen rural poverty.

In addition, as in all four of our countries, unemployment, estimated to be 14 per cent, remains a pressing social problem.

In our other three country studies, trends in poverty and social welfare during the reform period are much more complex. Jordan, Egypt and Morocco all started their reform programmes with a period of austerity under IMF stabilisation programmes. This involved cut backs in public expenditure, freezing of public sector wages and salaries and employment, reductions in subsidies and increases in taxation. In all cases this, not unexpectedly, led to an initial increase in poverty and a decline in social welfare. Egypt for example commenced her stabilisation programme in 1991 and poverty increased during the first half of the 1990s as did child malnutrition. This was partly due to the rapid stabilisation programme and partly due to the fact that the Government had not yet become sensitised to the issue of poverty. Likewise, Morocco commenced her reform programme in 1983 with a period of rapid stabilisation and poverty increased to over 20 per cent of the population. Again, as in Egypt there was little Bank or government focus on poverty during this period. It was in Jordan that the initial intervention of the Bank and the Fund led to the greatest increase in poverty. The twin banking and currency crisis that was precipitated by the early reforms of the capital account, exchange rate and financial sector along with fiscal austerity led to a sharp decline in social welfare with poverty increasing from 3 per cent in 1988 to 14 per cent in 1992. Although, as in Tunisia subsidy reduction was compensated for by the creation of a National Aid Fund this fund only covered 40 per cent of the poor at a time when informal as well as formal social safety nets were in decline.

After their initial stabilisation phase with its adverse effects on poverty and social welfare both Morocco and Egypt were able to generate periods of growth which led to an improvement in poverty. In Morocco between 1985 and the early 1990s strong labour intensive export-led growth emerged. In addition the agricultural sector grew due to favourable weather and the effect of reforms, whilst economic stabilisation also helped to attract in higher levels of remittances from migrant labour. All these factors led to a decline in poverty from 21 per cent in 1984 to 13 per cent in 1991. Likewise, in Egypt the second half of the 1990s witnessed a period of growth and improvements in poverty levels. Again, this can largely be explained by employment gains although unlike Morocco this was driven more by domestic demand and expansionary fiscal policies than by growth in the export sector. However, a regionally biased pattern of growth meant that poverty did not improve in Upper Egypt and the old rural/urban poverty divide in Egypt was replaced by a regional poverty divide. Jordan's growth spurt in the 1990s was much more short-lived than that in Egypt and Morocco and as a result the decline in poverty from 14 per cent in 1992 to 12 per cent in the late 1990s was less marked.

Egypt, Morocco and Jordan's growth phases were not sustained and as growth collapsed, poverty again increased in all three countries. In Morocco, the 1990s brought recession caused by periodic droughts, real exchange rate appreciation, and declining terms of trade. As a result, poverty increased dramatically from 13 per cent in 1991 to 19 per cent in 2000. In Egypt, between 2000 and 2004 recession, the effects on prices of devaluation and a decrease in subsidies all led to an increase in poverty whilst in Jordan low growth in the late 1990s and early 2000s also brought an increase in poverty with the government claiming that poverty is anywhere between 15 per cent and 30 per cent.

In summary, what our studies show is that the early phase of stabilisation under the IMF programme usually leads to a temporary increase in poverty. However, this is short-lived, as a successful stabilisation helps to eventually generate a period of economic growth. All four countries show that poverty reduction is closely associated with labour intensive periods of growth. But we have also seen that, with the exception of Tunisia, growth has not been sustained. As growth declines poverty again increases. We have shown that growth alone is insufficient to alleviate poverty. The pattern of growth is also critically important. The Tunisian pattern of growth has shown that intensive rather than extensive growth and growth in the tradeable rather than the non-tradeable sectors is crucial for a sustained improvement in poverty. Tunisia's ability to generate such a pattern of growth with sustained export led and labour intensive growth was due to the fact that she has a strong developmental state that was able to pick and support winning industries and preserve her social contract.

Civil society and faith-based welfare provision

We hypothesised at the start of our study that a retrenchment of state welfare provisioning under the reform programme might open up a space between the state and the family which faith-based and other civil society groups could fill with welfare provisions and the creation of social capital. Our analysis has again shown that reality is more complex than this. In Tunisia, it is clearly not the case that social welfare provisioning has declined, quite the reverse. In our other three countries welfare and poverty have experienced mixed trends during the reform period and although the quantity of state welfare provisioning has not necessarily decreased its quality certainly has.

Of our four countries, Tunisia has shown the least in terms of the growth of faith-based welfare provision and it is also the country which has seen the greatest improvement in poverty and state welfare. Morocco has seen a moderate increase in faith-based welfare provision coinciding with recession and an increase in poverty since the early 1990s whilst both Jordan and Egypt have seen a very marked increase in faith-based welfare during their reform periods as the quality of state welfare has declined. These trends lend some support to our hypothesis that there is a link between state welfare provision, poverty and the growth of faith-based welfare provision. However, we have also found that the trends are often closely related to country specific factors.

Both Tunisia and Morocco have shown a degree of state monopoly over the provision of social welfare and a tight control over civil society which has reduced the extent to which faith-based welfare provision could grow. In Tunisia the state tightly controls and infiltrates NGOs whilst religious based NGOs are effectively banned. The repressive nature of the state therefore leaves little room for the growth of civil society, either secular or religious. This is in contrast to the 1970s and 1980s when there was a fairly active civil society under the Bourguiba regime. Under Ben Ali, presidential programmes of social welfare are given a high profile, such as the National Solidarity Fund, The National Job Fund and the Back to School Programme. These Presidential initiatives are partly state funded and partly funded by private donations from the business community. The presidential and state monopoly over social welfare provision leaves little space for Islamic NGOs to operate or to gain political capital from welfare provision. Likewise in Morocco, the state in the form of the Monarchy has been dominant in welfare provisioning. The recently formed Mohammed V Fund and the Hassan II Fund along with the Slum Clearance Programme and the National Initiative for Human Development (INDH) are all high profile programmes fronted by the King. As in Tunisia, private individuals are compelled to contribute to the former two funds. These funds linked to the monarchy have extensive resources which significantly exceed those of the parallel state provisions for welfare. Although, especially since the political opening up from the mid-1990s onwards, Morocco has a more vibrant civil society than Tunisia and although Islamic groups in recent years have become more active in welfare provisioning, this faith-based welfare in Morocco has not become politicised, in contrast to Egypt and Jordan. The Islamic Justice and Development Party in Morocco, unlike the Muslim Brotherhood in Jordan and Egypt, does not possess a well developed network of social welfare provision, and welfare activities undertaken by Muslims tend to be in a private rather than a political capacity. Consequently, faith-based welfare provision is not a source of political support in Morocco, in contrast to Jordan and Egypt.

In Egypt and Jordan, there is a much longer history of faith-based welfare and social capital provision and this has grown dramatically during their periods of economic reform under the IMF and World Bank. In Jordan, there are 1,400 registered NGOs and many of these are Islamic. The Jordanian Muslim Brotherhood movement tries to unite all faith-based welfare activities under one structure in the form of the Islamic Society Charity Centre, although Imams in individual Mosques also carry out their own small scale activities. Until 1989 the state was the main provider of welfare in Jordan, but since then the Brotherhood has overtaken the state with its extensive network of services which have almost become a parallel state within a state. Hundreds of thousands of Jordanians benefit from their services compared for example to the 66,000 beneficiaries of the state's National Aid Fund with its limited budget of US$80 million per annum. The services provided by the Brotherhood are generally cheaper than other private providers and of better quality than those provided by the state and the Brotherhood also has funds to help the needy access their services. As in Egypt and Morocco, the provision of this faith-based welfare and social capital in Jordan is mainly concentrated in urban areas.

It is in Egypt that we found faith-based welfare provisioning to be most extensive and developed. It is not only the Muslim Brotherhood but various other Islamic groups and individuals who provide a variety of services, particularly in the areas of health and education. Civil society was suppressed under Nasser but from the 1980s onwards there has been resurgence. At the start of Egypt's adjustment programme in 1991 only one in five of the needy were covered by state social safety nets and a two-tier social welfare system was already well developed with private health and education services offered alongside those of the state. Although both health and education expenditures were protected during the reform period they remained lower as a percentage of GDP than in comparator countries and did not keep pace with population growth and maintenance needs such that the quality of state social welfare provisioning declined rapidly. In addition, state welfare such as subsidies were poorly targeted such that the ultra poor often did not benefit. The poor access to, and the declining quality of, state welfare has left a large gap which has been filled by both Islamic and Coptic groups as well as by secular civil society NGOs. At the start of the reform programme in 1991, 14,000 NGOs were registered. By 2000 this had risen to 20,000, many of them faith-based, and 20 per cent being part of the Muslim Brotherhood Movement.

In both Egypt and Jordan, unlike Morocco and Tunisia, Islamic political parties and movements have gained extensive political capital in the form of voter support from their welfare activities. These services are open to non-members and, indeed, to non-Muslims, and have clearly helped to 'win hearts and minds', as well as votes, in these two countries. Although in Egypt the Muslim Brotherhood is banned as a political party it puts forward candidates at the election either as independents or as members of other political parties. These candidates, however, are clearly perceived by the electorate to be Brotherhood candidates. In the post 1992 period, the Mubarak regime has cracked down on Islamic groups including the Brotherhood. Despite this, the Brotherhood won 88 seats in the 2005 election, making it the main opposition force in the country. Not only is the Mubarak regime hostile to faith-based welfare provision it is also wary of civil society groups in general and under Law 32 has sweeping powers to control NGOs. Such is the political success of the Brotherhood through its welfare activities that Mubarak's National Democratic Party has tried to emulate this in a much reduced scale sending physicians for example into poor communities.

In Jordan, the Muslim Brotherhood movement was supported by the regime until recently as a counter to Ba'athist, Communist and Leftist movements in the country. However it had no major political success until the mid-1980s. Since then it has gained political strength doing well in the 1989 elections and gaining a strong voice in the legislative enabling it to block or delay controversial reforms such as removal of food subsidies, privatisation and the introduction of the sales tax. However, in response to its growing political strength the Brotherhood Movement in Jordan has recently come under attack from the Government. Under King Abdullah II and in the post 9/11 environment, the Brotherhood in Jordan has been the subject of repression and control.

Although the Brotherhood movement in Jordan and Egypt are suppressed by the state, in both countries the movement is not revolutionary but has decided to work peacefully within the democratic system. The same is the case with the Justice and Development party in Morocco. In addition, our interviews with party officials especially in Morocco and Egypt showed that they were not necessarily hostile to the reforms advocated by the IMF and World Bank. Rather they had a mercantilist philosophy, derived from the fact that the Prophet himself was a merchant, and supported market led reforms so long as they did not exacerbate poverty and inequality. In fact, it has been the Trade Unions and leftist groups much more than Islamic groups which have been hostile to the economic reform programmes in our four countries. Despite this fact, Western donors, including the Bank, have been slow to engage with Islamic faith-based welfare provision. Hence, Islamic and other religious groups providing much needed social welfare services and helping to develop social capital to their populations have found themselves frustrated by government and ignored by donors. More recently, however, there are signs at least in Morocco and Egypt that the World Bank is more willing to engage with this important social phenomenon and this is to be welcomed. However, as long as incumbent regimes remain hostile to faith-based welfare provision, the extent to which donors can engage with it will be limited.

In all four of our countries there has been resurgence in Islam in the last decade or so. This is manifested by the increase in visible Islamic signs in the public sphere such as the wearing of the *hijab* by women and beards by men. We cannot ascribe this solely to the effects of declining state provisioning of social welfare and the increase in Islamic welfare provision since the trend has been manifest even in Tunisia where this did not occur. It seems that the causes of the increased Islamicisation of society are much more complex than this. Undoubtedly in Jordan, Egypt and more recently Morocco, the activities of Islamic groups in welfare provision have contributed to this trend. But in addition, especially in Tunisia, geo-political factors such as the Iraq wars, the War on Terror and the Palestinian conflict have also played a role. Also, the failure of both socialism and capitalism, the latter in the form of economic liberalisation, has contributed to the popularity of Islam as an alternative solution in Egypt, Jordan and Morocco where despite extensive IMF and World Bank programmes there has not been sustained economic growth and poverty reduction. Finally, in all four countries a corrupt and repressive pro-Western state has made Islam look increasingly attractive not only as a religion but as a solution to socio-economic ills.

Conclusion

In terms of the decline of state social welfare provision during the process of economic liberalisation, this was clearly not the case in Tunisia. In our other three countries, although the state often tried to protect social welfare and the social contract during the period of economic reform and liberalisation, this did not prevent a decline in the quality of state provisioning which along with poor targeting, problems of access and urban bias, left a space for faith-based welfare to fill. This opportunity was most extensively exploited in Egypt and Jordan, and to a lesser extent in Morocco. In all three countries, (although much less so in Morocco) this did provide political capital to Islamic groups who have had increasing success in legislative elections. We also found that this increase in faith-based welfare prompted a hostile response by the state in Egypt and Jordan, but less so in Morocco where the Islamic Justice and Development Party is a more accepted part of the political scene especially since the political liberalisation introduced by King Mohammed VI.

In all four countries, democracy is far from developed and the state remains repressive and dominant. This has drawn the Western backers of these countries into a hypocritical position. On the one hand, they advocate democracy as a way to 'win hearts and minds' in the region, and yet they continue to support repressive pro-Western states that violate human rights and suppress legitimate forms of Islamic opposition. At the same time, even in our most successful country, Tunisia, unemployment remains high, especially amongst the young and the educated in urban areas. This makes for a captive group for more radical forms of political Islam. Radical Islam is only a very small part of the rich Islamic tapestry we found in all four countries, but it remains a potential threat to their stability. Consequently, we would advocate that both incumbent regimes and their Western backers engage more positively with Islamic welfare provision in their countries. We have shown it to be an important source of welfare and social capital which has grown recently at a rapid pace in all countries except Tunisia. If the state and its backers do not positively support this growing social phenomenon as well as move to more democratic regimes with space for Islamic opposition groups, it is possible that faith-based welfare provision will be captured by more radical tendencies within the diverse Islamic movement.

Notes

1 Woltering, R. (2002), 'The Roots of Islamist Popularity' *Third World Quarterly*, Vol. 23, (No. 6), 2002, pp.1133–1143, defines political Islam as the desire for the Islamisation of society, which requires replacing the existing political system with a usually – undefined – Islamic one. The implementation of shari'a is a common goal although this term is more of a collective noun than a reference to a specific body or system of law. He contrasts political Islam with Christian-Democratic parties in Western Europe, Hindu parties in East Africa or the Jewish Shass party in Israel since the latter aim to work within the given political system they operate under whereas political Islam aims to overthrow the existing system in favour of 'something Islamic'.

2 Countries such as Kenya under President Moi and Malawi under President Banda experienced suspension of bi-lateral aid in the 1990s as a result of their unwillingness to embrace good governance, especially the move to multi-party democracy.

3 Putnam (2000 p.19) traces 'the first known use of concept' of SC in the writing of Hanifan, a state supervisor of rural schools in West Virginia in 1916. However, James Farr (2004) has traced the conceptual history to a much earlier period. His recent work represents so far (and by far) the most comprehensive exercise in tracing the conceptual history of the term SC.

4 As Zunes (2001 p.6) noted: 'In many respects, political Islam has filled a vacuum that resulted from the failure of Arab nationalism, Marxism and other ideologies to free Islamic countries both from unjust political, social, and economic systems and from Western imperialism.'

5 We are not assuming here that Colleta and Cullen actually introduced the term 'linking' SC. We cannot be sure of and confirm the first usage of the term 'linking' SC.

6 The full text of the presentation can be found in Richards and Waterbury, 1996 pp. 352–63.

7 While analysing the 20th century's most known impressive industrialisation achievement in South Asia, particularly by the so called Tiger economies of South Korea and Taiwan, the seminal work of Wade (2004) and Amsden (1989) shows that the key behind these countries' success was not the Washington Consensus' universal mantra of getting prices right and getting government out, rather by deliberately distorting prices and bringing the state further-in in order to achieve sustainable growth, development and social justice.

8 This is unlike the colonial church of the eighteenth century, which, contrary to general belief, 'played only a minor role in social service provision' (Cnaan et al, 2003 pp.26–7).

9 One often hears that, theoretically, Islam does not recognise separation between state and religion, and that makes Islam incompatible with modernity which tends to secularise tendencies (Fukuyama 1995). However, it is important to note here that the Islamic tradition did provide a powerful base for the separation between politics and religion. In his seminal work on democratic pluralism in Islam, based on a detailed analysis for the Koran itself, Sachedina (2001) shows how secularity, often attributed to the ingenuity of modern man, is embedded in Islam's essential and basic message originally used to remind the prophet of Islam (Muhammed) himself that his duty

is to deliver and not to enforce religion: 'There is no compulsion in religion' (*The Koran*, Chapter 2, verse 256).

10 The concept of SC itself is not new and its application was traced back to the early 19th century. As Putnam (2000 p.24) put it, 'Social capital is to some extent merely new language for a very old debate.' It was not before the work of Colman (1988) and Putnam (1995) that the term SC was put firmly on the development agenda. In recent years, the World Bank played an important role in enhancing understanding and measurement of SC, and in 1997 it launched The Social Capital Initiative that was funded by the Danish government. For details, see Grootaert and Bastlelaer (2002a chap. 1) and World Bank website: http://wordbank.org/poverty/scapital/. However, James Farr (2004) has recently offered by far the best and most comprehensive attempt to trace the conceptual history of SC.

11 The nature and extent of this debate is extensively discussed in the book by Partha Dasgupta and Ismail Serageldine, (Eds.), *A Social Capital: A Multifaceted Perspective*, World Bank, Washington DC, 1999.

12 Several chapters in Grootaert et al (2004) provide detailed information and several examples and case studies on the role of social networks and social capital in accessing information. On the informational role of SC among black community in the USA, see Glen Loury (1977), and in the Arab World in general, see Cunningham and Sarayah (1993).

13 This, of course, is contrary to the early literature on SC, which not only tended to 'romanticise' its effects, but also to underestimate its negative consequences (Narayan 1999 p.20, and Gootaert and Bastelaer 2002a p.138).

14 Some of these dimensions are both cause and effect at the same time. For example, a rise in the crime rate can reduce security and hence undermine social connectivity and visits as people prefer to stay at home for safety reasons. But the rise in the crime rate itself might have been caused by decline or erosion of SC. 'Endogeneity of social capital,' or determining the direction of causality, remains a key question in the analyses of SC (Grootaert and Bastelaer 2002a p.42). Several authors, however, have established the link to run from SC. See Grootaert and Bastelaer (2002a), Narayan (1999) and Narayan and Cassidy (2001).

15 Of course, it might have not have been called *wasta* under the Romans and Byzantines. But several historians show that such a phenomenon was very common and widely practiced at the time (see, for example, Cunningham and Sarayrah 1993).

16 It is important to note here that the British authorities, which sought to reduce Transjordan's (Jordan's name before independence in 1946) heavy dependence on the British subsidy, regarded the Mushi system as inefficient and the most serious impediment to raising production and hence tax revenues. By the mid-1930s, therefore, they sought to break it up by introducing a new property rights law to enhance production and at the same time state revenue. Although this process failed to raise production and state revenues, it managed to gradually undermine the *mushi* system.

17 More than 90 per cent of Jordan's land is arid. Some fertile areas exist in the Northern highlands, traditionally planted with wheat, but are without irrigation and are thus subject to the vagaries of rainfall. It is only in the Jordan Valley area where a commercial, reliable and irrigated agricultural sector exist.

18 Jreisat (1989 p.95) also noted that the dramatic increase in the number and heterogeneity of population did not evidently undermine economic growth, which remained relatively high during the 1950s and 1960s, with GDP and GNP between

1952 and 1966, respectively, registering 6.9 per cent and 7.5 per cent annual average growth rates.

19 As Peter Snow (1972 p.71–2), King Hussein's biographer, while describing the 1950s wrote: 'Nasser's militant campaign for Arab unity excited the minds of the masses throughout the Arab world and many Jordanians saw Nasser as their leader, not Hussein. Nasser's power seemed somehow born of the people, Hussein's did not. Nasser's fight to evict the British from the Middle East, in order to restore Arab dignity, was a striking contrast to Hussein's apparent wish to maintain and depend on continuing British presence.'

20 Yet, the majority of Palestinians did not stay in refugee camps or even registered their names with UNRWA. Even today, less than 26 per cent of all Palestinians in Jordan are registered with UNRWA. This could also provide another indication on the extent of support provided by the earlier immigrants, which, as Al-Hamarneh (2002 p.173) suggests was vital in enabling a large number of Palestinians to find jobs, housing and capital for either small business projects or simply for getting by in the new environment.

21 Again, labour movement from Jordan to the expanding oil Gulf States was beginning to gain momentum in the 1950s and 1960s, with thousands of Jordanians flocking to the region seeking higher paid jobs there.

22 This was also supported by the fact that the general Palestinian population of Jordan did not participate in the 1970–1 armed struggle itself. In fact, the large majority of the Jordanian armed forces at the time were made up of Palestinians who fought PLO fighters along side Jordanians.

23 Abu-Odeh (1999) defines those nationalists to consist of middle class Jordanians, a group of professionals, high ranked army and security officers, and relatives and friends of the former prime minister (Wasfi al-Tal) who was assassinated allegedly by the PLO in 1971.

24 Of course, this process was not only used to Jordanise the public sector, but also to penalise and undermine opposition to the regime from all ethnic backgrounds, including elements of the Jordanian society who were former members of the Baa'th, socialist or pan-Arabist movements.

25 Less than a year following the end of the 1970–1 clashes, Hussein stated that 'Last year's events with all its distress and suffering ... enhanced my conviction and belief in setting up a national union that brings together the people of the two dear banks and unites their efforts' (Hussein 1971).

26 Bel-Air (2002 p.157) also concluded that the regime deliberately constructed and fashioned 'a neo-patriarchal political system in Jordan' in order to increase 'allegiance' to itself and maintain communal loyalty.

27 While the exact number or share of Palestinians in the public sector is unknown, a study conducted by the Centre of Strategic Studies at the University of Jordan in 1996 suggested that Palestinian participation in the country's private capital amounted to 82.6 per cent, while Jordanian participation was only 11 per cent. The rest was owned by Jordan's main minorities, namely, Circassians, Armenians, Kurds, Syrians and Lebanese. See Abu-Odeh, 1999, p.196.

28 Also see Fathi, 1993.

29 This quotation is also interesting in that it suggests that the new post-1970 environment had put the pro-regime, Palestinian wealthy class that played an important role in moderating the political environment in the 1950s and 1960s in a difficult position and undermined their efforts in persistently soothing and calming the rising tension between the two communities in the post-1970 period.

30 Almost 98 per cent of Jordanian firms are small- and medium-sized. This may correspond well with Fukuyama's (1995) argument that societies with primary as opposed to generalised mutual trust do not develop large size firms.

31 While analysing the costs and benefits of SC among the US Asian community, Portes noticed a similar phenomenon taking place among prosperous Asian immigrants to America, who 'anglicized their names in order to divest themselves of communal obligations to subsequent cohort'. Cited from Woolcock and Narayan (2000 p.231).

32 As mentioned earlier, movement of labour has always been a major feature of the Jordanian economy. But there is some evidence, cited in Cunningham and Sarayrah (1993) which suggests that social networks, wasta, or SC was exerting excessive claims on more successful members of Jordanian society that they themselves opted for an exist strategy to the Gulf.

33 Within a mere 15 years between 1970 and 1985, the number of Jordanian civil servants increased by 300 per cent – from 27,000 to 74,000 (Jreisat 1989 p.99). By 1988, the size of the regular armed forces reached 85,000, from 25, 000 in 1956 (Satloff 1986 p.123 and 130). Most of these appointments were based on regional and tribal ties.

34 There is a big debate over the extent of poverty and unemployment in Jordan. Reflecting this debate, the 2002 Poverty Alleviation Strategy (Ministry of Social Development 2003 p.13) noted that 'Poverty is a serious problem in Jordan. Depending on the poverty line used, anywhere from 15 to more than 30 per cent of the population falls below that line' and anywhere between '13.7 per cent and 25 per cent' are unemployed.

35 According to Al-Oudat (1999 p.37), about 95 per cent of the returnees were of Palestinian origin.

36 There are 6 public universities in Jordan today and at least 13 private universities. While the latter are open to all students, the former tend to discriminate in favour of Jordanians. Reiter (2002, p.152–3) argues that more than 80 per cent of students in Jordanian public universities enter via some form of wasta, known as the 'quota framework' (such as the army quota, the Royal Palace Quota, and the Sons of the Deprived Quota), which are designed to favour Jordanian over Palestinian students.

37 A similar trend was also observed by the World Bank study (2002a, Local Level Institutions and Social Capital) in Bosnia and Herzegovina, where support provided by international community became a source of tension between various ethnic groups.

38 Amawi (1994) demonstrates how even involvement in trade was considered *ayeb* by most Jordanian families in the pre-independence period and was thus left for merchants who came mostly from outside the country.

39 Ten Palestinian refugee camps exist in Jordan, four of which were built after the 1948 war while the rest were built after the 1967 war. The majority of these camps (at least six) are located in the so-called Amman Metropolitan Area (AMA), which covers an area with a radius of 35 km. While almost 85 per cent of returnees settled in and near the refugee camps in AMA, another 13 per cent settled in Irbid where another large refugee camp, built in 1949, is located. However, less than 26 per cent of all Palestinians in Jordan are registered as refugees with UNRWA. For more details, see Al-Hamarneh, 2002 p.173–4, and Trooquer and Al-Oudat 1999 p.39.

40 According to Bileh (1991), only 10 per cent of the returnees were taken in by relatives.

41 This happened, for example, during the 1950s and 1980s when the Jordanian regime supported Islamic movements against Nasser and against the Ba'ath regime

respectively (for more details, see AUJRC 1997).

42 For example, interest on public debt alone comprised almost one-quarter of total expenditures, while another one-third represented expenditures on wages and salaries, pension and military.

43 Food subsidies were reinstituted again in 1988/89 following a rise in poverty. (See IMF 2004 pp. 100–16.)

44 Even in the U.S., the current level of religiosity is largely disputed. While some believe that Americans are more religious today, Putnam (2000), for example, contests this argument, and states that American sentiments are less tied to institutions and more self-defined instead.

45 In fact, the MBM insisted on meeting 14 conditions before they cast their vote of confidence to Mudar Badran's government in 1989–91 which they became part of one year later. These conditions were: exerting continued efforts to implement Sharia law; non-interference in the appointment of public servants by security apparatus; granting of educational scholarships, and licensing of charity organisations, clubs and professional associations; reversal of the martial law rule; extending support to the Palestine intifadah and liberation movements; enacting a law for holding all illegitimate financial gains accountable; restoring financial deposits smuggled out of Jordan through officials to finance development projects; cutting expenditures for government offices; cancellation of profit on small farmer loans and housing as an opening step towards doing away with the usurious system; allowing teachers to establish an association; withholding licenses and sale of liquor to Muslims and prohibiting alcoholic drinks in public places; granting permission to set up a Sharia' college as part of Yarmouk University and licensing of a Private Islamic University. The Badran's 1989-91 government was the only government that gained a vote of confidence by the MBM. Since then, the MBM has never given a vote of confidence to any other government (see Gharaibeh 1997 p. 49).

46 The ministers were: Dr. Abdullah Al-Akaileh education, Dr Ibrahim Zaid Al-Keilani (awqaf and Islamic Affairs), Dr. Adnan Al-Jaljouli (health), Dr Majid Khalifeh (justice), and Youssef Al-Adhem (social development). Their participation in government only lasted for 6 months.

47 Little work has been done on what really caused King Hussein to fire his Islamist minsters after such a short time in late 1990–early 1991. Some say that the regime felt that Islamists were politicising these sensitive posts to create a sharia law. One former Islamist cabinet member stated that 'this was not correct. I used to pray even during my working hours in my office. My staff used to see me and they started to do the same' (interview with the author, Amman October 2004). However, there were some well known Jordanian secular personalities, particularly women, who were forced to resign from their posts in some of the ministries which were dominated by Islamists (see AUJRC 1997).

48 As mentioned earlier in this chapter, the new Sales Tax was introduced in 1994, after four years of delay, at 7 per cent rate, rising to 10 per cent in 1995 and to 13 per cent in 1999 and after King Hussein died in February when it was converted to a General Sales Tax (GST). Similarly, privatisation in Jordan took off only after King Hussein died as well (for details see El-Said 2001 and 2002b).

49 Ironically, the IMF still claimed that Jordan's 'government was totally committed' to its policies, and that it was 'implementing faithfully the arrangement concluded with the IMF', even noting that 'in many respects Jordan had gone beyond IMF prescriptions' (quoted in Fanek 1997 p.3).

50 For example, on April 6, 1996, members of the MBM in the parliament voted against lifting food subsidies and many even boycotted the parliamentary session itself. On April 16, violence erupted for the third time in less than six years in the country following a decision by the government to lift all bread subsidy (Al-Rab'eh 2004 p.169).

51 Members of Islamic-based organisations in Jordan, Morocco, Egypt and Tunisia complained during interviews with the authors that members of their organisations and their operations have been subjected to enormous restrictions and limitations in recent years as part of what they perceive to be pressure from the US government.

52 Sabry (2005 p.38) has estimated that the Social Aid and Assistance payouts for a family of one woman, her disabled husband and three children would represent only 6 per cent of the poverty line whilst for a widow and two children at the most it would provide 22 per cent of the poverty line income. In addition, paperwork which requires an identity card and birth certificate excludes many – an estimated 55 per cent of women do not have an identity card and illiteracy extends to almost half the population.

53 Income distribution worsened slightly for the country as a whole with the Gini coefficient increasing from 34.5 to 37.8 between 1995–6 and 1999–2000 but the coefficient improved for Lower Egypt which had pro-poor growth.

54 The Muslim Brotherhood was formed in Egypt in 1928 and is now active in almost every Muslim country. It combines political activity with social work and aims to establish an Islamic Caliphate across the Muslim world through stages designed to Islamicise Muslim majority nations through all lawful means available. In the 1950s it was officially banned in Egypt after carrying out a number of assassinations and assassination attempts. Sadat reinstated the Brotherhood which renounced violence, but following his peace treaty with Israel he was assassinated by Brotherhood members in 1981. Since then the movement has been subject to periodic mass arrests and harassment. However, with 88 seats in the People's Assembly compared to approved opposition parties who won only 14 in the 2005 election there is a revived debate in Egypt as to whether the Muslim Brotherhood should remain banned as a political party.

55 The Brotherhood made these gains despite the fact that they only put up candidates in one third of the constituencies. Following their gain in the national elections the 2006 local elections were postponed for two years for fear that the Brotherhood would again make large gains. In addition, there has been a clamp down on student elections resulting in student riots in 2006.

56 In 1984 the Brotherhood formed a tactical alliance with the New Wafk Party and won eight seats and in 1987 it formed a tripartite alliance with the Labour and Liberal parties winning 36 seats for the Islamists in the People's Assembly making them the main opposition.

57 Although the poor benefit from some of these expenditures they are not specifically targeted at the poor.

58 Expenditures per student in secondary schools are three times higher than expenditures per student in primary schools.

59 However, as the children of the rural poor rarely attend school the poverty impact is limited.

60 Stabilisation in the 1982–84 period was based upon a pattern of adjustment that favoured imports and demand compressions and this was recessionary whilst from 1985 onwards the model adopted was one of export and income expansion.

61 This result is based on the 1984–5 household consumption survey and the 1990–1 Living Standards Measurement Survey and is robust even when different poverty lines are used.

62 Social protection expenditure includes: training, employment and labour market policies; education and health; rural development; social assistance; and social insurance.

63 Unemployment was not a major issue in Morocco in the 1960s and 1970s as until 1980 the government guaranteed jobs in the public sector for university and high school graduates.

64 The exception was the 1986 US$150 million policy based loan for the education sector which aimed to put a break on the expansion of higher education and prioritise primary education particularly in poor rural areas. However this Education Sector Reform Programme met with little success due to government resistance.

65 The maps provided a clear indication of the geographical location of poverty across the country as it stood at the time of the 1994 census. A second set of urban poverty maps was issued in 2006 integrating data from the 2004 census and from a comprehensive household survey carried out in 2002.

66 In 2003, 900,000 households lived in sub-standard housing conditions, which equated to roughly five million people or one third of the urban population, of which 212,000 households were in urban slums.

67 There are decision-making bodies at local, provincial and regional levels consisting of an equal share of Government officials, elected officials and representatives from civil society.

68 This figure includes functional or interest group associations such as trade unions, professional associations, farmers' cooperatives, religious groups and women's organisations.

69 Increasingly NGOs are also being supported by the diplomatic community in the form of embassies and bilateral aid donors. Several donors, including the Germans, USAID, the World Bank and the EU have projects to help strengthen NGO capacity.

70 Although a constitutional monarchy since independence Parliament was suspended between 1965 and 1970 due to violent opposition protests to the rigging of the 1963 elections. This opposition was orchestrated by the trade unions and left wing parties as opposed to Islamic political parties. Following two abortive military coups in 1971 and 1972 Parliament was reopened. A new constitution was approved by popular vote in 1996 and elections to a bi-cameral Parliament were held in September 1997. The political opening initiated by King Hassan II was accelerated under King Mohammed VI after his accession in 1999 with elections in 2003.

71 It has been argued that support for Islamic political parties is higher than their number of seats in Parliament suggest due to the low turnout in elections and the fact that the Justice and Development Party did not field the maximum number of candidates (Galal and Lawrence 2003).

72 The fact that the INDH was launched as a Government attempt to counter the growing influence of both NGOs in general as well as faith-based NGOs is shown by the fact that despite the avowed aim of working closely with NGOs as part of the INDH, local government has been reluctant to transfer resources for projects to NGOs preferring instead to execute projects by their own means.

73 This chapter relies on a diverse source of statistical data, but the reliability of these data is unclear; for example there is limited information on data collection and sampling for household surveys, and inconsistencies have been found on data between different government institutions. Nevertheless, comparisons between different sources suggest that the general trend of the data we present is relatively consistent.

74 Support for political Islam has also taken more violent forms, as evidenced by the

different terrorist attacks in countries such as Egypt and Algeria; however, these constitute a minority of political Islamists, which tend to overshadow the complexity and diverse forms taken by political Islam across the globe (Esposito 1994).

75 It is important to recognise that motivations of most Islamic charity organisations are primarily socio-economic, and that their link to political Islam may be direct or indirect. For more on political Islam and Islamic charities see Benthall and Bellion-Jourdan (2003) for a critique.

76 For a comprehensive review of social policies in Tunisia see Ben Romdhane (2006)

77 Ben Romdhane (2006) however argues that the drop in education spending in the 1970s explains the human capital gap experienced by Tunisia today.

78 The World Bank measure has been considered more reliable in terms of the reference groups chosen and the constitution of basic needs basket of goods. See World Bank (1995), Ayadi et al (2001) and Saïdi (2002) for more details.

79 The structural reform can be separated into two periods: 1986–7 to 1992–3 and 1994–5 to 2002.

80 The discussion on social policy in this section draws heavily from the comprehensive review by Ben Romdhane (2006).

81 Ben Romdhane (2006) found that donations included 2 TD per worker per month by employers, regular gifts by farmers and fishermen equivalent to 1 per cent of wholesale price and other gifts made on special solidarity days, which the authors approximate to total 24 million TD per year.

82 Note however that the INS measure finds that poverty is mostly an urban phenomenon with an urban poverty rate of 4.9 per cent and a rural poverty rate of 2.9 per cent. The difference is largely explained by the fact that the INS poverty line measure has an estimated unit value of food in urban areas 70 per cent higher than in rural areas which is likely to be an exaggerated food price difference estimation. The INS measure also uses a higher share of non-food consumption for the urban basket as compared to the rural one (Ghali and Mohnen 2004, World Bank 1995).

83 This would suggest that the World Bank poverty measure is more closely related to capability poverty indicators than the INS measure.

84 Everything, however, does not remain equal, and women's entry into the labour market creates trade-offs in terms of women's own well-being (work burden and health) human capital reproduction (care of children) in particular when infrastructure for social reproductive activities are poor.

85 Of unemployed household heads 22 per cent are poor (World Bank 1995).

86 The government changed the definition and measurement of unemployment in 2005, so that the stagnation to 14 per cent in 2006 might in fact hide a rise in the proportion of unemployed.

87 Organisations interviewed: ADB, EU and UNDP, High ranking civil servants from the Ministry of Economic Development and the Euro med bureau.

88 Interviews with several NGOs directors, September 2006.

89 One can simply look at the different government sponsored website such as www.tunisie.com or www.tunisiaonline.com which all refer extensively to the programme. It is also repeatedly referred to in Ben Ali's speeches.

90 Interview Charity NGO director, September 2006. The director of that NGO also pointed out that there were attempts by the government to take over the organisation.

91 For a review of the types of repression different political opposition groups undergo in Tunisia see Amnesty International (www.amnesty.org/Tunisia), Hibou 1999 also provides an analysis of the nature of this repression.

92 Alexander (1997) points out that '[i]n the 1950s and the mid-1980s, Bourguiba discretely supported worker unrest against union leadership. On both occasions he supported break-away unions, and then reunited the labour movement under leaders who owed their position to Bourguiba rather than the rank and file' (p.4).

93 Alexander (2000) notes that even when the MTI planned a coup to remove Bourguiba, they did not do so through social uprising, but through an alliance with other opposition groups (themselves quite elitists).

94 Al Nahda has generally been classified as a 'moderate' Islamist group given R. Ghanoushi's extensive work on Islam and civil society, Islam and democracy, and the party's position on women's status (see Tamimi 2001).

95 Name of respondents and organisations are kept anonymous.

96 Note however that this return to a more 'traditional' expression of their faith does not mean a return to the way Islam was traditionally practised in Tunisia, but rather refers to a very modern phenomenon of returning to the 'tradition' (life) of the Prophet Mohammed interpreted within a modern context (Gharbi 2006).

97 The relationship between Islam in the State in Tunisia is complex, while very much a secular society since independence, Islam is the religion of the state, and the latter effectively controls all religious institutions, preventing any independent Islamic initiatives. Ben Ali has been simultaneously presenting himself as the defender of the Islamic faith and identity while at the same time repressing those too zealous in their religious expression.

Bibliography

Abdel-Khalek, G. and Tignor, R. (Eds) (1982). *The Political Economy of Income Distribution in Egypt*, London, Holmes and Meier Publishers.

Abdel-Latif, A. (2005). 'Dealing with a new reality', in *Al-Ahram* Weekly, 24–30 November, Issue No. 770.

Abootalebi, A.R. (1999). Islam, Islamist and Democracy, *MERIA*, Vol. 3, No. 1.

Abigail, B. *Social Dilemmas and Shame-based sanctions: Experimental Results from Rural Zimbabwe*, Oxford, Centre for the Study of African Economics, University of Oxford, June 2001.

Abu-Odeh, A. (1999). *Jordanians, Palestinians and the Hashemite Kingdom in the Middle East Peace Process*, Washington, DC, United States Institute of Peace Press.

Achouri, H. (2005). Advances in the Implementation of Social Security Lessons from Tunisia International Conference on Social Health Insurance in Developing Countries, Berlin, December 2005 mimeo.

Achy L. and Hamdouch, B. (2003). Economic Growth in Morocco: An Assessment of the Last Two Decades and Future Prospects, Rabat, INSEA Working Paper, June.

Al Abed, M. (2005). 'Corruption Has Become Institutionalised, say Deputies', *The Jordan Times*, Amman, July 19.

Al-Braizat, F. (2002). 'Muslim Democracy: An Empirical Critique of Fukayama's Culturalist Approach', *International Journal of Comparative Sociology,* Vol. 43, No. 3–5, pp. 265–99, London, Sage Journals.

Alderman, H. and von Braun, J. (1984). 'The Effects of the Egyptian Food Ration and Subsidy System on Income Distribution and Consumption', International Food Policy Research Institute, *Research Report No. 45,* Washington DC.

Alexander, C. (2000). 'Back from the Democratic Brink: Authoritarianism and Civil Society in Tunisia', *Middle East Report*, October–December 1997.

—— (1997).'Opportunities, Organizations, and Ideas: Islamists and Workers in Tunisia and Algeria', International Journal of Middle East Studies, 32, pp.465–490.

Al-Hamarneh, A. (2002). The Social and Political Effects of Transformation Processes in Palestinian Refugee Camps in The Amman Metropolitan Area (1989–99), in Joffe, G. (Ed), *Jordan in Transition 1990–2000*, London, Hurst.

Ali, A. and Crain, M. (2002). 'Institutional Distortion, Economic Freedom, and Growth', *Cato Journal*, 21(3).

Ali, D.B. (1997). 'Economic Adjustment and Political Liberalisation in Morocco', Chapter 9 in Handoussa, H., *Economic Transition in the Middle East: Global Challenges and Adjustment Strategies,* Cairo, The American University Press in Cairo.

Al-Jumrid, A.A. (Ed) (2000). *Evaluating External Economic Assistance to Jordan 1989–1999,* Amman, Centre for Strategic Studies, University of London.

—— (2002). *Evaluating External Economic Assistance to Jordan 1989–1999*, Amman, Centre for Strategic Studies.

Al-Oudat, R. (1999). From Kuwait to Jordan: The Palestinians' Third Exodus', *Journal of Palestinian Studies*, 28(3), Spring 1999, pp.37–51.

Al-Rab'eh, F. (2004). 'Democracy', Amman, Dar Al-Hamad (in Arabic).

Al-Urdunn Al-Jadid Research Centre (AUJRC) (1984). The Results of the Elections, Amman, Sindbad Publications, AUJRC (in Arabic).

—— (1997). Islamic Movements in Jordan, Amman, Sindbad Publishing House, Aljazeera News, http://www.radiosawa.com/article.aspx?id=881926, 20 May, 2006.

Amadouny, V. (1994). 'Infrastructural Development Under the British Mandate', in Rogan, E. and Tell, T. (Eds), *Village, Steppe and State: The Social Origins of Modern Jordan*, London, British Academy Press.

Amawi, A. (1994).'The Consolidation of the Merchant Class in Transjordan During the Second World War', in Rogan, E. and Tell, T. (Eds), *Village, Steppe and State: The Social Origins of Modern Jordan*, London, British Academy Press.

Ammor, M. (2003). 'Le Programme des Priorites Sociales BAJ' in *Bulletin Economique et Social du Maroc, Rapport du Social 2000*, Okad, Rabat.

Amsden, A. (1989). *Asia Next Giant: South Korea and Late Industrialisation*, Oxford, Oxford University Press.

Anani, J. (2002). 'The Political Sociology of Jordan: An Analysis for the Map of Gains and Pains', in El-Said, H. and Becker, K. (Eds), *Management and International Business Issues in Jordan*, London, The Haworth Press.

Arrow, K. (1972). 'Gifts and Exchanges', in *Philosophy and Public Affairs* Vol. I, No. 4, pp. 343–362.

Ayadi, M., Matoussi, M.S., and Vicroria-Feser, M.P. (2001). 'Putting Robust Statistical Methods into Practice: Poverty Analysis in Tunisia', *Schweizerische Zeitschrift fur Volkswirtschaft und Statistik/Swiss Journal of Economics and Statistics* 137(3), pp.463–82.

Ayubi, N. (1995a). *Distant Neighbors: the Political Economy of Relations Europe and the Middle East/North Africa,* London, Ithaca Press.

—— (1995b). *Over-Stating the Arab State*, London, I.B. Tauris.

BBC News (2005). Blair extremism measures, reaction 5 August, (http://news.bbc.co.uk/2/hi/uk_news/4748963.stm). Last seen on August 2, 2007.

—— (2006). The political leader of the Hamas militant group has said it could create a new Palestinian army following its surprise election victory, (http://news.bbc.co.uk/1/hi/world/middle_east/4658872.stm).

Babou, C.A. (2002). 'Brotherhood solidarity, education and migration: The role of the Dahiras among the Murid muslim community of New York', *African Affairs*, 101, pp. 151–170.

Badran, M. (1991). 'Competing Agendas: Feminism, Islam and the State in 19th and 20th Century Egypt', in Kandiyoti, D. (Ed), *Women, Islam and the State*, London, Macmillan.

Barr, A. (2002). From Strangers to Neighbours. Taken from Global Poverty

Research Group, How Does SC Form? Overview, March 3, 2005.(http://www.gprg.org/themes/t4–soccap-pub-socsafe/how=sc.ht).

—— (1998). *Enterprise Performance and the Functional Diversity of Social Capital*, Working Paper Series 98–1, Oxford, University of Oxford, Institute of Economics and Statistics, Processed, 1998.

Bayat, A. (2006). 'The Political Economy of Social Policy in Egypt', in Karshenas, M. and Moghadam, M. (Eds), *Social Policy in the Middle East: Economic, Political and Gender Dynamics*, Basingstoke and New York, Palgrave Macmillan and UNRISD.

Becker, G. (1993). *Human Capital: A Theoretical and Empirical Analysis, with Special Reference to Education*, London, University of Chicago Press.

Bel-Air, F. (2002). 'Household Politics to Domestic Policies: The Effect of Demographic Transition on Socio-Political Patterns of Domination', in Joffe, G. (Ed), *Jordan in Transition 1990–2000*, London, Hurst.

Benthall J. and Bellion-Jourdan, J. (2003). 'The Charitable Crescent: Politics of Aid in the Muslim World', London, I.B. Tauris.

Ben Hussein, M. (2007). 'House discusses legality of understanding between gov't, JEA,' in the *Jordan Times*, Amman, 19 February.

Ben Romdhane, M. (2006). 'Social Policy and Development in Tunisia: A Political Analysis', in Karshenas, M. and Moghadam, V. (Eds), *Social Policy in the Middle East*, London, Palgrave and UNRISD.

Berger, P.L. (2002). 'Globalisation and Religion', in Religion and Globalisation, 'The Hedgehog Review: Critical reflections on Contemporary Culture', summer, 4(2) (pp.7–20).

Bibars, I. (2001). *Victims and Heroines: Women, Welfare and the Egyptian State*, London and New York, Zed Books.

Bileh, V. (1991). *The Socio Economic Characteristics of Jordanian Returnees*. Amman, National Centre for Educational Research and Development, July, 1991.

Braizat, S. M. (1998). *The Jordanian Palestinian Relationship: The Bankruptcy of the Confederal Idea*, London, The British Academy, 1998.

Brand, L. (1994). *Jordan's Inter-Arab Relations: The Political Economy of Alliance Making*, New York, Columbia University Press.

—— (1995). Palestinians and Jordanians: A Crisis of Identity, *Journal of Palestine Studies*, 24(4), Summer, pp.46–61.

Briggs, X. de S. (1998). 'Doing Democracy Up Close: Culture, Power and Communication in Community Building', *Journal of Planning Education and Research*, 18, pp.1–13.

CAFOD (1998). *Taming Tigers: Social Impact of Crisis*, London, March, CAFOD.

Campell, D.E. and Yonish, S.J. (2003). Religion and Volunteering in America, in Smidt, C. (Ed), *Religion and Social Capital: Producing the Common Good*, Boston, Baylor University Press.

Cardiff, P. (1997). 'The 1995/96 Household Income, Expenditure and Consumption Survey: Final Report Analysis', Washington DC, USAID and US Bureau of Census.

Carothers, T.T. (2003). 'Promoting Democracy and Fighting Terror', *Foreign Affairs*, Vol. 82, No. 8, pp 84–97.

Cavallo, D. (2002). 'Développement et libéralisation économique en tunisie: éléments d'anlyse des discours de légitimation', in Lamlou, O. and Ravenel, B. (Eds), *La Tunisie de Ben Ali: la société contre le régime,* éd. L'Harmattan, Paris.

Centre for Strategic Studies (CSS) (2003a). Public Opinion Polls Regarding Democracy in Jordan, Preliminary Results, Amman, University of Jordan, June.

—— (2003b) Public Opinion Polls: Democracy in Jordan 2003, Poll # 33, Amman, University of Jordan, June.

—— (2003c) Ma'an: An Open Ended Crisis. Amman, University of Jordan.

—— (2005) Democracy in Jordan – 2005, Public Opinion Polls Unit, University of Jordan, September.

CERMOC (1997). *Jordanies*, Amman, Centre d'Etudes et de Recherches sur le Moyen-Orient Contemporain, December.

Charlton, S., Everett, J. and Staudt, K. (Eds) (1989) *Women, the State and Development*, New York, State University of New York Press.

Chekir, H. (2001). 'La qestion des affaires locales par la citoyens: une certaine forme de gouvernance', presentation at Colloquium, Gouvernance Urbaine, School of Law and Political Science, Tunis.

Chemingui, M.A. and Chokri T. (2001). Internal and External Reforms in Agricultural Policy in Tunisia and Poverty in Rural Areas, Paper written for the GDN Research Medal Competition.

Cnaan, R.A., Boddie, S.C., and Gaynor, I.Y. (2003). 'Bowling Alone But Serving Together: The Congregational Norm of Community Involvement', in Smidt, C. (Ed), *Religion and Social Capital: Producing the Common Good*, Boston, Baylor University Press.

Colleta, N. and Cullen, M. (Eds) (2000). *Violent Conflict and the Transformation of Social Capital: Lessons From Cambodia, Rwanda, Guatemala and Somalia*, Washington DC, World Bank.

Colman, J. (1988). Social Capital in the Creation of Human Capital, *American Journal of Sociology,* 94, pp.95–119.

Cornia, A., Jolly, R. and Stewart, F. (1987). *Adjustment with a Human Face*, Oxford, Oxford University Press.

Cornia, G. and Court, J. (2001). *Inequality, Growth and Poverty in the Age of liberalisation and Globalisation*, Policy Brief No. 4, World Institute for Development and Economic Research, United Nations University.

CRS (Catholic Relief Service) (1989) *The Effects of Food Costs on Family Behaviour*, Cairo, CRS.

Cunningham, R. and Sarayrah, Y. (1993). *Wasta: The Hidden Force in Middle Eastern Societies*, London, Prager.

Curry, J. (2003). Social Capital and Societal Vision: A Study of Six Farm Communities in Iowa', in Smidt, C. (Ed), *Religion and Social Capital: Producing the Common Good*, Boston,

Baylor University Press, pp.139–152.

DFID (2000). *Eliminating World Poverty: Making Globalisation Work for the Poor,* London, DFID.

—— (2001). Participatory Poverty Assessment in Jordan, Near East Foundation, DFID and Ministry of Social Development, Amman, 2001.

Dahlerup, D. (1987). 'Confusing Concepts – Confusing Reality: a Theoretical Discussion of the Patriarchal State', in Showstack Sassoon, A. (Ed), *Women and the State*, London, Unwin Hyman.

Dajani, D. (2007). 'NAF studying plans to increase level of monthly assistance', in *Jordan Times*, 3 July.

Dallas, R. (1999). *A Life on the Edge: King Hussein*, London, Profile Books.

Dann, U. (1984). *Studies in the History of Transjordan, 1920–1949: The Making of a State*, Boulder, Westview Press.

—— (1989). *King Hussein and the Challenge of Arab Radicalism: Jordan: 1955–1957*, Oxford, Oxford University Press.

Dasgupta, P. and Serageldine, I. (Eds) (1999). *Social Capital: A Multifaceted Perspective,* Washington DC, World Bank.

Day, A. (1986). *East Bank / West Bank: Jordan and the Prospects for Peace*, New York, Council on Foreign Relations.

Dieterich, R. (2000). 'The Weakness of the Ruled is the Strength of the Ruler: The Role of the Opposition in Contemporary Jordan', in Joffe, G (Ed), *Transitions in Contemporary Jordan 1989–2000*, London, Hurst, pp.127–147.

Dimassi, H. (2000). 'Le système éducatif Tunisian: bilan et perspectives', contribution to seminar organised by the Association Mohamed Ali de La Culture Ouvrière Dévelopment des Resources Humaines et Transition Libérales de l'Economie Tunisienne, Tunis, 3–4 March.

Dimitri, V. (1993). 'Options for Pension Reform in Tunisia', Policy Research working papers, No. 1154, Washington DC, World Bank.

Dunkley, G. (1997). *The Free Trade Adventure: The WTO, the Uruguay Round and Globalism – A Critique*, London, Zed Books.

Economist, The (2002a). 'An Unsparing New Report by Arab Scholars Explains why their Region Lags Behind so Much of the World', 4 July.

——, (2002b) 'Revolution Delayed', 5 September.

——, (2004). 'Rational Extremists; Economic Focus', 17 January.

El-Erian, M., Eken, S., Fennell, S. and Chauffour, J. (1996). *Growth and Stability in the Middle East and North Africa,* Washington, IMF.

El-Ghonemy, M.R., (1998). *Affluence and Poverty in the Middle East,* London, Routledge.

El-Laithy, H. and Osman, M. (1997). 'Profile and Trend of Poverty and Economic Growth in Egypt', *Egypt Human Development Report Research Paper Series,* Cairo, UNDP/Institute of National Planning.

El-Laithy, H., El-Khawaga and Nagwa Riad (1999). 'Poverty Assessment in Egypt 1991–1996', Economic Research Monograph, Cairo, Cairo University Economics Department.

El-Saharty, S., Chase, S., and Richardson, G. (2005). *Egypt and the Millennium Development Goals: Challenges and Opportunities,* World Bank Report No. 31705, Washington DC, World Bank.

El-Said, H. (1996). Jordan: The Political Economy of Industrialisation in a *Rentier* Economy, PhD thesis, University of Manchester, Department of Government.

—— (2001). Waiting for Privatisation in the Arab World, in El-Said, H. and Kip, B. (Eds), *Management and International Business Issues in Jordan*, London, The Haworth Press.

—— (2001) 'The Political Economy of Reform in Jordan: Breaking Resistance to Reform?', in Joffe, G. *Jordan in Transition 1990–2000*, London, Hurst.

—— (2002a). *The Social and Political Impact of Globalisation in the Arab World,* Business School, Manchester, The Manchester Metropolitan University.

—— (2002b). 'The Political Economy of Reform in Jordan: Breaking Resistance to Reform?', in Joffe, G (Ed). *Transitions in Contemporary Jordan 1989–2000,* London, Hurst, pp. 254–76.

El-Said, H. and McDonald, F. (2001). 'Institutions and Joint Ventures in the Middle East and North Africa', *Journal of Transnational Management Development*, 6(1 and 2), pp.65–84.

—— (2002). 'Institutional Reform and Entry Mode by Foreign Firms: The Case of Jordan', *Journal for Institutional Innovation, Development and Transition*, 6(1), pp.76–88.

Enhaili, A. and Adda, O. (2003). 'State and Islamism in the Maghreb', in *Middle East Review of International Affairs* (MERIA), 7(1), March, (http://meria.idc.ac.il/journal/2003/issue1/jv7n1a6.htm).

Ennaji, M. (2006). 'Social Policy in Morocco: History, Politics and Social Development', Chapter 4 in Karshenas, M. and Moghadam, V. *Social Policy in the Middle East: Economic, Political, and Gender Dynamics*, Basingstoke, UK, Palgrave Macmillan.

ESCWA (United Nations Economic and Social Commission on Western Asia) (1991). The Return of Jordanian Palestinian Nationals from Kuwait: Economic and Social Implications for Jordan, ID/WG1/GP3, Amman.

Esposito, J. (1994). 'Political Islam: Beyond the Green Menace', Current History, 19.

—— (2000). 'Political Islam', *Joint Force Quarterly Forum*, Spring.

Fafchamps, M. (2006). 'Development and Social Capital', *Journal of Development Studies*, special issue, 42(7), pp.1180–1198.

Fanek, F. (1997). *Jordan Economic Monitor, Monthly Newsletter*, Amman, March, Issue No. 3/97.

Farr, J. (2004). 'Social Capital: A Conceptual History', *Political Theory,* 32(6), pp.6–33.

Fathi, S. (1993). *Jordan: Tribe-State Dynamics and the Formation of National Identity*, PhD dissertation, Hamburg University, 1993.

Fine, B. (2000). *Social Capital versus Social Theory: Political Economy and Social Science at the Turn of the Millenium*, London and New York, Routledge.

Fisk, R. (2006). 'What I am Watching in Lebanon each day is an outrage', in the *Independent*, London, 15 July, pp.1–2.

Francis, P. (2002). *Social Capital at the World Bank: Strategic and Operational*

Implications of the Concept, University of East Anglia, UK.

Friedman, T. (2004). 'The ABC's of Hatred', in *The New York Times*, 3 June.

Friedrich-Ebert-Stiftung (1997). *Islamic Movements in Jordan*, Amman, Sinbad Publishing House.

Fukuyama, F. (1995). *Trust: The Social Virtues and the Creation of Prosperity*, New York, The Free Press.

Fukuyama. F. (2000). *Social Capital and Civil Society,* Washington, IMF, WP/00/74.

Galal, A. and Lawrence, R. (2003). 'Egypt-US and Morocco-US Free Trade Agreements', The Egyptian Centre for Economic Studies, Working Paper Series No. 87, Cairo.

Garçon, J. (2007). 'Des jihadistes contre Ben Ali', *Libération*, 10 January.

Garnham, D. and Tessler, M. (1995). *Democracy, War and Peace in the Middle East,* Bloomington and Indianapolis, Indiana University Press.

Gellner, E. (1994). *Conditions of Liberty: Civil Society and its Rivals,* London, Hamish Hamilton.

Gerges, F. (2000). 'The End of the Islamist Insurgence in Egypt?: Costs and Prospects', in *Middle East Journal*, Vol. 54, No. 4, Autumn.

Ghali, S. and Mohnen, P. (2004). 'The Tunisian Path to Development: 1961–2001', A Case Study from *Reducing Poverty and Sustaining Growth – What Works, What Doesn't and Why*, May 2004, Mimeo.

Gharaibeh, I. (1997). 'The Muslim Brotherhood Political and Organisational Performance', in Islamic Movements in Jordan, 1997, Friedrich Ebert Stiftung and Al-Urdun Al-Jadid research Centre, Sinbad Publishing House, pp.47–77.

Gharbi, I. (2006). 'Les Femmes Dans Les Mouvements Islamistes: Aliénation ou Tentative De Libération?', *Journal d'étude des relations internationales au Moyen-Orient*, Vol. 1, No. 1.

Ghazouani, S. and Goaied, M. (2001). 'The Determinants of Urban and Rural Poverty in Tunisia', ERF Conference 'The Analysis of Poverty and its Determinants in the Middle East and North Africa', Sana'a, Yemen (31 July–1 August).

Ghecham, A. 2005, *The Institutional Framework and Performance of Firms in Egypt*, PhD thesis, Business School, Manchester Metropolitan University.

Gittell, R. and Vidal, A. (1998). *Community Organising: Building Social Capital as a Development Strategy*, Thousand Oaks, California, Sage.

Gerges, F. (2000). 'The End of the Islamist Insurgency in Egypt?: Costs and Prospects', *Middle East Journal,* Volume No. 4, Fall 2000, pp.592–612.

Global Poverty Research Group (2005). How Does SC Form? Overview, March 3. Avaiable on website: http://www.gprg.org/themes/t4–soccap-pub-socsafe/how=sc.ht.

Goldstein, M. (2000). *IMF Structural Conditionality: How Much is Too Much?,* Paper presented at NBER Conference on Economic and Financial Crisis in Emerging Market Economies, Woodstock, Vermont.

Government of Morocco, Ministere des Affaires Economique et Sociale (1993). *Etude sur les Sources de Vulnerabilite et les Filets de Securite pour les Populations Defavorisees: La Promotion Nationale*, Rabat, Government of Morocco.

Government of Morocco (2002). Etat/Associations: Les Balises d'un Partenariat Perenne et Solidaire, Budget Department, Rabat, Ministry of Economy and Finance.

Granovetter, M.S. (1973). 'The Strength of Weak Ties', in *American Journal of Sociology,* 78, pp.1360–1380.

Grootaert, C. and Van Bastelaer, T. (Eds) (2002a). *Understanding and Measuring Social Capital: A Multidisciplinary Tool for Practitioners*, Washington, DC, World Bank.

Grootaert, C. and Van Bastelaer, T. (2002b). 'Qualitative Analysis of SC: The Case of Agricultural Extension in Mali', in Grootaert and Bastelaer (Eds), *Understanding and Measuring SC: A Multidisciplinary Tool for Practitioners*, Washington, World Bank, pp.85–107.

Grootaert, C., Narayan, D., Nyhan Jones, V., and Woolcock, M. (2004). *Measuring Social Capital: An Integrated Questionnaire*, Washington DC, World Bank.

Gubser, P. (1973). *Politics in Al-Karak*, Jordan. Oxford, Oxford University Press.

Habib, R. (1990). *Religious Protest and Class Struggle in Egypt*, Egypt, Dar Sinai.

Hamdouch, B. (1998). 'Adjustment, Strategic, Planning and the Morocco Economy', in Nemat Shafik, *Economic Challenges Facing Middle Eastern and North African Countries: Alternative Futures*, London, MacMillan Press, pp.13–24.

Hamzeh, A. (2006). 'Results of Pilot Study on Bribery Released', *The Jordan Times*, Amman, 8 March.

Handoussa, H. (1994). 'The Economic Dimension to Policies Affecting Women-Headed Households in Egypt', paper presented at conference 'Women-Headed Households', Cairo, Central Agency for Public Mobilisation, 20 March.

Hansen, B. (1990). *The Political Economy of Poverty, Equity and Growth in Egypt*, Washington DC, World Bank.

Hansen, B. and Radwan, S. (1982). *Employment Opportunities and Equity in Egypt*, Geneva, ILO.

Harik, I. and Sullivan, D. (Eds) (1992). *Privatisation and Liberalisation in the Middle East,* Bloomington and Indianapolis, Indiana University Press.

Harmassi, A. (1996). 'Le mouvement islamiste en Tunisie et en Algerie: éléments pour une analyse comparative', in *Cahiers du CERES* – Série Histoire no.6, Les mouvement sociaux en Tunisie et dans l'immigration, Tunis.

Harrigan, J., El-Said, H., and Wang, C. (2006). 'The IMF and the World Bank in Jordan: Elusive Growth and Social Instability', *Review of International Organisations*, 1, September, 236–251.

Harrigan, J., and El-Said, H. (2008). *Aid and Power in the Arab World: IMF and World Bank Policy-based Lending in the Middle East and North Africa,* Palgrave Macmillan.

Hatem, M. (1992). 'Economic and Political Liberalisation in Egypt and the Demise of State Feminism', *International Journal of Middle East Studies*, 24(2), 232–51.

Heresh, J. (2003). 'US Ambassador Visits Irbid's Al Hassan Industrial Estate' in *Jordan Times*, Amman-Jordan, October 21.

Herzenni, A. (2002). 'La Protection Sociale: Cas de la Population Agricole', in *Bulletin Economique et Social du Maroc,* Rapport du Social 2002, Okad, Rabat.

Hibou, B. (1999). 'Les marges de manoeuvre d'un 'bon élève'économique: la Tunisie de Ben Ali', *Les Etudes du CERI* 60.

—— (2006). 'Domination & control in Tunisia: Economic levers for the exercise of authoritarian power', *Review of African Political Economy,* 33(108), pp.185–206.

Hussein, Ibn Tala (1971). King Hussein Opening Speech, 1st Conference of the Jordanian National Union, Amman, 25 November. The speech can be found in The Ministry of Information, (1986), Complete Collection of HM King Hussein's Speeches, 1952–1985, Amman, 1971.

Ibn Khaldoun Centre (1995). *Grassroots Participation in Egypt,* Cairo, Cairo Office of UNICEF.

Ibrahim, S. (1993). 'An Assessment of Grass Roots Participation in Egypt's Development', Cairo, Ibn Khaldoun Centre for Development Studies.

IMF (2002). Tunisia: 2002 Article IV Consultation – Staff Report and Public Information Notice on the Executive Board Discussion, IMF, Washington DC.

—— (2004). Jordan: Selected Issues and Statistical Appendix, Washington, IMF, IMF Country Report, No. 04/121.

— (2006). Tunisia: 2002 Article IV Consultation – Staff Report, IMF, Washington DC.

Institut National de la Statistique, (INS) (various years). *Statistical Yearbook,* Tunis, Government of Tunisia.

International Crisis Group (ICG 2003a). The Challenge of Political Reform: Jordanian Democratisation and Regional Instability. *Middle East Briefing,* Amman/Brussels, 8 October.

—— (2003b). Red Alert in Jordan: Recurrent Unrest in Mann, *Middle East Briefing,* Amman/Brussels, 19 February.

IRIN (2006). http://www.irinnews.org

Islamic Society Charity Centre (2003). Annual Report, Amman, ISCC.

—— (2005). Annual Report 2005, Amman, ISCC.

—— (2006). Annual Report 2006, Amman, ISCC.

Jeune Afrique (2007). 'Ben Ali, les Djihadistes et la Presidentielle', Abdelaziz Barrouhi, *Jeune Afrique,* 21 January.

Joffe, G. (1992). 'The Changing Geography of North Africa', in Graham Chapman, P. and Baker, K.M. *The Changing Geography of Africa and the Middle East*, London, Routledge, pp.139–164.

Joffe, G. (Ed) (2001). *Jordan in Transition 1990–2999,* London, Hurst.

Jordan Times, The. Amman, 28 January.

—— (2005a). 'Editorial: High Expectations', Amman, 3–4 June.

—— (2005b). 'Combating Corruption', Amman, 20 July.

—— (2005c). 'Local Runners Shine in Marathons', Amman, 11 September.

—— (2006a). 'Poverty Alleviation Project Comes to an End', 10–11 March.

—— (2006b). 'Islamic charity referred to public prosecutor', Amman, 6 July.

Jordan Watch (2006). 'Jordan Islamists Ready to Take Over the Government', 31January, (httt://www.jordanwatch.net/archive/2006/1/17242.html).

—— (Ed) (2002). *Transitions in Contemporary Jordan 1989–2000,* London, Hurst.

Jreisat, E. J. (1989). 'Bureaucracy and Development in Jordan', *Journal of Asian and African Studies*, XXIV(1–2), pp.95–105.

Kahkonen, S. (2002). 'Does Social Capital Matter in the Delivery of Water and Sanitation?,' in Kanaan, T. and Kardoosh, M. (2002). *The Story of Economic Growth in Jordan: 1950–2000.* Amman, October, found on web site at: http://www.erf.org.eg/html/grp/GRP_Sep03/Jordan-develop.pdf.

Kanan, C. and Kardoosh, T. (20020. *The Story of Economic Growth in Jordan 1950–2000*, Amman, October, found on website at http://www.erf.org.eg/html/grp/GRP_Sept03/jordan–develop.pdf.

Kandil, A. and Nefise-Paris, B. (1994). *Non-Governmental Organisations in Egypt*, Cairo, Centre for Political and Strategic Studies.

Kashef, A. (1987) 'Egypt', in Dixon, J. (Ed). *Social Welfare in the Middle East,* Croom Helm, London.

Kazem, A.A. (1997). The Muslim Brotherhood: the Historic Background and the Ideological Origins, in Al-Urdunn Al-Jadid Research Centre (AUJRC). Islamic Movements in Jordan, Amman, Sindbad Publications, AUJRC (in Arabic).

Kéfi, R. (1999). 'Comment les islamistes ont été vaincus', *Jeune Afrique*, 11 May.

—— (2006). 'Le Hijab est-il islamique?' *Jeune Afrique,* 15 Jan.

Khachani, M. (2002). 'Les Conflits Sociaux Collectifs' in Bulletin Economique et Social du Maroc, *Rapport du Social*, Okad, Rabat.

Khalaf, R. (2003). 'Zoellick Criticism Sets Back Egypt Hopes on Free Trade', in *Financial Times*, 24 June.

Khalifah, L. (2005). 'The Beating of Teachers is Less Than a Phenomenon and More Than a Wrong Behaviour', *al-Ghad Daily Newspaper*, Amman, 16 September.

Khiari, S. (2002). 'Le renouveau de mouvement démocratique tunisien;, in Lamloun, O. and Favenel, B. (Eds) *La Tunisie de Ben Ali: la société contre le régime*, Paris, L'Harmattan.

Khiari, S. and O. Lamloum (1999). 'Tunisie: des élections en trompe-l'œil.' POLITIQUE AFRICAINE, pp.106–116.

King, S. J. (1999). 'Structural Adjustment and Rural Poverty in Tunisia', *Middle East Report,* Spring.

—— (2003). *Liberalization Against Democracy: The Local Politics of Economic Reform in Tunisia,* Bloomington, Indiana University Press.

Klare, M. (1998). "The Rise and Fall of Rogue Doctrine: The Pentagon's for a Post-Cold War Military Strategy', *The Middle East Report*, 1998, pp.12–15.

Knack, S. and Keefer, P. (1997). 'Does Social Capital Have An Economic Payoff? A Cross Country Investigation', *The Quarterly Journal of Economics,* November 1997.

Knauss, P. (1989). 'The Political Economy of Morocco', *Economic Development and Cultural Change,* Reviewer, pp.435–441

Korayem, K. (1987). *The Impact of Economic Adjustment Policies on the Vulnerable Families and Children in Egypt*, Cairo, The Third World Forum and UNICEF.

Kossaifi, G.F. (1998). *Poverty in the Arab World: Toward a Critical Approach,* Morocco, Mediterranean Development Forum, Economic Development and Poverty Reduction, Marrakech, 3–6 September.

Krishna, A. and Shrader, E. (2002). 'The Social Capital Assessment Tool: Design and Implementation', in C. Grootaert and T. Van Bastelaer (Eds), *Understanding and Measuring Social Capital: A Multidisciplinary Tool for Practitioners*, Washington DC, World Bank.

Kuehnast, K. and Dudwick, N. (2004). *Better a Hundred Friends than a Hundred Rubles? Social Networks in Transition – The Kyrgyz Republic,* Washington, World Bank.

Laskier, M. (2003). 'A Difficult Inheritance: Moroccan Society Under King Muhammad VI', in *Middle East Review of International Affairs* (MERIA), 7(3), (http://meria.idc.ac.il/journal/2003/issue3/jv7n3a1.htm).

Lerner, D. (1958). *The Passing of Traditional Society: Modernising the Middle East*, New York, The Free Press.

Ligue Tunisienne de Droits de l'Homme, www.fidh.org, accessed April 2007.

Lofgren, H. (1993). 'Economic Policy in Egypt: A Breakdown in Reform Resistance?', *International Journal for the Middle Eastern Studies*, No. 25.

Loury, G. (1977). 'A Dynamic Theory of Racial Income Differences', in P. A Wallace and A. LeMund (Eds) *Women Minorities, and Employment Discrimination*, Lexington, Mass. Lexington Books.

Lubeck, P.M. (1998). 'Islamist Responses to Globalization: Cultural Conflict in Egypt, Algeria, and Malaysia', in *The Myth of 'Ethnic Conflict': Politics, Economics, and 'Cultural' Violence*, Beverly Crawford and Ronnie D. Lipschutz (Eds), University of California Press, University of California International and Area Studies Digital Collection, Edited Volume #98, pp.293–319, http://repositories.cdlib.org/uciaspubs/research/98/9.

Macchi, V. (2006). '98.3 per cent of Jordanians have never been a political party member – poll', in *the Jordan Times*, 26 June.

Mackenzie, M. (1946). 'Transjordan'. *Journal of Royal Central Asian Society*, 33.

Mahfouz, M. (1992). 'Community Development in Egypt' unpublished MA thesis, American University of Cairo.

Malhas, A. (1993). 'al-Fasad al-Qanuni' (Legal Corruption), *al-Ra'i* Newspaper, Amman, 5 May.

Mansi, R. (1995). 'Child labour from the Insurance and Social Security Perspective', paper presented to Ministry of Labour and ILO and UNICEF conference, March.

Mansur, A. and Field, C. (2004). 'Fiscal Policy and Structural Transformation of the Jordanian Fiscal Structure', in *Jordan: Selected Issues and Statistical Appendix*, Washington, IMF, IMF Country Report, No. 04/121.

Marshall, I. and Keough, L. (2004). *Mind, Heart and Soul in the Fight against Poverty*, Washington DC, World Bank.

Marshy, M. (2005). *Freedom of Association with regard to Political Parties and Civil Society in the Middle East, North Africa, and the Gulf: A literature review*, Ottawa, International Development

Research Centre.

Migdal, J. (1988). *Strong Societies and Weak States: State-Society Relations and State Capabilities in the Third World*, Princeton, Princeton University Press.

Miguel, E. (2003). 'Comment on: Social Capital and Growth', *Journal of Monetary Economics*, 50, pp.195–198.

Ministry of Social Development (MSD) (2003). P*overty Measures in Jordan*, Amman, Jordan Poverty Alleviation Programme, Ministry of Social Development.

Mishal, S. (1978). *West Bank/East Bank: The Palestinians in Jordan, 1949–1967*, New Haven, Yale University Press.

Moghadam, V. (1992). 'Women's Employment in the Middle East and North Africa: The Role of Gender, Class and State Policies', Michigan State University Working Paper No. 229.

Morford, M. and Berman, E. (2003). 'Hamas, Taliban and the Jewish Underground', NBER Working Paper No. w10004 Issued in September, NBER Program.

Mosley, P., Harrigan, J. and Toye, J. (1995). *Aid and Power: The World Bank and Policy Based Lending,* Vols I and II, London, Routledge.

Narayan, D. (1999). *Bonds and Bridges: Social Capital and Poverty*, Washington, Poverty Group, PREM, World Bank.

Narayan, D. and Cassidy, M. (2001). 'A Dimension Approach to Measuring Social Capital: Development and Validation of Social Capital Inventory', *Current Sociology*, 49(2), pp.59–102.

Nassar, H. (1995). *Economic Aspects of Vulnerability in Children in Egypt*, Cairo, UNICEF.

National Economic and Social Forum, The, (NESF) (2003). *The Policy Implications of Social Capital*, Dublin, Forum Report No. 28.

Nemeth, R.J. and Luidens, D.A. (2003). The Religious Basis of Charitable Giving in America: A Social Capital Perspective, in Smidt, C (Ed). *Religion and Social Capital: Producing the Common Good,* Boston, Baylor University Press, pp. 107–20.

Niblock, T. and Murphy, E. (Eds) (1993). *Economic and Political Liberalisation in the Middle East,* London, British Academy Press.

Niva, S. (1998). 'Between Clash and Cooptation: US Foreign Policy and the Spectre of Islam', *Middle East Report*, Fall 1998, pp.26–29.

North, D.C. (1990). *Institutions, Institutional Change and Economic Performance,* Cambridge, Cambridge University Press.

Nowarah W. (2007). The Parallel State: The Shadow State, a paper submitted for the Second Forum on Democracy and Reform in the Arab World, Doha, 27–28, Sheraton Hotel, Qatar.

O'Donnell, G. (1993). 'On the State, Democratisation and Some Conceptual Problems', *World Development*, 21(8), pp.1355–1369.

Ohmae, K. (1990). *The Borderless World: Power and Strategy in the Interlinked Economy,* New York, Free.

—— (Ed) (1995). *The Evoloving Global Economy: Making Sense of the New World Order*, Boston, MA Harvard Business Review Press.

Ostrom, E. (1999). 'Social Capital: A Fade or Fundamental Concept', in Dasgupta, P. and Serageldine, I. (Eds), *Social Capital: A Multifaceted Perspective*, Washington DC, World Bank.

Owen, R. (1992). *State, Power and Politics in the Making of the Modern Middle East*, London, Routledge.

Peake, F.G. (1958). *History of Jordan and its Tribes*, Princeton, Princeton University Press.

Peccoud, D. (Ed) (2004). *Philosophical and Spiritual Perspectives on Decent Work*, Geneva, International Labour Office.

Perthes, V., (1998). 'Points of Differences and Cases for Cooperation: European Critique of US Middle East Policy', *Middle East Report*, Fall.

Pfeifer, K. (1996). 'Between Hard Rocks and Hard Choices: International Finance and Economic Adjustment in North Africa', in *North Africa: Development and Reform*, D. Vandewalle (Ed), New York, St. Martin's Press.

Pfeifer, K. (1999). 'How Tunisia, Morocco, Jordan and Even Egypt Became IMF Success Stories', *The Middle East Report*, pp.23–26.

Piro, T. (1998). *The Political Economy of Market Reform in Jordan*, Boulder, Rowman & Littlefield.

Pitner, J. (2000). 'NGOs' Dilemmas', *Middle East Report* (214), pp.34–37.

Portes, A. (1998) 'Social Capital: Its Origins and Applications in Modern Sociology', *Annual Review of Sociology*, 24, pp.1–24.

Putnam, R. (1993). *Making Democracy Work: Civic Tradition in Modern Italy*, Princeton, Princeton University Press.

—— (1995). 'Bowling Alone: America's Declining Social Capital'. *Journal of Democracy*, 6, pp.65–78.

—— (2000) *Bowling Alone: the Collapse and Revival of American Community*, New York, Simon & Schuster.

Putnam, R., Leonardi, R. and Raffaella, N. (1993). *Making Democracy Work*, Princeton, NJ, Princeton University Press.

Ravallion, M. and Lokshin, M. (2004). 'Gainers and Losers from Trade Reform in Morocco', *Middle East and North Africa Working Paper Series* No. 37, Washington DC, World Bank.

Reiter, Y. (2002). 'Higher Education and Sociopolitical Transformation in Jordan', *British Journal of Middle Eastern Studies*, 29(2), pp.137–164.

Richards, A. and Waterbury J. (1996). *A Political Economy of the Middle East*, Boulder and Oxford, Westview Press.

Right, R. (1996). 'Islam and Liberal Democracy: Two Visions of Reformation', in *Journal of Democracy*, 7(2), pp. 64–75.

Robins, P. (2004). *A History of Jordan*, Cambridge, Cambridge University Press.

Rogan, E. and Tell, T. (1994). *Village, Steppe and State: The Social Origins of Modern Jordan*, London, British Academy Press.

Roy, Sara (2000). 'The Transformation of Islamic NGOs in Palestine', *Middle East Report* (214), pp. 24–26.

Sabry, S. (2005). 'The Social Aid and Assistance Programme of the Government of Egypt

– A Critical Review', *Environment and Urbanisation*, Vol. 17, No. 2, Oct 2005.

Sachedina, Abdulaziz (2001). *The Islamic Roots of Democratic Pluralism*, New York, Oxford University Press.

—— (2002). 'Political Islam and the Hegemony of Globalisation: A Response to Peter Berger', in *Religion and Globalisation,* 'The Hedgehog Review: Critical reflections on Contemporary Culture', Vol. 4(2), pp. 21–29.

—— (2007a). Can there be Democratic Governance Without the Separation of Religion and Politics?, paper presented to the Seventh Annual Conference of the Center for the Study of Islam and Democracy (CSID), Washington DC, 6 May.

—— (2007b). *The Role of Islam in Public Square: Guidance or Governance*?, Charlottesville, Virginia, USA, University of Virginia, memorandum.

Sadowsky, Y. (1991). *Political Vegetables? Businessmen and Bureaucrats in the Development of Egyptian Agriculture*, Washington DC, The Brookings Institution.

Sahlins. M. (1972). *Stone-Age Economies*, Chicago, Aldine-Atherton, 1972.

Saïdi, R. (2000). 'La pauvreté en tunisie: presentation critique', in Lamloun, O. and Ravenel, B. (Eds), *La Tunisie de Ben Ali: la société contre le régime,* Paris, L'Harmattan.

Salibi, K. (1998). *The Modern History of Jordan*, London, I.B. Tauris.

Satloff, R. (1986). *Troubles on the East Bank: Challenges to the Domestic Stability of Jordan,* London, Praeger.

—— (1994). *From Abdullah to Hussein: Jordan in Transition*. Oxford, Oxford University Press.

Schirato, T. and Webb, J. (2003). *Understanding Globalisation*, London, Sage.

Shaban, R. Abu-Ghaida, D. and Al-Naimat, A. (2001). *Poverty Alleviation in Jordan: Lessons for the Future*, Washington DC, World Bank.

Shafiq, N. (Ed) (1998). *Prospects for Middle Eastern and North African Economies: From Boom to Bust and Back?* London, Macmillan.

Shahine, G. (2005). 'To be Worse', in *Al-Ahram Weekly* found on http://weekly.ahram.org.eg/index.htm, 24 –30 November 2005.

Singerman, D. (1997). *Avenues of Participation: Family, Politics and Networks in Urban Quarters of Cairo,* Cairo, The American University in Cairo Press.

Singh, R. (2002). 'Liberalisation or Democratisation? The Limits of Political Reform and Civil Society in Jordan', in Joffe, G. (Ed). *Jordan in Transition 1990–2000*, London, Hurst, pp. 66–90.

Sivan, E. (1998). 'Why Radical Muslims Aren't Taking Over Governments', in *MERIA*, 2(2). May.

Smidt, C. (Ed) (2003). *Religion and Social Capital: Producing the Common Good*, Boston, Baylor University Press.

Snow, P. (1972). *Hussein: A Biography*, London, Barrie & Jenkins.

Sobel, J. (2002). 'Can We Trust Social Capital?' *Journal of Economic Literature*, XL, March, 2002, pp.139–154.

Stewart, F. (2000). *Income Distribution and Development*, Working Paper Series #37, Oxford, Queen Elizabeth House, Oxford University.

Stiglitz, J. (2002). *Globalisation and Its Discontents*, London, Penguin Books.

Stoddard, (Ed) (2007). U.S. Islamic charities feel post 9/11 heat, *Reuters*, Jul 20. (http://www.reuters.com/article/domesticNews/idUSN1725413920070720?src=072007_1359_DOUBLEFEATURE_withdrawal_warning).

Sullivan, D. (1994). *Private Voluntary Organisations in Egypt: Islamic Development, Private Initiative and State Control*, Gainesville, Florida, University Press of Florida.

Sullivan, D. and Abed-Kotob, S. (1999). *Islam in Contemporary Egypt: Civil Society vs the State,* Lynne Rienner Publishers, London.

Swalem, M., al-Zayood, M., Rayan, M., and Sharabati, R. (2005). 'The Experience of Youth with Voluntary Work'. *Al Rai Daily Newspaper*, Amman, September 15.

Tamimi, A. (2001). Rachid Ghannouchi: *A Democrat Within Islamism*, Oxford, Oxford University Press.

Tawila, S. (2000). *The School Environment in Egypt: A Situation Analysis of Public Preparatory Schools*, Cairo, Population Council.

Tessler, M. (2003). 'Do Islamic Orientations Influence Attitudes Toward Democracy in the Arab World? Evidence From Egypt, Jordan, Morocco and Algeria', *International Journal of Comparative Sociology*, Spring.

The National Economic and Social Forum (NESF). The Policy Implications of Social Capital, Report No. 28, Dublin, 2003.

Trooquer, Y. and Al-Oudat, R.(1999). 'From Kuwait to Jordan: The Palestinians' Third Exodus', *Journal of Palestine Studies*, 3, pp.37–61.

United Nations Development Programme (UNDP) (2002). *United Nations Arab Human Development Report*, New York, United Nations.

—— (2204a). *Arab Human Development Report: Towards Freedom in the Arab World.* New York, Regional Bureau for Arab States.

—— (2004b). Stratégie de Réduction de la Pauvreté – Étude du phénomène de la pauvreté en Tunisie, Geneva, United Nations.

Vandewalle, D. (Ed) (1996). *North Africa: Development and Reform*, New York, St. Martin's Press.

Vatikiotis, P. J. (1967). *Politics and Military in Jordan: A Study of the Arab Legion, 1921–1957.* London, Frank Cass & Co.

Wade, R. H. (2004). Governing the Market: Economic Theory and the Role of Government in *East Asian Industrialisation,* 2nd edition, Princeton, Princeton University Press.

Walle, D. (2004). Do Basic Services and Poverty Programmes Reach Morocco's Poor? Evidence from Poverty & Spending Maps, Discussion Paper, Washington DC, World Bank, November.

Waterbury, J. (1983). *The Egypt of Nasser and Sadat*, Princeton, NJ, Princeton University Press.

Weitzman, B.M. (1997). The Islamic Challenge in North Africa', in *Middle East Review of International Affairs* (MERIA), 1(2), July, (http://meria.idc.ac.il/journal/1997/issue2/jv1n1a2.htm).

Wickham, C. (2002). Moderate Islam is the Mainstream, Emory Report, 9 September (http://www.emory.edu/emory.edu/EMORY_REPORT/erarchive/2002/September/er Sept.)

Wiktorowicz, Quentin and Farouki, Shuha Tahi, (2000). 'Islamic NGOs and Muslim politics: a case from Jordan', *Third World Quarterly,* Vol 21:4, pp 685–699.

Wilson, M. (1987). *King Abduallah, Britain, and the Making of Jordan.* Cambridge, Cambridge University Press.

Woltering, R., (2002). 'The Roots of Islamist Popularity', *Third World Quarterly,* Vol. 23, No. 6, pp.1133–1143.

Wood, R. (1997). Social Capital and Political Culture: God Meets Politics in the Inner-City, in *American Behavioural Scientist,* 50(5), pp. 595–605.

Woolcock, M. and Narayan, D. (2000). 'Social Capital: Implications for Development Theory, Research, and Policy', *World Bank Research Observer,* 15(2), pp.225–249.

World Bank (1989). *Arab Republic of Egypt: A Study on Poverty and the Distribution of Income,* a draft report for the Country Operations Division, report no. CDIII EMENA, Washington DC, World Bank.

—— (1991). *Egypt – Alleviating Poverty during Structural Adjustment,* Report No. 9838, Washington DC, World Bank.

—— (1994). *Kingdom of Morocco: Poverty, Adjustment and Growth,* Report No. 11918 MOR, Washington DC, World Bank.

—— (1995). *Tunisia: Poverty Alleviation: Preserving Progress While Preparing for the Future, Middle East and North Africa Region,* Report, World Bank, Washington.

—— (1996). *Tunisia's Global Integration and Sustainable Development,* World Bank, Washington DC.

—— (1997). *Kingdom of Morocco: Country Assistance Review,* Report No. 16326–MOR, Washington DC, World Bank.

—— (2000). *Republic of Tunisia, Social and Structural Review 2000, Integrating into the World Economy and Sustaining Economic and Social Progress,*World Bank, Washington, DC.

—— (2001a). *Egypt: Social and Structural Review,* Washington DC, World Bank.

—— (2001b). *Morocco: Country Assistance Evaluation,* Report No. 22212, World Bank, Washington DC.

—— (2002a). *Bosnia and Herzegovina: Local Level Institutions and Social Capital Study.* Washington DC, World Bank, Vol.1, ECSSD, June, 2002.

—— (2002b). *Arab Republic of Egypt – Poverty Reduction in Egypt: Diagnosis and Strategy,* Vol. 1 Main Report, Report No. 24234–EGT, Washington DC, World Bank.

—— (2002c). *Kingdom of Morocco: Social Protection Note,* Report No. 22486–MOR, World Bank, Washington DC.

—— (2003). *Kingdom of Morocco: Findings and Recommendations of the Cereals Working Group: A Critical Review,* Washington DC, World Bank.

—— (2004a) *Jordan: Economic Development in the 1990s and World Bank Assistance.* World Bank, Washington DC.

—— (2004b). *Arab Republic of Egypt – A Poverty Reduction Strategy for Egypt,* Report No. 27954–EGT, Washington DC, World Bank.

—— (2004c). *Kingdom of Morocco Poverty Report: Strengthening Policy by Identifying the Geographic Dimension of Poverty,* Report No. 28223–MOR, World Bank, Washington, DC.

—— (2004d). *Jordan Poverty Assessment,* Washington DC, World Bank.

—— (2005). *Kingdom of Morocco: Country Assistance Strategy 2005–2009,* Report No. 31879–MA, Washington DC, World Bank.

—— (2006a). *Project Appraisal Document on a Proposed Loan in the Amount of US$100 Million to the Kingdom of Morocco for a National Initiative for Human Development Support Project,* Report No. 36973–MOR, Washington DC, World Bank.

—— (2006b). *Kingdom of Morocco: Poverty and Social Impact Analysis of the National Slum Upgrading Programme,* Report No. 36545–MOR, Washington DC, World Bank.

—— (2006c). World Development Indicators, Washington DC, World Bank, ESDS database.

—— (2006d). World Development Indicators (WDI) online database.

World Faith Development Dialogue (WFDD) 1999. Bulletin No.3, Oxford.

World Institute for Development Economics Research – United Nation University (WIDER – UNU) (2006), World Income Inequality Database V 2.0a June 2005, United Nations, the Hague, http://www.wider.unu.edu/wiid/wiid-introduction-2006-1.htm

Wuthnow, R. (2003). 'Can Religion Revitalise Civil Society? An Institutional Perspective', in Smidt, C. (Ed). *Religion and Social Capital: Producing the Common Good,* Boston, Baylor University Press, pp. 191–210.

Yorke, V. (1988). *Domestic Politics and Regional Security: Jordan, Syria and Israel: The End of An Era?,* Sydney, Gower.

Zakharova, D. (2004). 'Development of Social Protection Institutions', in IMF, *Jordan: Selected Issues and Statistical Appendix,* Washington, IMF, IMF Country Report, No. 04/121.

Zisser, E. (2000). 'Hizballah: New Course or Continued Warfare', in *Middle East Review of International Affairs* (MERIA), 4(3), (http://meria.idc.ac.il/journal/2000/issue3/jv4n3a3.htm).

Zunes, S. (2001). 'US Policy Toward Political Islam', in *Foreign Policy in Focus,* 12 September.

Zureik, E. (1996). *Palestinian Refugees and the Peace Process,* Washington DC, Institute for Palestinian Studies.

Index

Note: 'n' after a page number refers to a note on that page.

Abdullah II, King 36, 57, 58, 74, 75, 182
Abdullah, Prince 34
Abdullatif, Abu Qourah 56
Afghan War 138
Aga Khan Foundation 25
Al Nahda 166, 168, 169, 170, 171, 172, 173, 174, 175
al-Banna, Sheikh Hassan 21, 98
Algeria 3, 5, 6, 7, 13, 14, 16, 106, 135, 138
al-Khateeb, Abdual Kareem 136
Al-Qaeda 16
American University of Cairo 100
Amnesty International 7
Arab Archive Institute 52
Arab Bank 38
Arab Socialism 79, 138

Bank Development Policy Loan 129n
Ben Ali, General Zine 147, 154, 161, 163, 164, 165, 166, 169, 170, 171, 173, 174, 175, 180
Blair, Tony 6
Bosnia and Herzegovina 55
Bourguiba, President Habib 148, 164, 168, 180
Bretton Woods 146, 147, 163
Bush, President George W 6

Carey, Archbishop George 24
Centre for Strategic Studies 46, 47, 48, 51, 72
Coptic Church 79, 97, 98, 102, 103, 104, 105, 181
Country Assistance Evaluation 126, 143
Czechoslovakia 106

economic liberalisation programmes 1
Economic Recovery and Structural Adjustment Programme (ERSAP) 78, 79, 80, 81, 82, 83, 85, 86, 88, 89, 91, 92, 95, 96, 100, 101, 109, 110
Ethiopia 107
European Union 5, 6, 121, 142, 146, 161, 173, 174

Farouq, King 98

Ghanoushi, Rashid 169, 170, 171, 172, 173, 174
globalisation 2, 4, 5, 6, 22, 24, 28, 67
Gulf 36, 44, 45, 46, 52, 53, 61, 71
Gulf War (1990/1), 45, 52, 78

Hamas 5, 15, 106
Hassan, Prince 16, 21
Hassan II, King 112, 113, 119, 132,136, 137, 139, 140, 180
Hizb'Al Nahda see Al Nahda
Hungary 106
Hussein, King, of Jordan 36, 39, 40, 41, 42, 44, 57, 68, 69, 71, 74

National Initiative for Human Development (INHD) 130, 131, 140, 142, 180

Indonesia 6
infitah 80, 82
Inter-American Development Bank 25
International Crisis Group 7
Iraq 35, 45, 138, 172, 183
Islamic Salvation Front 106
Islamic Tendency Movement 169

Jordan Human Development Report 46

Khomeini, Ayatollah 8
Koran 19, 99, 168
Kuwait 53
Kyrgyz Republic 50

Latin America 1, 106
Lebanon 15, 16, 35, 36, 40, 75

Mauritania 3
Mohammed V, King 112
Mohammed VI, King 128–32, 183
Mubarak, President Hosni 5, 79, 98, 104, 107, 110, 181, 182
Muslim Brotherhood 5, 9, 15, 21, 22, 39, 42, 54, 56, 57, 59, 61, 63, 65, 67, 69, 71, 73, 75, 77, 98, 104, 107, 110, 136, 139, 180, 181, 182

Nasser, President Gamal 79, 80, 98, 181
New Institutional Economics (NIE) 29, 31

Ottomans 21, 33, 34, 35

Palestine 5, 15, 35–46, 48, 49, 52, 53, 54, 59, 69, 76, 106, 138, 145, 147, 172, 174, 183
Parallel State, the 15
Philippines 25
Poland 106
Poverty Reduction Strategy 26, 79, 109

Sadat, President Anwar 80, 82, 98, 106
Saudi Arabia 6
Senegal 15
September 11 attacks 7, 92, 94, 108, 182
Social Priority Programme 127
Society of Muslim Brethren 97
Structural Adjustment Loan (SAL) 1, 2, 119
sub-Saharan Africa 1, 2, 3, 7
Sudan 3, 16
Suez Canal 78
Syria 3, 35, 36, 56

Tocqueville, Alexis de 12, 15
Transjordan 35, 36
Transparency International (TI) 52
Turkey 2, 3

Uganda 25
United Nations Development Programme (UNDP) 31, 46, 47, 48, 49, 50, 51, 62, 86, 129, 158, 160, 162, 163
United Nations Relief and Works Agency (UNRWA)
USA 1, 2, 5, 6–8, 13, 15–8, 20, 22, 36–9, 44, 48, 53, 64–6, 68, 69, 71, 73–6, 100, 172
  USAID 108

Washington Consensus 1, 6, 15, 49
wasta 34, 35n, 36, 38, 43, 44, 51
Wolfensohn, James 24, 25
Wolfowitz, Paul 24
World Council of Churches 25
World Economic Forum 6
Yemen 3, 6
Young Men's Muslim
  Association 98, 103
Yugoslavia 16, 54
Zimbabwe 37

The manufacturer's authorised representative in the EU is Springer Nature Customer Service Centre GmbH, Europaplatz 3, 69115 Heidelberg, Germany. If you have any concerns regarding our products, please contact ProductSafety@springernature.com

Printed and bound by CPI Group (UK) Ltd, Croydon, CR0 4YY
30/10/2026
02242619-0007